DICTATORS WITHOUT BORDERS

DICTATORS WITHOUT BORDERS

POWER AND MONEY
IN
CENTRAL ASIA

ALEXANDER COOLEY & JOHN HEATHERSHAW

YALE UNIVERSITY PRESS
NEW HAVEN AND LONDON

For information about this and other Yale University Press publications, please contact:

U.S. Office: sales.press@yale.edu   yalebooks.com
Europe Office: sales@yaleup.co.uk   yalebooks.co.uk

Typeset in Adobe Caslon Pro by IDSUK (DataConnection) Ltd
Printed in Great Britain by Gomer Press, Llandysul, Ceredigion, Wales

Library of Congress Control Number: 2016962066

ISBN 978-0-300-20844-3

A catalogue record for this book is available from the British Library.

10 9 8 7 6 5 4 3 2 1

For Nicole and Greta
and
for Julia, Grace and Sam

CONTENTS

FIGURES AND TABLES

PREFACE

In April 2016, the offshore world hit headlines across the globe when records from the Panamanian law firm and company provider Mossack Fonseca were leaked online. The 'Panama Papers' – by far the largest data leak in the history of the secretive world of tax havens, with 11.5 million documents released – captured the public consciousness and caused oligarchs, politicians and celebrities the world over to lose sleep. A whole series of revelations ensued about tax avoidance and suspected money laundering in high-value real estate. The front page of the *Guardian* told of 'the London skyscraper that is a stark symbol of the housing crisis' with apartments owned by a Russian billionaire 'whose business partner is a close ally of Vladimir Putin's', a Nigerian banker and ex-minister, and a 'former MP and vodka tycoon' from the Central Asian republic of Kyrgyzstan.[1] These three examples were among many which demonstrate that both West and East, North and South, are connected via offshore jurisdictions.

In the public consciousness, it was the effect the offshore world might have on the sacrosanct right of modern Westerners to own a home which really touched a nerve. But researchers at Global Witness, supported by students from the University of Exeter, had already linked central London properties to the offshore accounts of Central Asian oligarchs such as the former son-in-law of President Nazarbayev of

Kazakhstan.[2] Campaigners at London's Transparency International and the New York headquarters of the Open Society Foundation saw new opportunities to force tax havens to publish registers of beneficial owners. One academic colleague had the unusual experience of flying business class to preparatory meetings for David Cameron's May 2016 anti-corruption summit at the expense of the very offshore jurisdictions that he had studied for many years. For us and these colleagues of ours, the questionable claim about the inflation of Western real estate markets was merely the tip of the iceberg.

As this book details, autocrats and their cronies use Western financial, legal, policing and political systems to both extend their power back home and to selectively access Western institutions, status symbols and legal protections. Tajikistan's largest state-owned enterprise opaquely diverts the proceeds from its aluminium industry into accounts in the British Virgin Islands (BVI). The elite of Turkmenistan hold personal dollar-dominated accounts managed by Deutsche Bank. Relatives of Uzbekistan's strongman president accepted bribes from several international telecoms providers via offshore accounts in Gibraltar and stored the proceeds in several different foreign bank accounts. The Kazakh government routinely uses the international policing organisation Interpol in their politically motivated pursuit of former high-ranking officials and their associates who have become exiled opponents of the regime, while members of the Kazakh elite themselves purchase luxury real estate holdings around the world via shell companies. The Tajik regime has used its BVI account to apparently dodge reporting requirements to the Justice Department regarding its lobbying of US Congress.

And Central Asia is not exceptional. Much of the world is governed for the benefit of a small number of people who hide their profits in offshore accounts. In short, the whole system of international law, universal human rights and global governance has been undermined by secretive offshore jurisdictions, leaving researchers, journalists and advocates to assess the extent of the damage.

These stories are some of many detailed in this book about those Central Asian republics that gained independence in 1991, and therefore became sovereign in the era of globalisation. *Dictators Without Borders* tells this very modern story of Central Asia. It thus differs from many other books on the region you might have read, with their tales of the Orient, the ancient silk routes and fractious clans, or warnings of Islamism and ethnic conflicts. We avoid discussion of these pre-modern themes as they are frankly far less important to the true nature of Central Asia than the high-tech finance and low-tech politics detailed here.[3] Central Asia is not predestined to corruption by its past, its culture, its religion or its traditional social ties. Rather, Central Asia's dictators and their allies are able to abuse power and pilfer their countries' resources because of the fact that international bankers accept their business and foreign politicians don't properly enforce their own laws. We explore the contours of this modern marriage of self-serving power politics to the increasingly sophisticated global financial and legal architectures and the professional intermediaries who manage them.

We use 'dictators' and 'autocrats' interchangeably in this book. 'Dictatorship' refers to trenchant systems of *authoritarian rule* and *neo-patrimonial relations*. 'Authoritarian rule' refers to systems in which political authority is concentrated in the hands of the few and exercised without effective accountability to parliament, the judiciary, civil society or a free press. 'Neo-patrimonial relations' refer to the means by which leaders (patrons) lock in junior allies (clients) in modern states via networks which typically provide financial rewards but demand absolute political loyalty. There is a huge amount of academic literature on these two concepts within our field which we will not explore here. Occasionally, when referring to the economic dimensions of dictatorships we refer to them as 'kleptocracies' (a term used to highlight dictators' abuse of office to enhance personal power and wealth) and their behaviour in the global market as 'crony capitalism' (a term used not to imply an aberration but a common form of capitalism across many regions including Central Asia).

The 'without borders' of this book's title is a play on the *sans frontières* phrase in the names of Médecins Sans Frontières (MSF), Dentistes ... (DSF), Educateurs ... (ESF), Reporters ... (RSF), etc. Modern autocrats have effectively taken on this mantra to subvert the idealised version of globalisation as transnational humanitarian action. But to say they are *dictateurs sans frontières* is not to say they have complete freedom of movement without the encumbrance of national borders and sovereignty. In fact, their actions beyond borders are often in the use of their sovereign status and power to get things done overseas. There are three senses in which dictators are 'without borders'.

First, and in the traditional liberal understanding, dictators are without borders in that they operate *without moral and legal limits* on their use of power. This is not to say they do not operate within their own laws – they sometimes do, they sometimes don't. They remake their laws to allow themselves to run for office as many times as they wish, extort the independent private sector (to the extent that it often ceases to exist) and pilfer from the public purse. At times they simply break national and international law by torturing their opponents or pervert the law to declare their non-violent enemies to be 'terrorists' or 'criminals' in order to eradicate them. Such actions actually often take place at the scale of *domestic* or national authoritarian government. There are plenty of examples of this old-fashioned style of dictatorship in this book.

Second, and less well known though nothing new, dictators operate *beyond borders*. Today's hidden offshore companies are yesterday's private Swiss or London accounts kept by dictators as their insurance against the rebellion they always fear might come. Today's use of rendition and extraterritorial assassination by Central Asian regimes has its precedent in the abductions and executions by the Russian Tsarist and Soviet secret police of their opponents. Consider the NKVD's killing of Trotsky in Mexico in 1940. This is *international* authoritarianism and authoritarian cooperation. Diplomatic relations with other states and personal diplomatic immunity are the products of sovereignty which have enabled this extension of dictatorial power into other states via cooperative relations with their governments or the use of national and intelligence services overseas.

The use of the word 'rendition' also highlights that it is not just autocrats that act beyond borders in this way. Journalistic, academic and congressional investigation revealed the extent of the CIA's extraordinary rendition programme under the Bush administration.[4] Such methods continue to this day as liberal democracies like the US and UK extrajudicially execute their citizens suspected of terrorism through drone strikes overseas.[5] But the refrain that 'they're all the same' simply won't do. There is a qualitative distinction between the national security rationales of the US and UK (questionable though they are) and the regime security rationales of Central Asian states. In an autocracy, there is no such thing as an opposition and even opponents in exile are fair game.

Third, and a novel phenomenon of globalisation, dictators operate *across borders*. In particular they subvert the very instruments of global governance that were ostensibly set up to keep them in check. This is *global* authoritarianism and is importantly different from the international mode noted above. Here we are not merely interested in the possession of foreign accounts or in the strategy of extraterritorial assassinations, but in the elite and even cosmopolititan networks that have enhanced the international status of these autocrats and safeguarded the privacy of their dealings. Brokers and intermediaries with global lives make the connections between post-Soviet dictators and the real estate agent who will sell them a London property, or the Washington lobbyist who will pursue regime agendas in the corridors of power. Transnational organised crime networks – with which many post-Soviet security professionals have relations – enable attacks on, disappearances and assassinations of exiles.

But it's not just about individuals. Networks of intermediaries, company service providers and bankers are embedded in an industry which exists to serve the world's dictators and politically connected oligarchs. These networks, which we refer to as 'transnational uncivil society', embed autocrats within a dense network of institutions, legal protections and global spaces that are intended to obfuscate their transgressions back home and conceal the origins of their personal fortunes. Courts struggle to cope with the opacity of the details in the cases brought before them. Enforcement agents lack the resources to investigate and prosecute even a fraction of the cases they face. Politicians shy away from offending powerful allies from friendly kleptocracies. In this way, informal practices are allowed to subvert anti-money-laundering and anti-corruption laws. The industry itself has its own cultures, norms and self-justifications. 'Well, otherwise they'd take their business elsewhere', is the common refrain. A 'don't ask, don't tell' culture emerges.

The revelations following the Panama Papers leak reveal that these attitudes are both morally wrong and factually selective. Many laws are already in place but are not implemented properly. In other cases enforcement does take place when it suits. A public register of owners – now accepted in the UK and some other states but resisted by tax havens – is a realistic possibility if the political will is there. The European Court of Human Rights is at least partially effective in reversing cases of the abuse of extradition treaties and revealing renditions. There are any number of points of leverage that can be used by governments and campaigners, from public shaming right through to 'blacklists' that would make potential purchasers of property and offshore accounts go through prohibitively demanding checks. These opportunities for change now present themselves. Anti-corruption initiatives must not lose momentum as the attention recedes.

ACKNOWLEDGEMENTS

A book such as this is the product of a certain amount of personal endeavour and a great deal of learning from the insights and labours of friends and colleagues. Many of these have been fellow travellers in a process which included two workshops at Columbia University, New York (in 2013 and 2016), presentations at Harvard University's Davis Center, Vilnius University and the University of Glasgow (2015), a panel at the meeting of the International Studies Association in San Francisco (2013), and a book conference at the University of Exeter (2015). They include Zulfia Abdullaeva, Fiona Adamson, John Agnew, Olivia Allison, Nils-Christian Bormann, Asel Doolotkeldieva, Saipira Fürstenburg, John Helmer, Alisher Ilkhamov, Edward Lemon, David Lewis, Tom Mayne, Ronen Palan, Jason Sharman, Kemel Toktomushev, David Trilling, Bill Vlcek, and Monica Whitlock. Many of these people read chapters in detail. We also thank four anonymous reviewers appointed by Yale. Authors of articles in the special issue of *Central Asian Survey* in 2015 on 'Offshore Central Asia' made their own important contributions to getting tax havens and extraterritoriality on the agenda of the study of the region. Stacy Closson, Charles Dainoff, Erica Marat, Jennifer Murtazashvili and Adrien Fauve as well as Doolotkeldieva, Sharman and Toktomushev helped inform our own work. We also thank Deniz Kandiyoti and, subsequently, Madeleine Reeves for their support.

ACKNOWLEDGEMENTS

Research collaboration and assistance has had a direct effect on this book. We must especially recognise Sharman and Doolotkeldieva again for their co-authorships with Cooley[1] and Heathershaw[2] respectively of material that in revised form has made its way into the succeeding chapters. Heathershaw's earlier work with Nick Megoran partially inspired this book's attempt to change the conversation about security in Central Asia.[3] Mayne's early reporting for Global Witness (GW) on Central Asia's offshore connections was path-breaking and his advice on sources invaluable. A team of student researchers from the University of Exeter then worked with Mayne and Chido Dunn to trawl through Land Registry records in earlier research published by GW.[4] Journalists and officials in Kyrgyzstan who shall remain unnamed helped in the background research, and the equally courageous Sean Daley shared his experiences of his attempted assassination during the time of the Bakiyev administration. We learnt from the investigative instincts of journalists John Helmer, David Trilling, Bernt Gran and the legal expertise of Scott Horton. Eve Bishop, Rosa Brown and Juliana Angeles Ruiz at Exeter worked with speed and efficiency on the production and review of the Central Asian Political Exiles Database. Over a dozen human rights activists reviewed the database and provided invaluable comments. Sarah Calderone, Casey Michel and Max de Havalang of Columbia University provided excellent research assistance. The talented Seth Farkas produced the illustrative graphics.

Finally, we must thank our friends and family. They may now have heard enough of *Dictators Without Borders*, but without their support and sacrifices this project would have not come to fruition.

INTRODUCTION

CENTRAL ASIA BEYOND BORDERS

In early 2007, a report by the anti-corruption watchdog Global Witness revealed that the Central Asian dictatorship of Turkmenistan had secretly accrued $8 billion in foreign reserves, most of which were held in US dollars by Deutsche Bank in undisclosed and offshore state accounts.[1] Revealingly, the report that a Western bank had acted as a personal treasurer to the Turkmen president was not met with universal shock and outrage in official circles. One US diplomat declared in 2008, just prior to the global financial collapse, that the '[presidential] fund has always been officially acknowledged', vigorously defending the bank's actions by noting that 'Deutsche Bank adheres to gold-standard international accounting, and thus *any corruption takes place before the money reaches the bank*' (our emphasis).[2] However, anti-money-laundering guidelines also make it clear that, if bankers and middlemen do not check or report their suspicions about the corrupt origins of capital, they are just as much part of a global network of corruption as government procurement bosses. Since 2008 Western governments have begun to recognise the problem of absolute financial secrecy. The US diplomat's defence of Deutsche Bank appears in this light to be either rather naïve or deeply cynical.

President Niyazov preferred to be called Turkmenbashi, the father of the Turkmen. He was the first leader of independent Turkmenistan, overseeing the state's transition, before his death in December 2006, from being the most southerly Soviet republic to one of the harshest and most secretive dictatorships in the world. In the central square of Ashgabat, the capital and shimmering storefront of the new sultanate, a golden statue of the great man revolved with the sun. Niyazov's image adorned almost every public building in the country, while he renamed some months after himself and members of his family. Niyazov even wrote his own 'holy book' of wisdom and philosophical musings, the *Ruhnama*, which became the core of the curriculum at all levels of education in Turkmenistan and an important part of civil service exams. The personality cult left no room for freedom of expression or any kind of political opposition, leading Freedom House to rank Turkmenistan among its 'worst of the worst' of human-rights-abusing countries,[3] and to give the country the lowest possible score for political rights and civil liberties every year since the mid-1990s.[4] The anti-corruption NGO Transparency International consistently ranks Turkmenistan in the world's ten most corrupt countries.

It is easy to dismiss Niyazov's Turkmenistan – as many Western media accounts routinely did – as a despotic and secluded desert oasis that was nonetheless fortunate to sit on vast reserves of natural gas. Indeed, the potential for large energy exports seemed to constitute its major link to the wider world. Niyazov's paranoid government banned international media, restricted foreign travel for citizens and closed almost all externally sponsored schools and universities. Turkmenistan's official foreign policy of neutrality, eschewing membership of military alliances or international organisations, has also promoted this image of isolationism. After his death, Niyazov was rapidly succeeded by the similarly autocratic but more difficult to pronounce Gurbanguly Berdimuhamedov.

Little has changed. Turkmenistan has gone from dependence on exporting gas along pipelines via Russia to a fresh dependence on new Chinese-built pipelines to the east, making Ashgabat desperate to start exporting gas southwards to Pakistan and India under the Western-backed but ill-fated TAPI project.[5] What would, however, spur the Central Asian state's development is political reform and liberalisation of its state-dominated and corruption-prone economy – none of which seem anywhere near the distant horizon.

However, as the Deutsche Bank story shows, this picture of isolation, autarky and eccentricity is incomplete. Beyond the public view we find Turkmenistan entangled in transnational networks of businesspeople, global bankers and cosmopolitan fixers. Germany may not officially be an ally of Turkmenistan or a supporter of its authoritarian practices, but some of its leading companies play major roles in the country's economy and finances. Deutsche Bank has been operating in Turkmenistan since 1994 and holds the accounts of the Central Bank of Turkmenistan. Its representative in Turkmenistan effectively serves as banker to the regime, managing its accounts.[6] Deutsche and another German bank, Commerz, as class-A European banks, are the only banks able to offer financial guarantees on the holdings of foreign companies working in Turkmenistan.[7] Other German businesses, including Mercedes and Siemens, and many other foreign companies, such as French construction giant Bouygues, have established themselves as preferred suppliers to the Turkmen government due mainly to 'good relations with the highest-ranking government officials'.[8] All these businesses sell in hard currencies, which Turkmenistan needs to purchase foreign technology for its industry and high-end consumer goods for its elite.

'Offshore' accounts are not to be confused with the foreign currency reserves typically held by national banks to pay debt and support foreign exchange stability. They are, however, vital to dictators like Turkmenistan's now-deceased Saparmurat Niyazov, allowing them both to shelter the spoils of power within the international financial system and, in turn, to use these spoils to promote political goals at home and gain influence overseas. Turkmenistan's gas revenues are not simply kept in its local currency, the manat, but are exchanged for dollars through state accounts held offshore. These accounts are off-budget, opaque and may hold as much as 50 per cent of annual hard-currency revenues. They are personally controlled by key regime figures who apparently use them for both personal gain and political purpose, which often coincide in the form of vainglorious state infrastructure projects and their generous kickbacks. If these offshore revenues declined due to the falling price of gas (as they are likely to have done in recent years), or if these accounts were frozen as part of corruption investigations, the very survival of the regime would be threatened. Politically, payments from these accounts fund foreign lobbying and international arbitrations over key state projects. Meanwhile, elites battle over such funds. Indeed, the desire to control them has been a main driver of intra-regime purges in Kazakhstan and Uzbekistan, post-civil war politics in Tajikistan, and the deposing of two governments in Kyrgyzstan.

This book tells the fascinating stories of Central Asia's *dictators without borders*. Their tales are at once local and global – and not infrequently gruesome. Far from operating in isolation, even the most closed Central Asian states have embedded their transactions, or at least their most significant transactions, in a set of informal transnational networks with global reach. The so-called 'local' familial, ethnic and regional networks of power and wealth in the region are often also globalised, as Central Asia's dictators play out their legal and power struggles overseas. This involves concealing their transactions through the use of shell companies, targeting and defeating their enemies abroad and accruing their winnings partly through this network of bankers, lawyers and lobbyists in Frankfurt, London, New York and other financial and political capitals.

How is it that the majority of policymakers, analysts and scholars ignore or disregard these links? Putting aside the cognitive dissonance of policymakers and any conspiracy theories that might explain their silence, there are three myths which undergird the assumption that Central Asia is a distinctly onshore region. Our analysis vigorously challenges all three.

Myth #1: the distant heartland of Asia

It is understandable that Central Asia is typically viewed in the West as a distant 'heartland', isolated from global influences and processes, beset by homegrown political repression and economic stagnation. There is a grain of truth to this image. Central Asia is sparsely populated and landlocked, with Uzbekistan one of only two doubly landlocked countries in the world.[9] The poverty-stricken states of Kyrgyzstan and Tajikistan have both suffered cycles of violence and 'revolution' largely of their own making. The idiosyncrasies of the resource-rich dictatorship of Turkmenistan and the brutally repressive tactics of its neighbour Uzbekistan seem to confirm the view that Central Asian despotism is far from the ways of the West and best left alone. Only Kazakhstan – also abundant in hydrocarbons and relatively 'open' for business – with its 'skilful leadership' is lauded as a modernising state worthy of attention and investment.

However, the relative public ignorance about Central Asia beyond its borders is no fault of Central Asians themselves, the majority of whom have considerable awareness of international affairs. Most adult Central Asians speak at least one European language – typically Russian – and many are remarkably knowledgeable about global popular culture, foreign exchange rates and contemporary events, particularly in the former Soviet states. But whilst in the aftermath of independence those former Soviet republics farther north received greater attention in English-language media, the southern states of Central Asia were largely ignored as very few global media outlets or major newspapers established bureaus there. Even today, there are few places to study Central Asian languages beyond the region, few major cultural exports from the region, and precious little coverage of its events. It is little wonder that Central Asia was perceived as particularly obscure. In Sacha Baron Cohen's *Borat*, John Cusack's *War, Inc.*, and countless other movies, TV shows and novels, Central Asia is an easy object of humour, whose states are treated as new instances of Ruritania, or simply those crazy '-stans'. In each of these cases, it is the ignorance of foreign publics and diplomats that is satirised, but in each case the image of Central Asia as unknown or obscure is also reproduced.

Western officials and experts are often little better informed. Diplomats, security professionals and analysts have routinely argued that Central Asia is disconnected from global political and economic transformations.[10] Following the region's newly acquired independence in the 1990s, most global powers were slow to establish embassies and committed few resources there. Central Asia was not considered part of the 'developing world' like sub-Saharan Africa,[11] nor the source of security threats like the Middle East, nor of global economic importance like East Asia. International oil and gas companies moved more quickly, but their interest was naturally narrow. Following the events of 9/11 and the US-led military campaign in Afghanistan, the region was securitised as a critical front in the Global War on Terrorism. But this new relevance seemed to only further popularise, rather than dispel, these myths as the Pentagon and its contractors justified funnelling additional resources to regime affiliates and their cronies.[12] As Chapter 6 shows, the West's military campaign in Afghanistan actually spawned new transnational networks and offshore schemes that enriched and empowered Central Asia's supposedly disconnected rulers.

The apparent obscurity of Central Asia thus became a self-fulfilling prophecy. It leads many of those who dabble in the region for the first time to fall back on the monikers of 'lost', 'hidden' and 'heartland' that were deployed in the nineteenth century by Russian and Western players of the 'great game'. This imperial struggle to control and otherwise cajole the political leaders of the territories between Russia in the north and British India to the south, between Persia and the Ottoman Empire in the west and China in the east, entered the public imagination via the memoirs, travelogues and reports of heroic European explorers.[13] Imperialist thinking was given academic credence in the British political geographer Halford Mackinder's early-twentieth-century claim to the Royal Geographic Society that the Central Asian space was a 'geographical pivot of history'. The centre of the Eurasian landmass, 'the Heartland', was, Mackinder argued, the key to global strategic preeminence.[14] These imperial perspectives on Central Asia have a lasting legacy in the apparent inability of many foreign analysts to think of Central Asians as both fully modern and agents of their own polities.

On closer inspection, rather than isolating the region, Central Asia's contemporary geography instead determines *how its ruling elites access specific transnational networks*. Oil-rich Kazakhstan and Turkmenistan, on the shores of the Caspian Sea, enjoy energy resources like Kashagan, the largest new oil and gas field discovered in the last half-century. The field itself has proved enormously challenging to extract, while intense corporate and international competition have also shaped external interest and its consortium dynamics. The whole region holds mineral

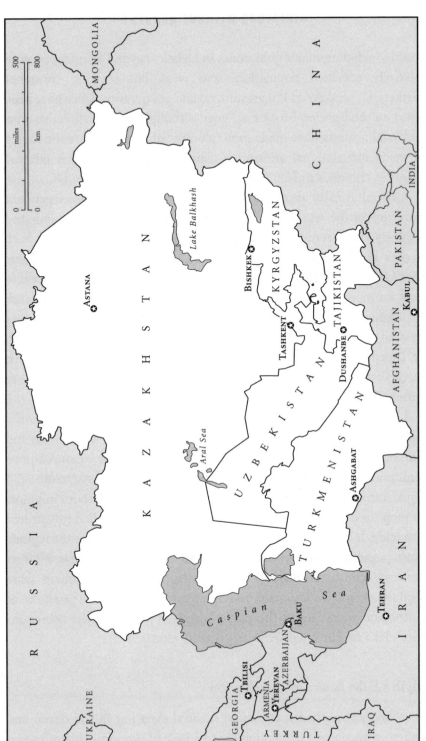

Figure I.1 Map of Central Asia

wealth, including major gold mines in Uzbekistan and Kyrgyzstan, with relatively educated populations and weak but growing consumer markets. Central Asia's largest mineral and energy companies have been listed on the London Stock Exchange, although forced nationalisations and local protests have made mining politically risky and are the source of many international arbitration claims against the region's governments in tribunals in London, Stockholm and Washington, DC.

Central Asia is also home to the two most migration-dependent countries in the world, the mountainous republics of Kyrgyzstan and Tajikistan. The remittances of Tajik and Kyrgyz labour migrants back to their families constitute about one-half and one-third of these countries' GDPs respectively. Kyrgyzstan is also the only state in the world to host, for more than a decade, both Russian and American military bases. Tajikistan is one of few countries to receive both a UN peacekeeping mission and a Russian-led one – the latter through the Commonwealth of Independent States (CIS), the international organisation which succeeded the Soviet Union. Both Kyrgyzstan and Tajikistan serve as entrepôts for China's re-export trade to the rest of the CIS.

Uzbekistan sits in the geographic and economic centre of Central Asia. It lies between the oil-rich deserts and steppe of Kazakhstan and Turkmenistan on the one hand, and the relatively resource-poor, remittance-dependent and mountainous states of Kyrgyzstan and Tajikistan on the other. Uzbekistan also relies heavily on labour migrants to prop up its autarkic economic model of state-controlled investment and trade. It benefits from modest oil and gas exports and, as the region's most populous country with around 30 million people, has a larger domestic consumer market than its neighbours. Downstream from Tajikistan's and Kyrgyzstan's mountain rivers, it is also a producer of cotton and wheat and is the single biggest opponent of the two countries' plans to dam their rivers to generate electricity.

Myth #2: the failure of liberalisation

A second entrenched myth about Central Asia lies in the donor and policy professional's perception that its lack of economic liberalisation has been largely responsible for its economic challenges and endemic governance problems. For the first two decades of independence, Central Asia was not only viewed as geographically isolated, but was widely judged as detached from global governance, the international economy and the process of globalisation. The solution offered to this problem was liberalisation, both political and economic, in the form of market reform, financial deregulation, privatisation and land reform, along with free and fair elections, multiparty politics, and open space for civil society between families and the state. In Central and Eastern Europe, with the carrot of European Union membership promised in the near future, such market and political reform appeared to be working. More importantly, most of the states on Europe's borders had a long history of independence, and the new elites who emerged after the end of the Cold War had no problem labelling the Eastern bloc as a Soviet imperial project to be disavowed wholescale. However, these conditions – massive international aid and inducements, and an elite committed to reform – were completely absent in Central Asia.[15] Despite the absence of these factors, the liberal reform blueprint was offered to Central Asia as if these political factors might be incidental to a largely technical process of creating new markets and electoral systems.

On paper, a considerable number of landmarks were achieved, as Central Asian countries initially mimicked post-communist states in 'transition'. In the heady days of their new-found independence, Central Asian leaders were willing to sign up to ambitious new statutes. Laws governing property and trade were written, with the liberalisers Kazakhstan, Kyrgyzstan and Tajikistan eventually introducing market economies to replace Soviet-era planning. The old Soviet–Russian ruble was unceremoniously abandoned and new currencies introduced by these states, while Western experts advised on how to privatise property and build financial institutions from scratch.

But, unlike in most of Central and Eastern Europe, such privatisations were not governed by the rule of law, but by the principles of neo-patrimonial relations, where ruling elites provided assets to relatives and allies in return for their absolute loyalty and a cut of the spoils. Elsewhere, this has been labelled 'crony capitalism', a well-established feature of many emerging economies including some of the most successful in terms of economic growth. According to David Kang, crony capitalism during the East Asian economic miracle occurred where politics drove economic policy choices, where bureaucrats lacked autonomy from politics, and where 'business and political elites wrestled with each other over who would reap the rents to be had'.[16] In Central Asia, a similar process occurred. However, as governments established themselves as consolidated autocracies, the spoils of the market reforms of the 1990s were seized and secured through new global financial connections, hidden bank accounts and offshore networks.

When economic and political transition in Central Asia was declared dead in the early 2000s the pathologists carrying out the post-mortem were clear that the Central Asians were laggards in market and democratic reform compared to their post-socialist brethren in Eastern Europe. Failure, it was widely acknowledged, was largely due to their domestic conditions. Anders Åslund, who advised Russia and Kyrgyzstan on their reforms, argued that the failure to reform Soviet systems was simply due to a lack of political will on the part of the Central Asians.[17] Thomas Carothers, who was critical of the presumptions of Åslund and his colleagues, identified some Central Asian states as 'feckless reformers' while others simply remained authoritarian.[18] Few acknowledged the distinct difficulties of the Central Asian states' starting conditions, which were completely wanting in the preconditions of capitalism including private property, their own currency and a modern history of free trade beyond the borders of the former Soviet Union.

But even fewer considered an alternative possibility – that the hasty promotion of financial deregulation may have actually hindered wider economic and political 'reform'. With hindsight, a closer look at the economies of Central Asia reveals that their problems are *not those of the complete failure of liberalisation, but rather its partial and selective adoption.* In particular, their acute difficulties arise out of the coincidence of authoritarianism and capitalism – a lack of democratic reform but considerable convergence with the global market economy, enabling transnational networks of kleptocracy and capital flight. These states, which have partially adopted financial and economic liberalisation while remaining authoritarian, are characterised with labels such as 'hybrid regimes', 'electoral authoritarianism' and 'authoritarian neoliberalism'.[19] Liberal reformers like Åslund simply dismiss this liberalisation as mere crony capitalism.[20] However, during the 'globalisation era' of the 1990s, this kind of cronyism became the norm in many so-called emerging markets, which adopted globalising reforms such as floating currencies, seeking foreign direct investment (FDI) and removing capital controls.

Further, these countries embed many of their transactions and dispute adjudication in foreign law, thus making their legal personas global, even as insider elites retain operational control of these companies. Elites wield liberalisation initiatives as instruments to advance their narrow economic and political interests. Instead of reducing state predation and elite enrichment, financial liberalisation has enabled these practices on a more global scale. Small wonder, then, that even a 'laggard reformer' like Tajikistan in 2011 experienced an estimated capital flight of over 60 per cent of its GDP, according to the IMF.[21] In Central Asia, crony capitalism is the *only* capitalist game in town, resourced by correspondent relations with major world banks, advice from law firms and auditors, and cooperation with the World Bank, IMF and other leading institutions of global financial regulation. Rather than being innocent bystanders to this slide, many great global financial institutions and major foreign companies were complicit in the emergence of crony capitalism.

Two inescapable truths of Central Asia's experience of transition have made reform near impossible and corruption a natural part of politics and business. First, the region is characterised by the blurring of politics and economics and public and private sectors to the extent that the boundary between them is completely absent. In Central Asia, if you are ahead in politics, you are ahead in business, and vice versa. This basic axiom is strongly implied by the fact that all members of Central Asian legislatures enjoy some degree of immunity from criminal prosecution. Most Central Asian presidents are wholly above the law, enjoying immunity from prosecution, formal designation as 'leader of the nation', and, with the absence of term limits, the effective power to remain president for life. Second, today's dictators and their cronies are deeply integrated into global business and finance. They may not be able to manage their currencies, control inflation or operate efficient state enterprises, but this is not to say they are not eager players in the hidden world of investments, assets and wealth management.[22] They don't need reconnecting to the global economy: they are already connected through webs of offshore companies, company service providers and brokers.

Not coincidentally, the emergence of this globalised crony capitalism coincided with the region's worsening authoritarianism. Electoral democracy was constitutionally enshrined in Central Asian countries, but competitive politics remains rare. In fact, during the 2000s basic civil liberties in all the regional states deteriorated. Turkmenistan established a de jure president for life, whilst three of the other four republics have followed this path – removing term limits and other constitutional barriers – without yet codifying this status. Uzbekistan experienced a brief flourishing of political opposition before this was crushed by its dictator Islam Karimov, who has ruled since the Soviet era. Tajikistan and Kazakhstan saw nascent multiparty systems overcome by authoritarian presidents who also trace their political careers to the Soviet period. In Tajikistan, this was justified by elites as the price of stability after the country's brutal civil war of the 1990s. In Kazakhstan, it was enabled by economic growth on the back of the country's immense oil and gas wealth coming online. Only Kyrgyzstan, despite suffering from periods of authoritarian rule and persistent cronyism, has seen the emergence of multiparty politics and, finally, in 2011 the peaceful relinquishing of power by one leader (interim president Roza Otunbayeva) for another (Almazbek Atambayev). Space for politically engaged civil society tenuously remains in Kyrgyzstan and to a lesser extent in Kazakhstan. Elsewhere, it has disappeared entirely.

The onset of the so-called 'colour revolutions' from 2003 to 2005 further equated the practice of democracy promotion with regime instability, a fear that in May 2005 informed the Uzbek government's bloody crackdown on thousands of demonstrators in the eastern city of Andijan. Since then, all Central Asian states have cracked down on independent media and imposed restrictions on civil society. Meanwhile in the aftermath of the Arab Spring, Central Asian security services further targeted social media and unleashed yet another wave of restrictive laws against 'foreign agents', with international NGOs and foundations accused of fomenting dissent and encouraging 'non-traditional' behaviours. Gender and sexual identity remain heavily circumscribed within highly conservative laws, norms and political discourse, while Western-style liberal values are now routinely discredited in public in favour of local 'cultures', state sovereignty or 'traditional' morals.[23] All the while, Central Asian ruling families have acquired foreign luxury real estate in cosmopolitan hot spots like London, Paris, Geneva, Los Angeles and New York. Their robust and active transnational networks stand in stark contrast to their countries' weak, demonised and underfunded civil societies.

Myth #3: Central Asian localism

Finally, we have the myth that Central Asia's political predicament has local or cultural causes. 'Okay,' the argument goes, 'these guys have a few offshore bank accounts and Western PR consultants but they get to the top and stay there because of factors internal to Central Asia.' This is the argument of 'localism'. It has two variants: the vulgar and the nuanced. In the nuanced version, where local actors are placed in their global contexts, localism is no myth at all, but the means by which Central Asia is shaped as a region. However, in the vulgar version, localism is a deeply deceptive lens through which Central Asia becomes a mere problem to be solved.

Vulgar localism, as championed by popular commentators, posits that there is a clear divide between the region and the outside world. Central Asia is the source of a series of problems for the wider world associated with its supposed multiethnic discord, its religious ferment and its history of tribal and clan-based organisation. Chief among these is Islamism, which is said to be 'resurgent' in Central Asia following the collapse of the Soviet Union.[24] Such localist analysis ironically fails to take account of the particular history of Central Asia. The region's Muslim societies were highly secularised by the Soviet experience and therefore remain infertile ground for widespread radicalisation.[25] Central Asia has not experienced a major armed conflict for twenty years, despite predictions to the contrary.[26] Mercifully, terrorism and political violence – despite kleptocratic governance – are rare compared to neighbouring regions of South Asia, the Middle East and the Caucasus. From 2001 to 2013, just 0.1 per cent of global terrorist attacks took place in Central Asia – a region with around 1 per cent of the world's population.[27]

For some prominent commentators and analysts, Central Asia's internal problems should be considered threats to the Western world. According to Thomas Barnett, professor of warfare analysis at the US Naval War College, Central Asia is part of a 'non-integrating gap' (including most of Africa, the Middle East, South America and Pakistan/Afghanistan, but not Russia or Europe), that is dangerous to the 'core' of globalisation because of its disconnectedness from it.[28] For Chris Seiple, director of the Washington think tank the Institute for Global Engagement, using an expression coined by former US Secretary of State Zbigniew Brzezinski and popularised on a famous *Time* magazine cover, Central Asia sits 'atop the crescent of crisis that rises from North Africa to Central Asia before descending into Southeast Asia'.[29] In a similar vein, former US defence secretary Donald Rumsfeld identifies a 'broad arc of instability that stretches from the Middle East to Northeast Asia' and which threatens critical US interests.[30] The affiliation of these writers is significant, illustrating the circulation of ideas among agenda-setters in Washington – a phenomenon also found in other Western policymaking centres.[31]

Nuanced localism is a very different beast. It has been the main means by which social scientists in the field of Central Asian Studies have explained the region over the last ten to fifteen years. Political scientists such as us, who undertook fieldwork in the region following the fall of the Soviet Union, found that local informal institutions trump formal constitutional arrangements. 'Clans', ethno-regionalism and patron–client ties were all identified as significant. In the best work, the ties that bound clans were never presented as purely those of blood.[32] The fictive kinships of business relations and bureaucratic solidarities were shown to expand and update 'clans' during the Soviet and post-Soviet periods. To some authors, localism (*mestnichestvo* in Russian) was itself a product of the Soviet multinationalist (or colonial) state project.[33] By this account, 'localism' was the product of a profoundly modern political order. This version of Central Asian affairs has been extremely helpful in our understanding of how local patterns of governance have emerged in the region. For example, such bottom-up analysis provides the best explanations for the end of the civil war in Tajikistan, the 'revolutions' in Kyrgyzstan and the tensions in the border regions of the Ferghana Valley.[34] Such field-based research was a corrective to an earlier generation of scholarship from a time when the Soviet republics had been inaccessible and were largely viewed by Western researchers from afar.

However, the study of the international politics of Central Asia still lacks many of these nuances. Commentators often struggle to see how the internal and external affairs of Central Asia are connected. Only a handful of studies have ventured to the region's hidden offshore and extraterritorial spaces. This is striking as few questions of government, international relations, development, business and state formation can be answered without acknowledging the offshore dimension. The timing of Central Asia's independence in the globalisation era of the 1990s was crucial as it allowed this localism to rapidly scale up and embed itself in transnational networks. In Kyrgyzstan, for example, both in the capital Bishkek and in the villages of Talas Province, localism combines with an awareness of the price of gold on the global market and an aspiration to the modern lifestyles and wealth seemingly enjoyed overseas.[35] More importantly, however much regional clans may structure national politics, they require a further set of connections to brokers and middlemen beyond their borders in order to convert their power into secure financial reserves.

Why have both policymaking and academic worlds been reluctant to identify the offshore dimension? One important consideration is that the full reality of the entangled nature of our global economic and financial relations is a very inconvenient truth indeed. It is uncomfortable for Western governments (and academics) to admit that the same banks that are protected by generous taxation regimes are also laundering the money of organised crime networks. It is unpleasant to recognise that our strict regimes of asylum and immigration make exceptions for high-net-worth investors – often oligarchs – whose 'worth' is based on the plundering of their home economies. It is embarrassing to recognise that Companies House in London registers both major high-street brands and shell companies whose beneficial owners are legally unknown and might include organised criminals. And it is inconvenient to admit that the system of deregulation, tax avoidance, legal globalisation and offshore havens which has been advanced by successive British and American governments is the very system which facilitates corruption on an unimaginable scale. In the West, at least, we are schooled to think our political and economic systems are ultimately governed by the rule of law and are therefore relatively free from corruption compared to political systems outside of the Organisation for Economic Cooperation and Development (OECD). The realisation that our systems may provide the opportunities and vehicles for large-scale corruption is a difficult pill to swallow.

Perhaps the greatest casualty of this focus on Central Asian localism has been that we have missed how Central Asian political contestation – even so-called clan politics and intrafamilial struggle – has itself gone global. The Kazakh state had targeted a number of estranged political dissidents and opponents abroad through appeals to foreign law enforcement and the use of Interpol arrest warrants, even including the now-deceased former son-in-law of the Kazakh president. Uzbekistan's ruling family has played out a high-profile international drama involving former President Karimov's once powerful daughter Gulnara Karimova, now under house arrest in Tashkent, and her public spats with her sister Lola. And, as Chapter 7 explores, both the Uzbek and Tajik regimes, no longer satisfied with monopolising 'clan power' and repressing opposition domestically, have taken more aggressive measures to target political opponents and opposition communities residing abroad through a number of extraterritorial instruments. Simply put, even if we privilege the importance of local, familial and regional political identities and loyalties, the setting in which they play out is increasingly global.

Central Asia and the 'offshore' world

As Nicholas Shaxson, a tax haven specialist, notes in his book *Treasure Islands*, 'capital no longer flows to where it gets the best return but to where it can get the best tax subsidies, the deepest secrecy, and to where it can best evade the laws, rules and regulations it does not like'.[36] Perhaps more than half of world trade, half of all banking assets and a third of foreign direct investment are routed offshore, yet rarely do we associate these offshore trends with developments in Central Asia.[37] Redirecting our focus away from formal trade flows to the more hidden offshore world and institutions of contemporary finance, we see, in fact, multiple links between the Central Asian region and the global economy, often via post-Soviet business networks, elite bank accounts, third-party brokers and lawyers who connect supposedly isolated Central Asian elites with global centres of power and wealth. These ties and deals have considerable political and security implications.

This interconnectedness may begin in the financial realm but it has economic and political, domestic and international ramifications. Over the past two decades, Central Asian elites have learned to use global financial institutions and offshore vehicles to split the legal personality of nominally state-controlled assets. They have also laundered money through shell companies and structured side-payments from their dealings with external actors, including telecommunications companies, energy multinationals and even foreign militaries.

As researchers, we are only now beginning to comprehend the breathtaking scope and analytical import of these activities. An increasing number of cases have come before Western courts, been the subject of parliamentary investigations or appeared in the international press. In Central Asia, these include Kazakhgate, the Baker Hughes and Kazakhmys cases in Kazakhstan,[38] Asia Universal Bank and Manas jet fuel contracts in Kyrgyzstan,[39] the National Bank and Talco cases in Tajikistan,[40] various examples from Turkmenistan's gas sector,[41] and the ongoing investigation into TeliaSonera in Uzbekistan.[42] In all cases, the use of offshore companies allowed Central Asian regimes to either hide financial transactions or divert state funds into the accounts of leaders and their cronies. These cases are probably the tip of the iceberg. Today, some of the world's biggest banks provide offshore services to Central Asian regimes, as the case of Turkmenistan's presidential Deutsche Bank account shows. But the origins of Central Asia's offshore connections are altogether more ad hoc and adventurous.

One of the earliest and most notorious brokers operating in the region was the American James Giffen, the key figure in Kazakhgate. In the early 1990s, Giffen became a close adviser to the man who remains Kazakhstan's president, Nursultan Nazarbayev. Giffen organised introductions to international energy companies, brokered large deals and acted as a fixer for the ruling family during the first years of independence, eventually earning himself a Kazakh diplomatic passport. He reportedly structured at least six large international oil deals involving American companies that included Texaco, Amoco, Phillips Petroleum and Mobil Oil.[43] He allegedly used a complex network of over thirty offshore bank accounts and shell companies to direct unlawful payments from these oil companies to the personal Swiss bank accounts of 'very senior' Kazakh officials.[44] In 2003, he was arrested at New York's John F. Kennedy airport and indicted for wire and mail fraud, money laundering and violations of the Foreign Corrupt Practices Act (FCPA). In 2010, he pleaded guilty to one violation of the FCPA.[45]

Though Giffen was the quintessential broker, similar roles are now played, though perhaps not with the same public persona, by groups of lawyers and accountants who are skilled in both negotiating contracts and structuring their terms. Particularly notable in the last two decades is the entry of prominent Western law firms who have opened offices in the region, as well as the increasing tendency of local lawyers to have US or English law qualifications, or at least to take a temporary placement at a firm in one of these two countries.[46] The academic literature on kleptocracy suggests that unscrupulous lawyers are usually a key node in transnational laundering networks.[47]

Other stories remain untold, hidden from view. The offshore world provides secrecy and security but it also proffers personnel and advice that enables dictators and their cronies to manage and enhance their ill-gotten gains. Some of this activity is perfectly above board: offshore companies do serve legitimate purposes. They may protect a buyer seeking to make several purchases at once of similar commodities from price-gouging by sellers. More controversially, they enable tax minimisation in order to attract foreign investment. In this sense, the offshore world is integral to the functioning of the world economy, with all of its immense prospects for growth and its deepening inequalities. But there is also a darker side to the offshore realm, not just in the loss of legitimate public funds in the form of tax avoidance, but in the illegal activities it facilitates. These include illicit tax evasion, money laundering and the secret financing of illegal activities such as terrorism and violent rebellion.

As our chapters explore, networks of shell companies have been critical in structuring a range of financial transactions involving Central Asian elites. Shell companies have served as crucial intermediaries in new global networks, supplying the West's intervention in Afghanistan, providing links between Western banks and transnational organised crime in Kyrgyzstan and Tajikistan and facilitating the foreign-financed corruption of the oil and gas sectors of Turkmenistan and Kazakhstan – all the while concealing actors' identities and hiding ownership structures. And as Chapter 1 discusses, Western countries are actually more likely to enable the establishment of anonymous companies than so-called tax havens. So while Western diplomats blame the region's economic problems on a supposed 'disconnectedness', they are usually oblivious to the fact that Western intermediaries, shell company providers and professional brokers have actually set up the legal and financial architectures that facilitate Central Asia's economically destructive capital flight and money-laundering networks.

These, then, are the global links that help produce the greatest security threat for the people of Central Asia: the survival and longevity of predatory regimes that are bleeding their countries dry. In short, Central Asia has been placed at the centre of world politics through a partial process of liberalisation which has connected it to the hidden global financial system of tax havens and shell companies. Central Asia's 'offshore' links are a critical, yet unacknowledged, part of its inherently intertwined domestic and international politics.

Challenges of research

The recent Panama Papers leak notwithstanding, the global industry of tax avoidance and evasion for the super-rich rarely enters the public spotlight. Much of the reason for the lacuna may be that gathering basic facts on the offshore world is no easy task. As Palan, Murphy and Chavagneux remark, there are greater barriers to research on this topic than most:

> They say in financial circles 'those who know do not talk and those who talk don't know'. In tax matters, those who know talk, some-times, but those who do not know talk a lot. The world of tax havens is opaque, confusing and secretive. It is a world that is saturated with stories, rumours and anecdotes. Yet the veritable flood of informa-tion can sometimes hide a dearth of solid data.[48]

In embarking on a book such as this it is very important to be humble about the limits of what can realistically be discovered, in order to avoid simply becoming 'those who talk'. Basic methodological problems of access to sources, reliability of data and validity of findings are particu-larly pronounced in the study of the offshore world. And as Peter Andreas reminds us, the study of the illicit global economy is not only methodologically fraught, it is intertwined in the political agendas of international organisations and bureaucrats who have incentives to selectively engage with the issues.[49] We have faced such obfuscation from potential informants – often Western interviewees who do not want their dubious connections and clients' manoeuvres exposed. We have also seen surprising candour and openness – sometimes from post-Soviet officials alarmed that the regulators of London and New York are so relaxed about money laundering taking place on their watch.

Three qualifications about research methods should be made before we proceed further.

First, there is the dearth of data. It is hard to get documentary sources: offshore transactions are not published and the beneficial owners of companies are not disclosed. Where documents do become available, they often reveal only part of a complex series of transactions. These documents may be leaked or released for political purposes. Company service providers and lawyers are usually bound by professional confidentiality or non-disclosure agreements. Therefore, only fragments of this world are accessible to us, with sources typically becoming available only as the ownership or the legality of transactions are questioned in the courts. Most of the cases covered in this book emerged after legal action such as that against James Giffen,[50] quasi-judicial investigations such as the Tierney report on Kyrgyzstan for the US Congress,[51] or audits requested by international organisations such as the Ernst & Young review of Tajikistan's National Bank.[52] Publicly available data is therefore limited but it is growing with much smaller data leaks preceding that of 2016. In the future, massive data leaks such as that of the Panama Papers will be all the more vital to exploring the general trends and specific cases of the offshore world. In the study of the regulation of tax havens and the offshore world there are many more sources and a 'rhetorical contest', in Sharman's terms, which can be studied; regulators and public officials may also consent to be interviewed.[53] But for this study, we have chosen to stick strictly to public sources and openly available legal records, so that our study is fully replicable: we hope this work will motivate others to delve deeper.

Second, there is the question of the reliability and quality of data. In the complex and multiparty case in the London Court of International Arbitration that addressed the tolling arrangements of Talco, Tajikistan's state aluminium company, many of the disclosed sources were questioned by judges for their reliability. The case dragged on for four years and became the most expensive in British legal history at the time, without coming close to resolution, as multiple judges requested further information. Nine years after the beginning of the initial case, a Swiss court found in favour of a United Company Rusal-owned company but against the position argued by Rusal's lawyers in the earlier trial. When documents are presented in this way through the judicial process we can question whether they are representative and whether they constitute full disclosure. Fragments of data may mislead as much as they lead to reliable conclusions. For these reasons, WikiLeaks' Public Library of US

Diplomacy, otherwise known as PlusD, has been extremely valuable in plugging political-economic analysis into financial data holes.

Third, there is a question of the validity of findings given the unavoidable compromises that must be made in terms of the principles of research design. The hidden nature of offshore communities means that only certain questions can be answered, even then tentatively. The immediate, topical and policy-focused questions of journalists and the regulatory concerns of officials are often not those of academics who consider conceptual questions of the nature of international political economy, the state and regime dynamics. Sources cannot be selected to achieve a representative sample and it is not possible to select cases in a scientific manner; cases arise and only become known as a result of a regime's fall or a struggle between power-holders and their rivals. We may not be able to generalise about the whole of the iceberg from the study of its tip. Academic research in this area can often resemble investigative journalism or the reports of advocacy organisations, or rely on such reporting as a major source. Research by the journalists Steve LeVine, John Helmer and David Trilling and by the NGOs Global Witness and Transparency International *inter alia* has greatly added to our knowledge of the offshore world and provides much of the groundwork that inspired this volume.[54]

These problems of research also beget opportunities for the small band of analysts who study the offshore world.[55] This study requires productive partnership between academics, activists and investigative journalists. We hope this book bears witness to the benefits which such collaboration brings. In working closely with groups such as Global Witness on the offshore economy of tax avoidance and money laundering, and Amnesty International and Human Rights Watch on countering the mechanisms of extraterritorial repression, we have both learnt a great deal about how dictators operate within and beyond borders. Through our information-sharing with investigative journalists, we have better understood complex problems such as Tajikistan's aluminium trading and Kyrgyzstan's fuel contracts. More collaboration across the boundaries of journalism, academic and policy research will be required to push the study of the offshore world forward.

A final challenge, both methodological and ethical, is in the use of deception in research. Experimental, path-breaking research by Jason Sharman, his colleagues and others into the effectiveness of the global anti-money-laundering regimes has involved the impersonation of high-risk clients seeking to set up anonymous companies via offshore jurisdictions or major world financial centres.[56] It is innovative, hard work and great fun – and all the more important in that their findings show that compliance with the global anti-money-laundering regime is weaker in London and New York than in jurisdictions like the British Virgin Islands and the Caymans. The UK Channel 4 programme *From Russia with Cash* involved a similar set-up, with investigative journalists impersonating Russian buyers of high-end West London property, and making it clear that the source of the money for the purchase was corrupt.[57] In this case, all five representatives of leading London real estate agents were apparently ready to proceed with the sale, making no attempt to report to the UK's National Crime Agency, as required by law. The practically ethics-free zones of wealth management and luxury property seem fair game for research but such deception must be done carefully so as not to lead participants towards law-breaking (to confirm a suspicion and hypothesis), and with the public interest in mind.

Our argument

In this book we argue that Central Asia is best understood by focusing on the sprawling, informal transnational links between elites from Astana to London and Bishkek to Beijing. Four of the five Central Asian states are dictatorships whose autocratic presidents rule with an iron fist both at home and abroad. They and their associates use anonymous companies to move money and extraterritorial practices to track down and stifle their opponents. Wherever you are reading this book you may not be far from the registered address of an anonymous company they've used, a PR consultant they've employed, a lobbyist they've contracted, a property they've invested in, or an exile they've had tracked down, arrested, detained or disappeared. More specifically, *Dictators Without Borders* has three aims.

First, we intend to throw light on Central Asian politics writ large – the means by which autocrats operate beyond their borders with money laundering, political influence and brutal violence. We do not assume their targets are necessarily innocent victims. Only a few have been found guilty of law-breaking in an environment where they may receive a fair trial, but it is clear from these cases that Central Asian regimes sometimes have good cause to want to see their opponents behind bars. In other cases, it is very clear that an innocent victim has been targeted because she or he fell out with the wrong people back home. More often it is hard to discern the rights and the wrongs of a given case. But what is clear is that to understand what's going on in Central Asian politics we must stop thinking about these cases as simply 'what goes on in those countries'.

In most cases, the struggles we observe are between the regime and a former insider whose alleged crimes took place as a natural function of being in the very government that is now accusing him of corruption. Mukhtar Ablyazov has been found guilty by a British court of failing to disclose his global network of assets, while Kazakh authorities insist that he embezzled billions of dollars as the head of Kazakhstan's largest bank (see Chapter 2). But what we know from the revelations of the James Giffen affair is that such theft was rife among 'senior Kazakh government officials', right to the very top. The former management of the Tajikistan Aluminium Company certainly did make all kinds of side payments but such corruption is routine in Tajikistan (see Chapter 3). For it to count as corruption surely there has to be some kind of alternative, non-corrupt state of affairs? But no one can imagine the Tajik regime holding together without such payments from clients to patrons and the receiving of favours in return. Uzbekistan's Gulnara Karimova's alleged corruption and power-grabbing may have become so obvious as to endanger the regime in Tashkent but it is this obviousness which is evidently the problem, not the alleged corruption itself (Chapter 4). There is undoubtedly some political motivation for some of those who want to see Maxim Bakiyev behind bars in Kyrgyzstan, but there is also a considerable amount of evidence to suggest that he both provided the political cover for the development of a money-laundering system centred on Kyrgyzstan and conspired in the attempted murder of a rival, a well-known British businessman (Chapter 5).

Second, we aim to highlight the need for regulatory changes in national and global governance to prevent endless repeats of the stories of *Dictators Without Borders*. If this sounds naïve, let us begin with a simple thought: for corrupt money to be laundered it needs a laundry of clean US dollar or euro bills. Without this, it is just corrupt money and worth little to anyone. Laundering is not necessarily straightforward and can be made considerably more difficult with relatively minimal international action, such as minor changes to the law and proper enforcement of existing regulations. The US and UK, despite much positive rhetoric about 'anti-corruption', could do more – much more. Simply increasing the budget and mandate of the UK National Crime Agency's International Corruption Unit may make a big difference. Whilst the UK has increasingly good, but improperly enforced, laws, the US has many loopholes but its enforcers can come down on law-breakers very heavily indeed. Moreover, the operation of offshore finance and international criminal justice cooperation fall inevitably under the purview of international regulators who can change their rules. The offshore economy would be a good deal more transparent and protected from abuse if it were agreed that each jurisdiction should hold a register of beneficial owners. In the security realm, the extraterritorial arm of Central Asian security services can be evaded if foreign govern-ments provide better legal protections and more rapid provision of safe havens to legitimate refugees while cooperating fully to enable prosecu-tion of exiles who are guilty of crimes at home. This is a difficult balance. We will explore some specific recommendations to global governors and regulators in the conclusion of this book.

Third, and finally, we call for a fundamental reassessment of the nature of politics in Central Asia. We need to get beyond the perceived binary division between domestic affairs and foreign affairs. No longer should we think of authoritarianism as overseeing merely internal repression, and foreign affairs as being about strategic interests and geopolitics. Domestic politics also takes place overseas among the regime's opponents who have fled abroad. Foreign affairs also takes place at home as the great games of external powers play out within domestic politics. The book is thus a call to our colleagues in universities to open up their study of both the international relations and comparative politics of Central Asia to consider the inside-out and outside-in dynamics of its political economy.

After presenting an explanatory framework for how Central Asia interacts with the forces of globalisation in the next chapter, across Chapters 2–5 the book tells a series of stories that illustrate these dynamics in four of the five Central Asian states.

As in Turkmenistan's opaque Deutsche Bank accounts, the boundary between domestic and foreign, public and private is blurred in each of these cases from the four other republics. Each case explores the interaction between political and economic developments inside and outside the region. Political contestation, so frequently absent within these authoritarian systems, now takes place beyond their territory. This is as true for more globalised Kazakhstan (Chapter 2), whose government has targeted a number of exiled political opponents residing in London, Los Angeles, Geneva and Cannes, as it is in closed and autarkic Uzbekistan (Chapter 4), where a series of international investigations into alleged money-laundering activities involving the president's daughter appear to have fatally weakened her at home and encouraged her house arrest. It is as critical to remember when observing how Tajikistan's ruling elites (Chapter 3) have battled to consolidate political power and monopolise state wealth, as it is in Kyrgyzstan (Chapter 5), where previous authoritarians and their families now safely reside in exile with their accumulated wealth, perversely using the West's own international legal and humanitarian protections to prevent their own confrontation with justice.

In the final two chapters we turn our attention to international development and security affairs, which are also characterised by the outside-in and inside-out dynamics observed in politics and business.

In Chapter 6, we show how grand geopolitical schemes, as developed by the United States and China, to resurrect the Silk Road and 'connect' the region, both misdiagnose the sources of Central Asia's development problems and ignore the existing informal networks that connect local, regional and global actors with their external patrons. We show how offshore vehicles have been key in facilitating the logistical contracts that have helped to supply the Afghanistan War, including a study of how Russian, Kyrgyz and US officials colluded to produce a fuel-smuggling ring to supply the Manas air base. In the case of China, we show how the country's major acquisitions of Central Asian energy assets, usually structured through offshore intermediaries, were loosely monitored by central authorities and appear to have encouraged shady transactions and local elite corruption schemes, and how these activities are now enmeshed in one of the largest corruption scandals to hit the country. Both Washington and Beijing's plans to promote connectivity by funding large-scale infrastructure projects may actually exacerbate the region's governance problems and further fuel the shadow networks that link the region's kleptocrats and their intermediaries with the world.

In Chapter 7, we demonstrate that in states such as Uzbekistan and Tajikistan where the political opposition has practically disappeared, politics now takes place offshore, as dictators use international institutions such as the Commonwealth of Independent States (CIS) and Interpol to track down, arrest and detain their exiled opponents. When they fail to legally extradite adversaries who would face long prison sentences and torture at home, dictators are able to adopt overseas many of the tactics of arbitrary arrest, violence and kidnapping that they may use at home. This is done by allies in the post-Soviet security networks and contracted agents who have entrapped, maimed and killed in Istanbul, Sweden and further afield. Domestic politics here works inside out. Central Asian dictatorships not only stifle political competition at home but also seek to wipe it out abroad – with varying degrees of success.

Our Conclusion addresses how better enforcement and minimal extension of existing international regulations can close down the offshore and extraterritorial spaces that the region's autocrats now use and abuse. But before then it is vital that we properly understand how Central Asia operates beyond borders. It is to the development of an analytical framework to make sense of these practices and their sources, variations and implications that this book turns next. Our account of how Central Asia went global points to the international linkages and informal transnational networks that we in the West have long ignored.

1

INSIDE-OUTSIDE, ONSHORE-OFFSHORE
HOW CENTRAL ASIA WENT GLOBAL

Central Asia's post-Soviet state-building was part of a broader wave of post-communist transition that coincided with the rapid rise of globalisation. The post-communist states, in Claus Offe's famous formulation, confronted a 'triple transition': from a Communist Party that monopolised politics to a more plural democracy; from a planned economy to a market; and from state-controlled social sphere to an independent civil society.[1] But a generation following the independence of the post-Soviet Central Asian states, this globalised transition, unlike in Eastern Europe, has failed to produce states and polities that conform to the liberal-ideal type of marketised democracies. Politically, the Central Asian states, with the exception of Kyrgyzstan, are all described as 'consolidated authoritarian' by Freedom House in 2016,[2] with regimes steadily accumulating power by shoring up their clients and security services, and cracking down on all forms of political opposition. All of the Central Asian states score poorly on global indicators of economic governance, with corruption, patrimonialism and state predation common practices.[3] And civil society remains embattled throughout the region, facing increasing crackdowns and restrictions on its foreign funding and activities, even as Central Asian elites themselves become more globalised and actively use Western banks, company service providers and legal systems, and acquire luxury real estate.

A tale of two post-communist globalisations: how Central Asia became more authoritarian and more global

This alternative understanding of Central Asia's state-building and global integration is at odds with many assumptions about post-communist pathways. Focusing disproportionately on the relatively successful transition experiences of Eastern Europe, scholars and policy-makers have assumed that all 'liberal' processes and reforms reinforce each other – global integration promotes political and economic reform, which in turn supports and expands civil society. But a brief comparison between the state-building experiences of post-communist Eastern Europe and Central Asia illustrates how their experiences with extrication, international orientation and bargaining with the West differed strikingly; in the Eastern European case, the international environment mostly promoted reforms, while in Central Asia it reinforced global authoritarianism.

First, while Eastern European states created competitive political party systems in an attempt to decisively move away from communism, Central Asians were far more ambiguous about shedding the Soviet past. In Eastern Europe, former communists were either almost instantly discredited through lustration campaigns or had to join reformist parties, property was quickly privatised, and civil societies were empowered. Severe political disruptions from market reforms did not, for the most part, engender political backlashes, as some theorists predicted, while these processes were benchmarked against the standards of neighbouring European democracies.[4]

By contrast, in Central Asia the Soviet Union was abandoned, not overthrown, as Central Asian elites initially feared political life without Moscow's guidance, protection and economic subsidies.[5] Former communist republican parties, led by former party bosses, clung to power, now at a new national level, with little incentive to actually implement political and economic reforms. Only Kyrgyzstan, which had endured an elite purge in late Soviet times, showed signs of genuine political and economic liberalisation, electing a former academic as president.[6] As the 1990s progressed, Central Asian rulers consolidated power, forged large bureaucracies and strengthened the coercive and surveillance capabilities of their loyal security services. Rather than allow competitive political parties, they increasingly marginalised and then banned opposition movements, monopolised power under new nationalist discourses, and structured their political economies to personally take advantage of state assets through insider privatisations. Most political contestation took place through informal channels and networks, rather than the formal party system, while high levels of corruption became entrenched in their weak legal systems.[7]

Second, Eastern Europe and Central Asia's varying geographical contexts and referents produced different experiences of the purpose and form of globalisation. In Eastern Europe, the prospect of joining the European Union as a national project and 'undividing' Europe became a political focal point.[8] In the economy, foreign direct investment from Western Europe surged into the East, as international companies took advantage of newly nearby cheaper labour, as well as anticipating the region's overall future integration into Europe.[9] This European influence was critical in nudging even the laggards of Eastern Europe to undertake more comprehensive institutional changes in the early 2000s. Thus, for ruling elites, mainstream political opposition parties and the public at large, to be global and modern were synonymous with returning to Europe. By contrast, the Central Asian states did initially join broader European institutions such as the Organization for Security and Cooperation in Europe (OSCE), and ratified major human rights treaties, but these actions appeared to be driven more by the need to avoid international opprobrium and to pay lip-service to liberal values.[10] Over time, the Central Asian states were also subject to influence from non-European external patrons and models, most notably Russia and China, which included them in a number of regional economic initiatives such as the Eurasian Economic Union and the Shanghai Cooperation Organisation;[11] from 2000 to 2010, official Central Asian trade with China grew from under $1 billion to over $30 billion, while Russian trade expanded from $5 billion to over $25 billion.[12] In turn, these new regional organisations openly challenged Western liberal democratic norms.[13] China also steadily displaced the West and Western-led financial institutions as the main provider of regional development assistance, infrastructure investment and emergency lending.[14] At the same time, Central Asian elites themselves became more adept at using the global financial institutions, shell companies and legal entities for their own benefit and to structure many of those insider deals that involved state assets.

Finally, the bargaining dynamics between the West, on the one hand, and Eastern Europe and Central Asia in the 2000s helped to reinforce Eastern Europe's liberal trajectory, while fuelling Central Asia's global authoritarian practices. Once they committed to join the European Union, EU conditionality mandated that over 20,000 of the EU's legal standards or the *acquis communautaire* had to be passed by domestic legislatures in almost every area of political, social and economic life. In many cases, this offered lawmakers their political cover to pass unpopular reforms such as liberalising land ownership or protecting minority rights. The EU's strict rules on complete capital account convertibility also ensured that Eastern Europe was rapidly and comprehensively integrated into global financial markets and flows.[15] Eastern European candidate countries had no choice – to join the club they had to accept the strict membership rules and institutional changes mandated by Brussels.[16]

The situation in Central Asia again differed strikingly. Not only was Central Asia untouched by any remote prospect of EU membership, but also the West's leverage in promoting liberal values was undermined by geopolitical developments. Following the attacks of 9/11, the Central Asian states became critical hubs in the US and the International Security Assistance Force's (ISAF's) military campaign and reconstruction efforts in neighbouring Afghanistan. Uzbekistan, Kyrgyzstan and Tajikistan provided logistical military bases for Operation Enduring Freedom (OEF), and all of the Central Asian states provided transit rights for resupply and refuelling.[17] In return, Central Asian rulers overnight became new allies in the Global War on Terrorism and were given unofficial quid pro quo in the form of military assistance and lucrative logistics contracts to support the campaign in Afghanistan; as an extension, both the EU and the US muted criticism of their increasingly authoritarian and rent-seeking tendencies.[18] Supporting the Central

Asian regimes and providing them with the incentives to maintain their security cooperation and maintaining basing access became the overwhelming regional priority of Western governments including the United States, UK, Germany and France.

As geopolitical competition across the region intensified over the 2000s, authoritarianism and governance deteriorated. Under the presidency of Vladimir Putin, Central Asia once again became a strategic priority for the Kremlin, which promoted new economic and security organisations to reintegrate the Central Asian states within Russia's orbit. China too dramatically increased its engagement with the region, both bilaterally and through the SCO, as it attempted to stabilise its borders and crack down on the activities of Uyghur networks that it perceived as fomenting separatism in its adjacent western province of Xinjiang. Then, when a series of post-communist governments were deposed in the mid-2000s in the 'colour revolutions' following rigged elections and replaced by pro-Western alternatives, both Moscow and Beijing strengthened their support for Central Asia's authoritarian rulers and helped them push back against sources of 'destabilising Western influence', including democratic monitors and human rights NGOs. Over 2005 and 2006, all of the Central Asian governments introduced new restrictions on NGOs and the media, and increasingly accused the United States of fomenting instability in the region by promoting its 'values agenda'.[19] Central Asian rulers also invoked geopolitical competition as an excuse to reject external political conditions and supported Russian efforts to scale back the 'human' dimension of the OSCE's activities in the region, such as promoting rigorous and critical election monitoring.[20]

In short, Central Asia and Eastern Europe experienced post-communist extrication and the new international environment as independent states in very different manners. The Central Asian states were not transformed, as Eastern Europe was, by the forces of globalisation and interactions with Western states and international organisations. Quite the contrary, they innovatively used the new opportunities, institutions and legal tools offered by globalisation to pursue their private economic agendas on a more global scale.

Legal globalisation: shell companies and outsourced law

Let us consider more closely the area of legal globalisation. The conventional wisdom is that the globalisation of international law, similar to economic globalisation, improves overall efficiency, especially in conjunction with the harmonising effects of the EU.[21] But over the last two decades, the two prominent extraterritorial legal features involving the Central Asian states have been the central role of offshore registered companies in facilitating international transactions and the outsourcing of legal dispute settlement between contracting parties to international legal venues and third-country courts. Theoretically, the use of offshore subsidiaries by modern multinational enterprises is meant to minimise tax liabilities and move capital to lower-taxed jurisdictions from higher ones. Similarly, the outsourcing of dispute settlement is argued to be a reaction by commercial actors to uncertain institutional environments where the protection and enforcement of property rights is weak. Such institutional weakness was especially characteristic of the post-Soviet states where property rights remained ill-defined during the transition and transacting actors demanded the protections and certainty of Western common law.[22]

But the problem with these 'efficiency' explanations, when applied to Central Asia, is that they assume a private business that acts independently of the state and state-related power structures. However, in Central Asia's patronage-based and authoritarian systems, elite networks were fused with state institutions, and elites actively took advantage of unclear property rights jurisdictions, insider privatisation processes and regulatory bodies to extract private benefits and camouflage their own roles in extracting this wealth. In this type of domestic institutional environment, these legal instruments of globalisation have functioned not as protections *from* the state, but rather as instruments of elite patronage and political contestation *over* the state and its prized assets.

Offshore registries and round-tripping

Data on the use of foreign legal entities that actually conduct business is scarce in Russia, and even scarcer in Central Asia. The difficulties are compounded by the tendency of Central Asian companies to split and spin off portions of their companies to offshore jurisdictions, thereby creating patchwork assemblages of domestic and foreign incorporation and jurisdiction even within the same company. Another common practice involving foreign registered companies is that of 'round-tripping', or 'tolling' – the channelling of funds to special foreign-registered shell companies and legal entities, usually to minimise tax obligations or hide ownership structures, and the subsequent return of these funds to the local economy recorded as foreign direct investment. For example, according to Global Financial Integrity, in 2012 about $403 billion or 61 per cent of Russia's direct outward investment was held in tax havens, with Cyprus the consistently leading source and destination of Russian FDI.[23] In the Russian case, round-tripping has been correlated with the laundering of illicit proceeds and efforts at maintaining secrecy from corrupt regulators and authorities.[24]

The one Central Asian state whose central bank publishes data on investment inflows and outflows by country or place of origin is Kazakhstan and its investment profile is similar to Russia's in its use of the offshore registries of the Netherlands and the British Virgin Islands. In 2012, the Netherlands, one of the leading international centres for company incorporation, accounted for 42 per cent of inward foreign direct investment to Kazakhstan and 58 per cent of all outward flows.[25] The same year the BVI ranked as the third leading source of inward FDI and third biggest destination for outward flows. But these figures tell us very little about the actual national origin and destination of these flows' countries.

Shell companies have also been associated with facilitating high levels of grand corruption on behalf of Central Asian elites. As the case chapters will show, the strategic use of shell companies has been a key weapon used by Central Asian elites who have sought to conceal their own individual transactions and roles in corrupt or questionable deals. Whether used for concealing the extent of ownership of bank holdings from Kazakh regulators, hiding the beneficial owners of a telecommunications licence vendor in Uzbekistan, concealing the dealings of Tajikistan's largest source of export income, covering up the global money-laundering dealings of Kyrgyzstan's largest bank, or structuring Turkmenistan's lucrative but opaque energy trade, shell companies and offshore registries have been at the centre of questionable transactions, international corruption schemes and major acquisitions within the region. One report by Global Witness on Turkmenistan's intermediary energy trading companies found that:

> These companies have often come out of nowhere, parlaying tiny amounts of start-up capital into billion-dollar deals. Their ultimate beneficial ownership has been hidden behind complex networks of trusts, holding companies and nominee directors and there is almost no public information about where their profits go.[26]

In April 2016 the leak of 11.5 million documents of the Panama-based law firm and company provider Mossack Fonseca – now known as the Panama Papers – dramatically highlighted the sheer industrial scale of the use of secret shell companies by international banks, politicians and their agents. The investigation conducted by the International

Table 1.1 Foreign direct investment and round-tripping in Kazakhstan, 2012

Inward direct investment from top five sources			Outward direct investment to top five destinations		
	$ millions	Percentage		$ millions	Percentage
Netherlands	51,419	43%	Netherlands	11,274	51%
United States	12,853	11%	United Kingdom	5,969	26%
France	8,421	7%	Switzerland	835	4%
People's Republic of China (mainland)	5,308	4%	Russian Federation	599	3%
British Virgin Islands	3,862	4%	British Virgin Islands	597	3%
Total inward	119,944	100%	Total outward	22,928	100%

Source: IMF Coordinated Investment Survey, available at: http://cdis.imf.org

Consortium of Investigative Journalists (ICIJ) found nearly 214,000 separate companies that had been established across twenty-one different jurisdictions.[27] In the initial release, the family of Azerbaijan's President Ilham Aliyev was found to hold stakes in a variety of financial, media, insurance, construction and telecoms companies, as well as several luxury real estate holdings in Dubai.[28] A subsequent story by the Organised Crime and Corruption Reporting Project (OCCRP) explored how in Kazakhstan, despite President Nazarbayev's calls for Kazakh citizens to repatriate funds from abroad, 'the documents obtained by OCCRP show that members of the Nazarbayev family were regular users of these same tax havens'.[29] Of particular interest were the offshore holdings of Nurali Aliyev, grandson of Nazarbayev and son of the president's daughter Dariga and his deceased political opponent Rakhat Aliyev, who was found to be the beneficial owner of two BVI companies used for 'operating a bank account and a luxury yacht'.[30] Shortly after, Kazakhstan's prosecutor general ruled out investigating these allegations, arguing that 'there is no reliable information in these materials [the Panama Papers] concerning their source'.[31] In Uzbekistan, the leaks also revealed a 'string of companies' owned by Rustam Madumarov, the former boyfriend of the president's disgraced daughter Gulnara Karimova (Chapter 4), who was jailed in 2014 for ten years on corruption charges.[32] Surveying the importance of the papers to Central Asian elites, Paolo Sorbello and Bradley Jardine conclude that 'these developments suggest that western tax havens have played a crucial role in consolidating political power in the hands of Central Asian elites'.[33]

The politics of enforcing anti-money-laundering rules

But what of the international rules, guidelines and recommendations that have been devised to combat money laundering through secret shell companies? Specifically, the Financial Action Task Force (FATF) has drafted guidelines that include a recommendation that all providers of companies should obtain a notarised proof of identity from the purchaser and a current address. Should not the very attempt of Central

Asian elites involved in corruption-prone sectors such as energy serve as a warning to providers of shell companies and offshore registries?

Work conducted by Michael Findley, Daniel Nielsen and Jason Sharman provides dramatic and sobering results regarding the actual 'due diligence' that company providers around the world conduct to verify the identities of their clients.[34] In an extraordinary social science experiment, the authors sent over 8,000 email solicitations under fictitious identities inquiring about buying a shell company, critically asking whether the purchase could take place without providing internationally recognised identity documents (in violation of globally agreed rules set by the FATF that require company providers to obtain notarised copies of the registrant's identification documents). With this large sample size, the authors used proxy servers to solicit company providers in over 190 different countries, and impersonated potential clients from twelve countries, including four of the Central Asian states, of various professional backgrounds.

Tellingly, for our purposes, over 600 solicitations were sent under fictitious Central Asian names like Abdullo Ogorodov, who described himself as a 'consultant' from a Central Asian country involved in 'government procurement'. The solicitation contained myriad corruption-related red flags that any company provider should pick up on, providing further reason to carefully verify identity information before selling a company. However, the researchers found that the so-called 'Central Asia corruption treatment' made no difference whatsoever to the results – company providers were as likely to flout the rules with such prospective buyers as they were when approached by representatives from 'clean' countries.

Strikingly, the advanced industrialised democracies of the Organisation for Economic Cooperation and Development (OECD), were more likely to sell an anonymous company without proper documentation than providers based in developing countries, with the UK and the US the biggest culprits. The City of London and several US states have, in fact, long been havens for corrupt capital and are accustomed to turning a blind eye. More than that, they brazenly advertise themselves to those that demand secrecy and non-disclosure to law enforcers. The state of Nevada touts its 'limited reporting and disclosure requirements' and a speedy one-hour incorporation service via its website. As reported in *The Economist*, it does not ask for the names of company shareholders, nor does it routinely share the little information it has with the federal government.[35]

In fact, among OECD providers, the research showed that such high-risk figures would need to make only eleven approaches on average before being able to set up an account without the appropriate checks and documentation – what the authors refer to as the 'dodgy shopping count' – while the count for providers in developing countries was about twenty-five approaches.[36] With thousands of companies and brokers in the marketplace the determined money launderer has a high chance of success. This work suggests how relatively easy it is for Central Asian elites, and their designees, to purchase a shell company anonymously in this globalised market.

The failure of even OECD countries and jurisdictions to follow international rules designed to prevent money laundering can be usefully contrasted with how the Central Asian governments them-selves have often politicised anti-money-laundering (AML) norms, using them selectively as legal weapons to clamp down on political opponents and dissidents. One study of the application of AML in the post-communist countries finds that these governments are especially prone to 'using AML mechanism to target political opponents', including 'opposition leaders'.[37] The authors cite prominent examples such as the Uzbek government's targeting of opposition leader Sanjar Umarov in 2006 on counts of money laundering, as well as other leading Uzbek human rights defendants. Chapter 2 will show how the Kazakh government has consistently deployed accusations of money laundering and financial crimes in their efforts to extradite and freeze the assets of political opponents residing abroad. And in yet another unintended political consequence, new global guidelines on AML and terrorist financing have been used by Central Asian governments as justifica-tions to further restrict the activities of NGOs, especially those with foreign funding.[38]

Legal outsourcing and arbitration

Whilst foreign-registered shell companies have facilitated round-tripping, money laundering and secrecy, the outsourcing of legal jurisdiction and adjudication to foreign courts has shifted the sites of legal contestation over important Central Asian assets to outside of the region. Many of these international disputes feature litigants from the same country and within the post-Soviet region, even as they act through foreign-registered affiliates and designees. In turn, a host of international judicial actors and Western professionals have benefited from and encouraged this lucrative 'outflow' of legal proceedings.[39] Legal outsourcing has taken a number of transnational forms and modalities.

First, since independence, Central Asian elites and their foreign-registered companies have entered into a number of different commercial agreements that effectively outsourced their governance and adjudication to UK law. Though no official statistics are kept on national origins of litigants, one *Financial Times* report from late 2011 estimated that about half of all active cases in the English Commercial Court had connections to Russia and the former Soviet states,[40] while a High Court judge noted that from March 2008 to March 2013, out of 705 rulings by the Commercial Court, 61 per cent of litigants were from outside the UK, with many from 'Russia, Eastern Europe and Central Asia who amassed wealth following the break-up of the Soviet Union'.[41]

Jurisdictionally, cases can be brought under UK law in three main ways: if one of the litigants is physically present in the UK (regardless of whether she is a UK national or permanent resident) or if a company is registered or listed in the UK; by 'party autonomy' or mutual consent to have UK law govern the transactions; and by 'service out of the jurisdiction', which involves UK courts exercising discretion to assume jurisdiction, despite the objections of one or more of the parties, should the court find that it is the 'natural forum' (as opposed to the home country court) or determine that the home country court cannot provide justice in the case.[42] This designation was used to justify the proceedings of the *Tajik Aluminium Plant v Ermatov* case, described in Chapter 3, which became one of the most expensive cases in UK Commercial Court history.[43]

The second major institutional mechanism for outsourcing legal proceedings has been the activation of international arbitration clauses in bilateral investment treaties (BITs).[44] According to one survey, as of January 2013 the Central Asian states were parties to a total of 176 BITs, with Uzbekistan party to the most agreements (49), followed by Kazakhstan (42), Tajikistan (32), Kyrgyzstan (29) and Turkmenistan (24).[45] International arbitration judgments are enforceable through the New York Convention (1959), which permits damaged parties to seek to petition for the recovery of sovereign assets of the losing party in any third country that is a signatory to the treaty.

In the period following the ousting of Kyrgyzstan's President Kurmanbek Bakiyev, Kyrgyz authorities were taken to court nine times around the world, including formal legal proceedings in Ontario, Moscow, Paris and The Hague. Most of these cases involved legal disputes over alleged breaches of contracts in the area of mining and financial institutions, with the cumulative awards and legal fees amounting to nearly $1 billion dollars, about the equivalent of the annual Kyrgyz state budget.[46] The hearings included three cases of bank nationalisations, that of Manas Bank, owned by the Latvian businessman Valeri Belokon, Asia Universal Bank, site of allegations of money laundering (Chapter 5), and BTA Bank, subsidiary of Kazakh BTA. In the first two cases, Kyrgyz officials claim that these financial institutions were repurposed as money-laundering vehicles during the Bakiyev era. However, arbitrators in 2014 issued a $16.5 million judgment in favour of Belokon, brought under the Latvia–Kyrgyzstan BIT, while the Asia Universal case remained active into 2016.[47] With the Kyrgyz government unwilling and seemingly unable to pay these judgments, foreign investors, in turn, explored and initiated proceedings for claiming Kyrgyz sovereign assets in third-party areas, most notably Kyrgyz government shares in gold-mining joint ventures.[48]

Third, the Central Asian states have also entered into a number of regional and multilateral sets of rules governing investment, such as the general investment treaty of the Commonwealth of Independent States (also known as the Moscow Convention for the Protection of Investment Rights) and the Energy Charter Treaty, which provide for international arbitration for dispute settlement.

Fourth, domestic legislation within the Central Asian states has also allowed for foreign investors to refer disputes to an arbitration panel. For example, Kyrgyz legislation gives broad consent, even in the absence of a specific arbitration clause in an investment agreement, for the investor to initiate a dispute in the International Centre for Settlement of Investment Disputes (ICSID) or another UN-recognised commercial court.[49] One comprehensive review of Central Asian states' international arbitrations estimated that as of 2013, of the thirty-eight cases involving the Central Asian states, twenty-two were brought under a BIT, six were brought under the Energy Charter Treaty, and the rest were unclear.[50] Most of the cases involved disputes in the energy, mining, construction and telecommunications industries, with most claimants described as medium- and small-sized companies, as opposed to large multinational corporations, originating mostly from Western states and Turkey.

Diffusing law or a globalised legal Tower of Babel?

But far from clarifying investment rules and procedures, the onset of outsourced litigations appears to have further emphasised the fragmented and selective nature of Central Asia's relationship with international rules and standards. Though most of the hearings remain confidential, we do know from some completed cases with public records that a significant amount of time and resources in these proceedings are devoted to establishing the actual identity and nationality of the litigants, especially if the case is being adjudicated under a BIT. At times, the proceedings have highlighted the fragmented status of the parties' international legal personas, with disagreements over which language and texts should apply in arbitration proceedings.[51]

One other area of political and legal irony is the use of domestic corruption accusations to void the validity of international arbitration clauses. In *Metal Tech v Uzbekistan*, an Israeli mining investor tried to take the government of Uzbekistan to the ICSID for a forced expropriation that it argued clearly fell under the jurisdiction of the Israel–Uzbekistan BIT. However, the ICSID ultimately refused to consider the case because the claimant admitted to structuring a number of payments as bribes (amounting to about 20 per cent of the overall investment) to government-connected 'consultants', in violation of Uzbekistan's anti-bribery laws and international public policy norms against corruption.[52] In essence the decision meant that once a company admitted to bribing officials as part of its transaction with the host country – in this case Uzbekistan, which ranks very poorly on all international transparency and anti-corruption indicators – it essentially forfeits its right to an international arbitral claim. The case was the first ICSID decision to deny a BIT claim due to corruption.[53]

In sum, although legal globalisation has played a pivotal role in the legal and commercial landscape of the Central Asian states, it has not advanced global governance or standards of accountability. Instead, Central Asian litigants, elites and governments have actively wielded the law and legal proceedings for their own political and economic purposes, often mixing their private agendas with state obligations and protections.

Globalising Central Asia's elites: a transnational 'uncivil society'?

As Central Asian elites have enmeshed their transactions in a variety of global legal forums and institutions, they have embedded themselves outside the region by globalising their identities, citizenships and places of residence. Far from the stereotype of 'disconnected backwaters', Central Asian elites rank among the world's most active cosmopolitans and socialites, directing charities and foundations in parallel with their political and business activities. Stories of decadent parties and lavish lifestyles have grabbed occasional international media headlines, but it is worth thinking analytically about the legal processes that have allowed Central Asian elites to live and work abroad, often with perceived impunity.

Global citizenship and residence: diplomatic status, investor residences and asylum

First, diplomatic service is a common way for Central Asian elites to live overseas and cultivate their international networks. Diplomatic service also affords diplomatic immunity from international investigations and prosecutions of crimes, a perk that is especially appealing for Central Asian elites.[54] One of the most high-profile and controversial examples of a Central Asian elite diplomat is that of Gulnara Karimova, daughter of Uzbekistan's long-serving first president Islam Karimov (1991–2016). Karimova, as we explore in Chapter 4, has been connected to several money-laundering investigations around the world during the time she served in a number of diplomatic positions. Meanwhile, Gulnara Karimova's estranged sister, Lola Karimova-Tillyaeva, has served since 2008 as Uzbekistan's envoy to UNESCO in Paris, building a number of European-centred networks.

In Tajikistan, President Rahmon's eldest daughter Ozoda Rahmonova was appointed deputy foreign minister in 2010 after working for just two years in the ministry and then, in 2016, made chief of staff to the president.[55] The two daughters of Turkmenistan president Gurbanguly Berdimuhamedov resided in London and Paris as a result of their spouses receiving official diplomatic appointments. The eldest, Guljahan, is married to Dovlet Atabayev, who rose spectacularly through the state's energy sector and was appointed as director of the London head office of the Turkmen State Agency for Management and Use of Hydrocarbon Resources.[56] A US embassy cable reported that Atabayev subsequently became the target of an internal investigation in Turkmenistan, noting that 'Supposedly, the young man is in trouble for having acquired some nice real estate in the London area.'[57]

A second method of gaining global citizenship and residency is to openly purchase a passport or to obtain a residency through one of a number of blossoming investor-residency programmes. The 'second citizenship' market appears to be growing as a result of demand from elites and private actors to increase their global mobility.[58] The pioneering provider in this area is the Caribbean island state of St Kitts and Nevis, which sells passports without even a residency requirement. The passport is appealing as it provides visa-free travel to much of the OECD, including Canada and the EU.[59] An array of Central Asian fugitives accused of embezzlement and corruption have produced passports from the island state to apply for political asylum overseas.[60]

Central Asian elites and oligarchs have also acquired overseas residences, passports and citizenship by participating in a growing number of investor-residency programmes. Since the great financial crisis, more than half of all OECD countries have instituted new or refashioned residency-for-purchase programmes.[61] Portugal, Cyprus and Malta openly award passports to investors which, once obtained, afford the holders free movement and rights of residency in the European Union's Schengen Area.[62] Since its adoption of a similar 'golden visa' programme in 2010 for external investors in property or financial institutions, Latvia, a member of the EU's Schengen zone, has become the favoured overseas destination for Russians and Central Asians; according to one report, from 2010 to 2015 the Latvian government awarded 1,525 such visas to Uzbek nationals.[63] A number of private law firms and second-citizenship consulting agencies also appear to be expanding their business to introduce these programmes to high-net-worth individuals, some specifically targeting Kazakh and other post-Soviet clients.[64]

Another popular destination for investor visas has been the United Kingdom. According to UK authorities, between 2011 and 2013, under the revamped Tier 1 Investor Residency programme, forty-one Kazakh nationals were afforded UK residency, ranking the UK the sixth largest single country recipient of such permits.[65] The programme, according to the UK Home Office, 'is for people with high net worth to make a substantial financial investment in the UK' – as of 2016, no less than £2 million.[66] Under the programme, recipients are afforded a three-year residency with the possibility of applying for an additional two-year extension. Following a six-year period, they can then qualify for actual citizenship.

Finally, Central Asian elites have managed to secure residency abroad by successfully petitioning for political asylum. Given the fact that all of the Central Asian states, with the partial exception of Kyrgyzstan, have been governed by authoritarian regimes with poor human rights records, estranged officials and dissidents seeking to leave can make credible cases, under international human rights law, that returning to their native country would subject them to political discrimination and/or torture. As Chapter 2 shows, a slew of Kazakh elites, former government officials and insiders have secured residency and citizenship abroad by claiming political persecution by authorities in Astana. Once political asylum is granted, most countries offer subsequent pathways to permanent residency and even citizenship.

Even the son of ousted Kyrgyz autocrat Kurmanbek Bakiyev has managed to secure residency in the UK by credibly claiming that he would be subjected to persecution and unfair legal procedures in Kyrgyzstan, as Chapter 5 makes clear. Bakiyev, generally detested in Kyrgyzstan and convicted in Kyrgyz courts for embezzlement and ordering the murder of a British national in a gold-mining deal, has thus managed skilfully to use Western legal protections to shield himself from return to the small Central Asian state. According to one report, he currently resides in a £3.5 million Surrey mansion that was purchased by Limium, an 'anonymous company' registered in Belize.[67] He became eligible to apply for permanent UK residency in June 2015 and for UK citizenship in June 2016.[68]

The high-profile case of Rakhat Aliyev, the controversial former son-in-law of Kazakhstan president Nursultan Nazarbayev, illustrates how all three of these citizenship tools have been deployed by exiles to resist their return to Central Asia. Aliyev was married to the president's eldest daughter, Dariga Nazarbayeva, and in February 2007 was appointed as Kazakhstan's ambassador to Austria and permanent representative to the OSCE. After a falling out with Nazarbayev in May 2007, Aliyev was recalled and formally charged with fraud and abduction. However, the former diplomat successfully applied for political asylum in Austria and used his international contacts and standing to avoid return. He settled in Malta, where he obtained citizenship, during which time both Malta and Austria refused Kazakh requests for extradition on the grounds of human rights concerns. Living overseas, he became an outspoken critic of Nazarbayev, authoring the highly publicised exposé *The Godfather-in-Law* in which he made many allegations about the Kazakh regime's corrupt dealings and international criminal networks. In February 2015, he was remanded in Austrian custody after prosecutors there charged him separately for the murder of two former senior executives at Nurbank JSC in 2007.[69] Aliyev was found dead of an apparent suicide by hanging in his jail cell in Vienna in February 2015 while awaiting trial for murder. Though prison officials described his death as a 'clear suicide', his lawyer disagreed, stating that his client had shown no signs of suicidal tendencies the day prior to his death.

The politics of luxury real estate

Along with attaining global residence and citizenship, Central Asian elites have invested heavily in luxury real estate across the world, including in London, Paris, St Tropez, New York, Los Angeles, Miami and Geneva. A number of studies by NGOs and transparency watchdogs have explored how real estate investments are often used to assist in money laundering. Possible red flags include the purchase of real estate by designated shell companies registered offshore as well as purchase prices significantly exceeding asking prices.

Real estate is viewed as an increasingly useful way of laundering ill-gotten proceeds because of the generally more lax rules associated with settling transactions in cash. For example, in the United States, real estate brokers are exempt from 'know thy client' regulations mandated on banks conducting transactions, while in London, the world's premier luxury market, such due diligence, while legally mandated for sellers, is not required at all of purchasers.

Appendix 1, compiled from public news sources and investigative reports, details some of the more high-profile purchases by Central Asian elites and oligarchs. These include a $32.75 million Beverly Hills mansion bought by Lola Karimova – President Karimov's second daughter – and her husband that, according to an industry estimate, constituted the most expensive sale in the Los Angeles area real estate market in the year 2013.[70] During her diplomatic postings, Gulnara Karimova purchased luxury properties, including an $18 million villa in Geneva in 2009, and acquired properties in France and Hong Kong (see Chapter 4).

Perhaps most dramatically, the purchase of the Duke of York's Berkshire estate by Kazakh presidential son-in-law Timur Kulibayev for

£15 million (£3 million over the asking price) is just one of many acquisitions made by Kazakh oligarchs in the UK luxury market.[71] Chapter 2 explores how the Kazakh tycoon Mukhtar Ablyazov purchased luxury properties in London's Hampstead and an estate in Surrey, both via shell companies registered in offshore jurisdictions. And, following the mysterious death of Rakhat Aliyev in his Austrian prison, the London-based watchdog Global Witness released a report claiming that a network of offshore companies linked to the Kazakh tycoon acquired £147 million of London properties, which included 221 Baker Street, site of the legendary 221B Baker Street address of fictional detective Sherlock Holmes.[72]

A transnational 'uncivil society'

Central Asia's globalised elite provides a strong counter to stereotypes of the region's 'isolation' or purported lack of global connections. The point can be pushed further to argue that it is precisely this group of Central Asian oligarchs and government officials, entangled in these international networks, business activities, multiple residencies and luxury real estate holdings, who are the most 'globalised'.

Taken as a category, they constitute what we might term, playing on Stephen Kotkin's revisionist formulation, a post-Soviet transnational 'uncivil society' – a group of elites and entrepreneurs who operate beyond borders, but who do not hold the liberal principles or share the democratic agendas normally associated with members of 'civil society'.[73] Oligarchs and political elites may fund international charities and cultural events, but their political attentions are primarily dedicated to image-crafting and asset protection. Kotkin's double term also finds a transnational counterpart in contemporary Central Asia and the way scholars have used formulations such as 'transnational networks' and 'civil society' to describe the region's fledgling liberal activist networks and embattled civic organisations.[74] Though myriad NGOs were initially created across the region, they have been demonised as unwelcome foreign forces, their political role has been increasingly marginalised, and they have been subjected to ever-greater funding and registration restrictions: their actual sustainability is now in doubt.[75]

Hunted overseas: opposition politicians go global

As Central Asian elites have globalised their private lives and activities, they have also turned their sovereign power abroad to target political opponents. While the authority of Central Asian rulers remains unchallenged at home, decades of domestic authoritarianism has generated an increasing number of disaffected former government elites, political allies and family members who have fallen out with regimes and fled abroad. Political opposition and political contestation mostly operates from exile. In the case of Kazakhstan, as Chapter 2 explores, a host of former regime officials – including a prime minister, national security chief and presidential son-in-law – who have clashed with the iconic President Nazarbayev during his twenty-five-plus years in power have sought refuge abroad. In some cases, such as that of the banking tycoon Mukhtar Ablyazov or former Almaty mayor Viktor Khrapunov, they have even actively supported opposition movements from abroad and funded oppositional media to broadcast within their home country.

Critically, Central Asian governments have not passively accepted the rise of this 'opposition in exile'. Rather, they have responded by conflating their battles with political opponents with matters of state, and have used international state mechanisms and law enforcement tools to target their critics abroad. The diplomatic priorities of the Central Asian states, rather than pursuing national interests, have often become global projections of these authoritarian agendas. These are explored in more depth in Chapter 7, but here we briefly note four broad categories of such authoritarian foreign policy practices: regional security treaties; international litigations; diplomatic image-crafting; and extraterritorial actions by security services and their agents.

First, all of the Central Asian governments have institutionalised new extraterritorial powers to more easily extradite political dissidents living abroad through the use of new regional security and anti-terror treaties such as the Minsk Convention and SCO Counter-Terrorism Convention. The SCO Counter-Terrorism Convention, signed and ratified in 2009 by its member states (China, Russia, Kazakhstan, Kyrgyzstan, Tajikistan and Uzbekistan), grants broad authority to governments to demand the extradition of individuals living abroad simply based on accusation (without accompanying asylum hearings), gives security services of one state signatory the right to conduct investigations on each other's territory, and allows for the creation of a common blacklist of 'extremists, terrorists, and separatists' without accompanying procedures for review or delisting.[76] Human rights groups have criticised the impact of these treaties on safeguarding international human rights commitments, while some monitors have observed that Central Asian prosecutors and government authorities have justified the extradition of wanted political opponents as obligations to these regional treaties, noting that they violate basic international humanitarian norms such as the principle of non-refoulement.[77] As Russian investigative journalists Andrei Soldatov and Irina Borogan have noted, these new regional security treaties have enabled a number of renditions and extraditions across Eurasia, effectively ending the use of Russian territory as a 'safe space' for Central Asian political opponents.[78]

Second, Central Asian authorities have also marshalled a variety of international legal tools and law enforcement procedures to attempt to secure the extradition of political opponents and to target their assets. Central Asian governments have been among the most active users of the Interpol Red Notice system. Interpol, the International Criminal Police Organization founded in 1923, is charged with coordinating and networking the activities of its more than 190 member states. Interpol itself has no global enforcement powers, but it provides a number of tools to its members to aid in the cooperation against transnational crime, provided that they remain in accordance with countries' own domestic laws and the spirit of the United Nations Universal Declaration of Human Rights. Chief among these is its issuing of colour-coded warnings known as the 'notice system', in which 'Red Notices' function as a criminal designation akin to an international arrest warrant that empowers member countries to detain and extradite individuals for crimes committed in third-country jurisdictions.[79] However, as revealed in a recent report by the watchdog Fair Trials International, the system is ripe for abuse by authoritarian countries, which routinely list political opponents and activists as international criminals.[80]

Central Asian governments and their agents have also utilised the authority of the state in order to initiate international legal proceedings against exiles on financial crimes charges. Political scientist Keith Darden has argued that in post-Soviet states where corruption is pervasive, the use of *kompromat* and blackmail over financial crimes is an essential tool of control and compliance by presidents over their elites.[81] Darden's analysis can be usefully extended extraterritorially, as regimes can use state institutions such as financial agencies and the prosecutor's office to accuse exiled political opponents of financial crimes and target them with anti-money-laundering investigations, asset freezes, Interpol Red Notices and international litigations. Given that a large group of these exiles are estranged former government officials who amassed their fortunes through insider privatisations, especially in countries where property rights and the rule of law are weak, the accusations of economic crimes are plausible, if unremarkable. Nevertheless, they serve as a useful basis to reach out to regulatory counterparts in countries hosting exiles such as the UK, Switzerland, France and the United States.

Other international legal actions are more obviously orchestrated purely for political purposes. In 2011, Lola Karimova sued a French news site for libel for calling her the Uzbek 'dictator's' daughter. In the ruling against Karimova's claim and request for damages, the judge ruled that the article was 'entirely true to reality'.[82] But the proceeding also seemed to backfire when it drew attention to the fact that the EU had funded some official project assistance for Karimova's charitable activities, leading to a backlash among European MPs.[83] In a similar spirit, in 2014, the Kazakh government initiated a legal proceeding in a New York federal district court, under a US federal statute, against the opposition newspaper *Respublika*, in an effort to close down the newspaper's website for leaking classified documents while attempting 'to pry personal information about *Respublika* employees and volunteers'.[84]

Third, Central Asian governments have become increasingly adept at leveraging overseas representatives and envoys both to promote positive images of their countries and to designate political opponents as 'criminals', as opposed to political dissidents. Often, these campaigns have directly targeted legislators and officials in countries that host exiled opponents, such as Switzerland.[85]

But a more informal, indirect type of political influence and lobbying has also emerged – what journalist Casey Michel has referred to as 'free agent diplomacy'.[86] This involves a set of policy institutions, analysts and academics who appear to have close ties to or contracts with Central Asian governments and their official positions, but fail to disclose them when writing commentaries and op-eds or presenting projects about the region. One journalistic investigation into influence activities on behalf of Talco Management Ltd (TML), the management company of the Tajik Aluminium Company registered in the BVI, found that TLM had contracted Fabiani & Company to formally lobby for Western support for a dam project and to paint a favourable picture of Tajikistan in the US media.[87] Among these activities, Fabiani admitted to paying a writer for upbeat pieces about the corruption-ridden Central Asian country in publications like *Forbes* (see Chapter 3).[88] Other reports have documented the Kazakh government's funding of research and analysis by reputable Washington-based think tanks – including the Center for Strategic and International Studies and the Atlantic Council – that paint it in a glowing light, including an event at the Atlantic Council commemorating the twentieth anniversary of Kazakhstan's independence that was entirely sponsored by the Kazakh government.[89] In Brussels, Kazakhstan funded the establishment of a new think tank, the Eurasian Council of Foreign Affairs, with a high-profile board including the former UK foreign secretary Jack Straw.[90] In addition, Astana has funded a number of international sporting, cultural, educational and diplomatic events and activities whose primary purpose is to promote a positive image of the country and its leadership.[91]

Finally, in a certain category of cases, usually when these legal tools and channels of influence have proven insufficient, Central Asian rulers have sent their security services abroad to forcibly return home or even to attempt to eliminate opponents. From 2001 to 2005, Central Asia was a hub for the practice of 'extraordinary rendition', the forcible abduction of suspected terrorists, extremists and political dissidents carried out by the United States, China and Russia in collaboration with Central Asian security services.[92] Yet Central Asian security services have gone further, with mounting evidence of extraterritorial activities against exiled political dissidents becoming routine. Chapter 7 recounts the increasing extraterritorial renditions, surveillance activities and assassinations carried out against political opponents residing abroad, with a focus on the political refugees who fled Uzbekistan following the Andijan crackdown in May 2005, as well as the campaign against Tajikistan's exiled political opponents in Russia and Turkey. As Central Asia's oppositional politics has become more globalised, the Central Asian regimes and their security apparatuses have relentlessly followed suit.

Globalised, connected – and unapologetically authoritarian

Purchases of luxury real estate, the strategic use of shell companies for business transactions, the carrying of multiple passports, the outsourcing of legal disputes to international courts, and active security service campaigns targeting exiled opposition leaders: these are not typically thought of characterising Central Asia's purportedly isolated elites and disconnected governance structures.

Yet the conventional wisdom is simply and spectacularly wrong. Central Asia has become significantly globalised and embedded into a number of transnational networks, but not in the manner that is typically thought of by globalisation theorists and Western policy officials. The region's politics have become increasingly authoritarian and restrictive, even as these governments have increased their interactions with global institutions and transnational networks. Central Asian elites have deployed the resources of the sovereign state extraterritorially, while using the protections and services provided by institutions of global governance to safeguard their own individual safety.[93] Politics, like economic transactions, have been taken offshore. The remarkable case of Mukhtar Ablyazov, a Kazakh political insider turned economic fugitive and leading critic of the Kazakh government, dramatically demonstrates these trends.

KAZAKHSTAN'S MOST WANTED

ECONOMIC FUGITIVE OR DEMOCRATIC CHAMPION?
THE CASE OF MUKHTAR ABLYAZOV

Since independence, Kazakh politics has revolved around the rule of its first and only president Nursultan Nazarbayev.[1] The last Communist Party boss of the Kazakh Republic in late Soviet times, Nazarbayev was elected first president of independent Kazakhstan in 1991 and since has been re-elected four times, most recently in 2015. In 2007, Nazarbayev signed a constitutional amendment allowing him to stay in office for an unlimited number of terms. The president's supporters argue that he remains a highly popular figure domestically and has shown a skilful and steady hand, effectively cultivating Kazakhstan's new identity, developing a modern and stable state, and establishing the newly independent country as a crossroads of civilisations in the heart of Eurasia.[2] His political opponents and critics maintain that this carefully crafted image belies a record of ruthlessly targeting political opponents and using the resources of the state to promote the fortunes of his family and well-connected insiders.[3] Scholars have noted the relative skill and sophistication through which the Kazakh regime has itself pioneered new techniques of image-crafting, media manipulation and clientelism, distinguishing its 'soft authoritarianism' from the country's more overtly repressive regional counterparts.[4]

Kazakh elite politics under Nazarbayev is frequently, and persuasively, characterised as 'patrimonial' or 'neo-patrimonial', emphasising that the ruling regime monopolises power by dispersing selective bene-fits, drawn from state assets and state positions, to loyal supporters via formal and informal channels.[5] But irrespective of how we choose to characterise the form and legitimacy of Kazakhstan's ruling regime, to exclusively focus on political trends and patronage dynamics *within* Kazakhstan in the 2000s risks missing some of the most important actual developments in Kazakh elite politics – the global exile of Kazakhstan's political opposition. As the political space within the country and the region has shrunk and power has increasingly become centralised, political opponents and disaffected officials have fled the country. In some cases, these exiles have agreed not to enter the political sphere, but in others they have energetically funded and supported opposition movements and media outlets from abroad. In turn, the Kazakh government has vigorously pursued these overseas political opponents using a mix of international legal tools, including anti-money-laundering laws, asset freezes and extradition requests, and direct diplomatic pressure exerted on foreign governments and law enforce-ment agencies.

This chapter focuses upon the political fortunes of one of the most intriguing and controversial figures of this Kazakh 'offshore opposition' – that of the billionaire tycoon Mukhtar Ablyazov. Once Nazarbayev's trusted political ally, having served as minister of energy, industry and trade in the late 1990s, Ablyazov dramatically fell out with the president after he involved himself in oppositional politics, co-founding the Democratic Choice of Kazakhstan movement in 2001. He was convicted and imprisoned in 2002, but was released in 2003 after allegedly agreeing to cease political activities and focus on business affairs. Ablyazov then left Kazakhstan for Russia, but returned again in 2005 to become chairman of BTA Bank, the country's largest financial institution. Following the onset of the financial crisis and a crash in value of many of the bank's holdings and derivatives, Ablyazov was accused of one of the most elaborate financial crimes of our era, as he allegedly embezzled billions of dollars from Kazakhstan's largest bank through a complex array of offshore legal schemes.[6] He then proceeded to claim political asylum in Western Europe and present himself as a democratic champion and opponent of Nazarbayev's rule, while Kazakhstan relent-lessly pursued his arrest and extradition.

Almost every aspect of the Ablyazov case is contested. Public opinion in Kazakhstan and abroad is sharply divided over whether Ablyazov is a political dissident and whistleblower or a fugitive who cynically presents himself as a democratic activist. His struggle against the long transnational reach of the Kazakh government is inextricably bound with a broader campaign to democratise and depersonalise the Kazakh political system. From his perspective, the Kazakh regime has ruthlessly targeted him at home and abroad, stripping him of his BTA Bank hold-ings through a predatory nationalisation and deploying the long arm of Kazakh law enforcement and the foreign service apparatus against him in what he insists is a personal vendetta. In legal proceedings, Ablyazov has consistently proclaimed his innocence, insisting that all charges of financial crimes levelled against him are politically motivated, while his supporters maintain that his cardinal sin was to violate a pledge to Nazarbayev that he would stay out of politics after he was released from prison in 2003.

Yet, evidence from the legal hearings suggests that the Kazakh banker had personally designed a vast complex of offshore vehicles in order to mask his ownership of certain assets. Moreover, international courts have consistently ruled against Ablyazov in his fierce interna-tional legal battles with BTA, now under de facto Kazakh state control, while a UK court found him in contempt for failing to fully disclose his assets and violating a court freezing order. Subsequent attempts by the new BTA management to recover his assets revealed an array of global holdings, including lavish properties in London and Paris. After his capture and arrest by French authorities in 2013, his extradition hear-ings attracted intense international attention.

For the Kazakh government, Ablyazov is a clear-cut financial criminal, who has styled himself a democrat to deflect international attention from his alleged transgressions. The regime maintains that the billionaire's framing of his personal actions as part of a broader democratic crusade is nothing more than a cynical attempt to manipu-late international public opinion and find allies among Western governments, international organisations and NGOs, eager to criticise Kazakhstan's political practices.

Still, this official characterisation fails to account for the sheer zeal and significant state resources that have been deployed in the international effort to fight Ablyazov. A more convincing explanation for the government of Kazakhstan's obsession may be found in the fact that Ablyazov's acts took place while he was part of the country's political and business elite. His story reveals a great deal about how this elite operates at home and abroad and is therefore hugely embarrassing to the regime. Moreover, in its unrelenting campaign against the tycoon the Kazakh government has severely compromised its own credibility: Astana has cracked down on media outlets and political organisations that Ablyazov has supported and been associated with, while authorities have targeted Ablyazov's family and associates with a broad range of international legal and extralegal tools. Moreover, the campaign waged against Ablyazov has been mirrored by similar campaigns launched against a group of exiled Kazakh elites who once were close to the presidential regime, including a former prime minister, a national security chief and, most dramatically, the president's own former son-in-law. Thus, the Ablyazov case, while unprecedented in terms of the scale of its financial dealings, is part of a broader global political struggle between the Kazakh government and its exiled opponents.

Kazakhstan's 'Enron': the fight for BTA and Ablyazov's offshore dealings

Ablyazov's first forays into business coincided with the new opportunities brought by Kazakhstan's independence. In 1992 he founded Astana Holdings, a private equity company. In 1998 he led a group of investors in acquiring Bank TuranAlem (BTA) through a voucher privatisation, just after he had successfully restructured an electricity company. Following his imprisonment and exile in Russia from 2003 to 2005, Ablyazov was invited back as chairman of the board. Initially, the bank appeared to thrive, wooing foreign investors and institutional clients and presenting itself as Kazakhstan's dynamic flagship financial institution. But as the global real estate bubble popped and financial crisis hit in 2008, many of BTA's deals went sour and the bank was effectively nationalised in February 2009, when the Kazakh sovereign wealth fund injected liquidity to keep it afloat.

Ablyazov and his lawyers have denied allegations of embezzlement and fraud; however, they have admitted to designing hundreds of offshore deals between 2005 and 2009 to restructure the bank's holdings in order to conceal their ownership from Kazakh regulators.[7] Further, it appears that the pattern of Ablyazov concealing the extent of his ownership goes back even further. At an arbitral hearing under the auspices of the ICSID, Ablyazov revealed that in 2002, when he first went to jail, he had temporarily re-assigned all of his shares in BTA to his associate Yerzhan Tatishev to 'prevent a seizure by President Nazarbayev'.[8] In turn, this allowed Tatishev to allegedly make 'a public announcement that Mr. Ablyazov no longer had any shares in BTA'.[9]

The BTA scandal

Kazakh authorities, and several international financial media reports, present the BTA scandal as a case of clear fraud and embezzlement, one of the most audacious and complex ever committed.[10] BTA's new management accused Ablyazov of defrauding the bank of billions by lending money to a number of shell companies of which Ablyazov was the beneficial owner, and assigning assets and loans on 'terms that were unfavorable to BTA'.[11] Between 2003 and 2007, the bank's outstanding loans grew by 1,100 per cent as it acquired an international reputation for aggressive investments that yielded eye-popping results; Western institutional investors – including Royal Bank of Scotland, Barclays and HSBC – poured about $10 billion into the Kazakh bank.[12] This reliance on foreign funds, as opposed to domestic deposits, raised BTA's reported loans-to-deposits ratio to 3.6:1 in 2007, reportedly 'one of the highest anywhere in the world'.[13] In total, BTA is estimated to have borrowed up to $15 billion from external sources, while according to BTA lawyers and Kazakh prosecutors, between $8 billion and $12 billion worth of loans – about half of its loan book – were funnelled to offshore shell companies that Ablyazov secretly controlled.[14]

Most of the funds appear to have been invested into ambitious real estate and infrastructure development projects in Russia and Ukraine, including Eurasia Tower, a 75-storey office building in Moscow.[15] According to a leaked US embassy cable, in a meeting with the US ambassador, the chairman of the Kazakh Central Bank, Grigori Marchenko, claimed to have advised Ablyazov to get out of his real estate holdings as late as 2007, when prices were still rising, but the Kazakh banker apparently suggested that the boom still had three years to run.[16] As the property bubble popped in 2008, Ablyazov reportedly still refused to sell these holdings, even while other Kazakh banks were selling at a loss and a deep financial crisis was unleashed throughout Kazakhstan's globally integrated financial system. Instead, as BTA's balance sheets turned red, Ablyazov started shifting loans and holdings to offshore entities.[17] The full extent of the damage done would only be uncovered after investigations into hundreds of deals, offshore shell companies and legal intermediaries. Western financial institutions that had aggressively poured money into the bank were forced to write off billions.[18]

Selective investigative reports and legal proceedings provide a window into a small but revealing sample of BTA's networks of offshore shell companies and how Ablyazov managed them. A UK High Court judgment, according to the *Wall Street Journal*, found that 'between 2006 and 2008 BTA had lent $1.4 bn to 17 companies incorporated offshore', which held 'few assets'.[19] According to presiding judge Sir Nigel Teare, these seventeen companies were 'owned or controlled by Mr. Ablyazov'.[20] One of these loans for $45 million, dated November 2007, was extended to Astogold Corp., a shell company registered in the BVI with a single nominee director in Cyprus and a balance sheet showing only $5,000 worth of assets. According to the court, these loans were only 'partly repaid', and were subsequently replaced by a new wave of loans, in excess of $1 billion, extended through another network of offshore companies.[21]

Another arbitration hearing, this time brought by Ablyazov against the Kazakh government for the expropriation of one of his holding companies as a result of the BTA takeover, provides a remarkably vivid account of the Kazakh billionaire's schemes.[22] Evidence from *KT Asia v BTA*, a case brought under the Dutch–Kazakh bilateral investment treaty (KT Asia was registered in the Netherlands), suggests that the Kazakh banker designed a vast complex of offshore vehicles in order to hide the extent of his ownership of BTA holdings from Kazakh authorities.[23] The panel found that Ablyazov had controlled 75.18 per cent of BTA, 'acquired in stages' and 'through a series of separate companies incorporated in different jurisdictions under the direction of trusted associates'.[24] The panel further determined that 'each of these companies beneficially owned by Abyazov held less than 10% of BTA shares' to avoid disclosure to Kazakh authorities.[25]

In a critical transaction (see Figure 2.1), in 2007 KT Asia purchased BTA shares from two shell companies registered in the BVI, Refgen Technologies Inc. (Refgen) and Tortland Productions Inc. (Tortland), which together constituted 9.86 per cent of BTA's shares. The panel found that at the time KT Asia was in the hands of a nominee director and 'never had any assets other than the shares in BTA and a bank account with a balance of approximately €18,000'.[26] As BTA management alleged, 'KT Asia acquired 808,321 shares in BTA for a consideration of approximately US$66,803,388', while the minimum value of

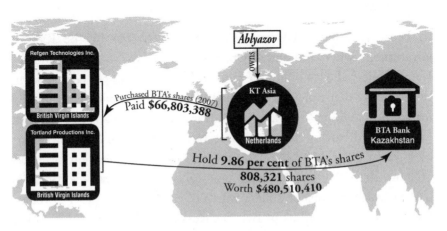

Figure 2.1 Ownership structure of KT Asia and relation to BTA Bank

those shares at the time was (according to the KASE index) almost eight times as much – $480,510,410. This was not disputed by Ablyazov's team.[27] Further, KT Asia never paid for these shares, as they were purchased using loans from the actual vendors (the BVI shell companies), and neither did it pay principal or interest payments to Refgen and Tortland.[28]

According to Ablyazov's lawyers, these elaborate structures were part of 'Project Aquila', designed by Ablyazov's financial advisers to facilitate the placement of BTA's shares in companies he owned and to 'achieve optimal tax efficiency' across the group of holding companies of BTA's shares.[29] The private placement of shares was preferred to an IPO because 'it would allow him to sell the shares at minimal risk of confiscation by President Nazarbayev'.[30] Ablyazov has maintained that the financial crisis that BTA found itself at the centre of had been deliberately engineered by Kazakh authorities in order to seize the bank after he steadfastly refused to turn over 50 per cent to the president himself.[31] But an investigation into global offshore networks by the International Consortium of Investigative Journalists found that Commonwealth Trust Ltd (CTL), a company provider registered in the BVI, had alone set up thirty-one companies as early as 2006 and 2007 for an individual who was later identified by UK courts as a frontman for Ablyazov.[32]

UK court cases and asset recovery

In February 2009, BTA was effectively taken over by the Kazakh government when the state-owned sovereign wealth fund Samruk-Kazyna injected $1.4 billion of funds into it for an 80 per cent stake in the bank. By that time Ablyazov had fled to London where he applied for political asylum: this was eventually granted in July 2011. A complex internal restructuring then took place, but at the core of the bank's troubles was a giant $10 billion hole in the balance sheet left by these offshore deals.[33] One particular unit called UKB6 was identified as having issued billions of dollars' worth of credits for property developments and other projects in Belarus, Russia and Ukraine.[34] According to one financial survey, as of 2013 BTA was still in the worst shape of any of the major Kazakh banks, reportedly weighed down by about $11 billion in non-performing loans.[35]

BTA's new management almost immediately began a vigorous international legal campaign to locate and reclaim about $6 billion of the bank's assets from Ablyazov. On the basis of a 2008 BTA transaction worth $285 million with a British shell company, Drey Associates, BTA's litigators established jurisdiction in the UK court system.[36] More than eleven separate legal proceedings have been held, with the Kazakh government hiring five law firms and more than a hundred leading lawyers for the case.[37] The cases themselves have proved to be enormously complex and even groundbreaking, reportedly adding twenty-three new points to the White Book, the UK's civil procedure rules.[38]

Overall, the outcomes of these legal proceedings have been unfavourable to Ablyazov. BTA achieved an important initial victory on 13 August 2009 when a court ordered the freezing of Ablyazov's global assets and directed him to fully disclose his holdings and to cease actively managing them. Ablyazov appealed against the ruling on the grounds that compliance with the court order might lead to his self-incrimination in legal proceedings in Kazakhstan, but the directive was upheld on appeal in October 2010.[39] Commenting on Ablyazov's initial lack of compliance with the disclosure order, Justice Teare observed that 'it can fairly be said that the deficiencies are extraordinarily inadequate'.[40]

BTA also successfully petitioned the court to appoint a receiver to preserve Ablyazov's assets, pointing to the defendant's use of complex networks of nominees and shell companies registered in jurisdictions 'renowned for their secrecy and light regulation', as well as his breach of the initial freezing order.[41] The court agreed and in August 2010 it appointed the international accounting firm KPMG to guard against the dissipation of assets prior to trial. In late 2010, the court added an additional 212 companies to the scope of the receivership order, finding 'good grounds for believing that they, and therefore any assets they held, were beneficially owned by Mr Ablyazov through his usual modus operandi of a nominee UBO', while in 2011 another 389 were added.[42]

In February 2012 Ablyazov was found guilty *in absentia* of failure to disclose assets and lying under oath. Justice Teare found him guilty of three counts of contempt of court, observing that the Kazakh 'chose not to disclose some of his assets, to lie on oath and to deal with some of his assets', adding that these contempts were 'so serious that nothing less than a prison sentence is appropriate'.[43] Ablyazov was sentenced to twenty-two months in prison, but had fled England, reportedly by coach to France, just hours before the ruling was handed out.[44] As a result, his political asylum and UK residency were revoked.

Following the contempt judgment, a November 2012 Court of Appeal ruling by Lord Justice Maurice Kay asserted: 'It is difficult to imagine a party to commercial litigation who has acted with more cynicism, opportunism and deviousness towards court orders than Mr Ablyazov.'[45] Later that month, the High Court entered new judgments against Ablyazov for two civil suits worth $2 billion. Overall, one account estimates a total of $4 billion worth of judgments against the Kazakh fugitive with interest accruing at about $1 million per day.[46]

These complex litigations have been accompanied by an international effort by Kazakh authorities and their agents to identify and reclaim Ablyazov's assets. In Kazakhstan, prosecutors allegedly amassed 1,000 volumes of evidence against him and his alleged associates, while seizing 20 houses, 9 office buildings, 3 aeroplanes, 106 cars, stakes in 22 companies and $20 million in cash.[47] In May 2012, a court in Almaty convicted twenty-one individuals of embezzling $2.1 billion, resulting in seventeen prison sentences.[48] Overseas, an asset recovery effort by BTA has revealed a global network of holdings held by the banker, including several luxury homes, stakes in energy and mineral companies, holdings of real estate projects and complexes in Russia, and stakes in BTA subsidiaries in Ukraine and Georgia. In May 2014, a judge ruled that BTA could seize and sell Ablyazov's $25-million London mansion, while in April 2015 a 100-acre country estate in Surrey was sold for $40 million.[49]

Kazakhstan's politics outside-in: offshore political opposition and the 'foreign element'

Ablyazov's main defence in the BTA case was to claim that he has been subjected to a relentless political assault by the Kazakh authorities for his defiance of President Nazarbayev and his support for Kazakhstan's fledgling democratic opposition. As a result, his defenders maintain, the very seizure of BTA was politically motivated, thereby also justifying Ablyazov's own elaborate ownership schemes and efforts to conceal his stakes in BTA via offshore vehicles.

By November 2001, the former minister had been playing an increasingly vocal and active role in politics. That month, along with Galymzhan Zhakiyanov, Ablyazov co-founded the political opposition movement Democratic Choice of Kazakhstan (DCK). According to scholars and analysts, at the time the DCK was a significant landmark in Kazakhstan's domestic political evolution.[50] The party, spanning clan and regional cleavages, drew upon a broad range of support from the business community and elites who had served in government, who viewed the organisation as a potential bulwark against the government's growing economic predation.[51] According to one study of the party's formation, 'the "who's who" of Kazakhstan's business and economic elite issued a joint statement announcing their commitment to the rule of law and democratization', declaring that 'Kazakhstan's stalled political reforms represented the most significant threat to the future of the country, economic development, and national security'.[52]

Anticipating the substantial political danger posed by the DCK, Kazakh authorities acted decisively against Ablyazov and his allies. Prime Minister Kassym-Jomart Tokayev condemned the party, warned of impending political chaos, and demanded the resignation of DCK members holding government positions. On 21 November 2001, a number of government officials with ties to DCK were removed by a presidential decree, including the deputy prime minister and deputy defence minister.[53] In March 2002, party co-founders Ablyazov and Zhakiyanov were arrested on criminal charges. Ablyazov was tried and convicted on charges of abuse of authority during his tenure as minister between 1998 and 1999. He was sentenced to six years in prison, with foreign observers widely condemning his trial as politically motivated.[54]

After serving fourteen months in prison, Ablyazov was pardoned and released in 2003 following a public campaign by international advocates including the European Parliament, human rights NGOs and Western governments. His release was reportedly part of a bargain struck with Nazarbayev to refrain from any further political activity.[55] Ablyazov left Kazakhstan for Russia, where he continued to support opposition movements and, according to his own admission, headed the DCK.[56] He lived there until returning to Kazakhstan in 2005, when he was invited back by Nazarbayev to take full control of BTA. Even upon his return Ablyazov covertly continued to support oppositional political activities. According to one of Kazakhstan's leading human rights lawyers, the intensity of Nazarbayev's political targeting of Ablyazov was rooted in a sense of repeated betrayal.[57]

Political exile and offshore opposition

After his flight to London in early 2009, Ablyazov's time was consumed with BTA-related litigations and he reinvigorated his oppositional activities against the Kazakh regime. From his position in exile, Ablyazov began practising 'outside-in' politics, attempting to influence developments in Kazakhstan by supporting the unregistered opposition political party Alga! and independent media, and networking with other banished Kazakh elites.

In his meetings with US officials, Vladimir Kozlov, the leader of Alga!, recounted that in London Ablyazov not only declared himself in 'open opposition' to the Kazakh government, but reached out to other exiled Kazakh political players including the former prime minister Akezhan Kazhegeldin and DCK leader Galymzhan Zhakiyanov. According to US officials, Kozlov also reportedly acknowledged that Ablyazov continued to fund Alga! from exile and involve himself in decisions on party policies.[58] In one US embassy cable from London, Ablyazov himself confirmed to US officials that he had privately supported Alga!, the United Democratic and Communist parties, or 'anyone who is against the President'.[59] Ablyazov also shared his plans to increase 'oppositional reporting' on his K-Plus satellite channel, which was set to transmit across the region and over the internet.[60] Commenting on Ablyazov's political organising in London, the human rights activist

Yevgeny Zhovtis stated that 'Practically all opposition leaders visited him in London.'[61]

From his new offshore perch, Ablyazov proceeded to launch a blistering public campaign to reveal the offshore dealings and alleged corruption schemes of Kazakhstan's ruling elite. In court papers filed for his defence in a BTA case, Ablyazov alleged that Timur Kulibayev, the president's son-in-law, had profited from selling off state assets for below market value, and that he controlled the sovereign wealth fund Samruk-Kazyna – which effectively acquired BTA in 2009 – and its subsidiaries, which included all of the country's 'major industrial prizes'.[62] The dramatic disclosure was released during the same week as Kazakhstan hosted a high-profile OSCE summit, the pinnacle of its much-touted years as the international organisation's chair. Ablyazov also alleged that Kulibayev and his associates had devised an offshore scheme, involving a BVI company, to pocket $166 million from a government sale of a 25 per cent stake in the national oil company Aktobe MunaiGas to the Chinese state-owned oil company CNPC in 2003.[63] Kulibayev and his partners have denied the allegations,[64] as has CNPC.[65] In a statement accompanying the allegation, Ablyazov declared: 'It is important that the Kazakh people understand how these shadowy transactions have been conducted and what sort of methods are being used by those close to the president to gain creeping control over the economy in order ... to enrich themselves.'[66] The core allegation in the story was subsequently published in the *Wall Street Journal*, along with a visualisation of how the complex deal involving shell companies was allegedly structured.[67]

As the allegations broke, Kulibayev reacted by taking aggressive measures to prevent the story's appearance in the Kazakh media. He asked for, and won, an injunction in a local Almaty court to halt national newspapers from publishing anything 'harming the honor and dignity' of Kulibayev.[68] The order also allowed authorities to confiscate the entire print runs of the four independent and opposition newspapers that had published the story, including *Respublika* and *Svoboda Slova*. Kazakh authorities had long viewed *Respublika* as a mouthpiece for Ablyazov: just a few months earlier, in September 2009, the newspaper had been fined and its print run confiscated for its critical coverage of the initial takeover of BTA by the Kazakh government.[69]

The crackdown at Zhanaozen and the politics of outside blame

In late 2011, the campaign against Mukhtar Ablyazov would take yet another dramatic turn, this time becoming entangled with the most repressive and lethal crackdown carried out by Kazakh authorities since the country's independence. On 16 December 2011, Kazakh police opened fire against protesting oil workers in the western city of Zhanaozen, near Aktau. The strikes had been ongoing since May 2011, as three different oil service companies' workers demanded higher wages and improved living conditions.[70]

The incident exacted a heavy human toll, but also proved deeply damaging to Astana's carefully crafted international image as an island of political stability in Central Asia. Overall, at least sixteen demonstrators were confirmed killed and sixty-four injured, whilst thirty-five members of the security services also sustained injuries. Initially, forty-eight civilians were indicted, with the first page of the prosecutor's report stating that 'Fired workers ... with the help of troublemaking youth created mass disturbances accompanied by pogroms, robberies, arsons, and violence toward the peaceful population and members of the police'.[71] Prosecutors also tried and convicted five police officers for using excessive force, all of them junior in rank, who in May 2012 were found guilty and received sentences ranging from five to seven years.[72]

Kazakh authorities seized upon the aftermath of Zhanaozen to implicate Ablyazov and further crack down on his political allies and opposition groups and media. On 23 January 2012, Kazakh authorities arrested both Kozlov and Igor Vinyavsky, editor of the opposition newspaper *Vzglyad*. Kozlov was convicted on 8 October 2012, after a trial widely criticised by international observers as deeply flawed, and sentenced to seven and a half years' imprisonment.[73] As one watchdog observed of the trial, 'at no point in the verdict did the court explain who started the violence on December 16. The defendants were convicted of "incitement of social hatred leading to grievous consequences" without any explanation of how the incitement caused the consequences.'[74]

Accusations that the defendants had close ties to Ablyazov and were part of an orchestrated foreign plot dominated the trial. Prosecutors presented Ablyazov as the founder of an 'organized criminal group' which Kozlov allegedly came to lead. As part of its closing argument, the prosecution showed a documentary film about how Ablyazov was planning to seize power in Kazakhstan; it was also shown on several Kazakh official television stations following the 8 October verdict.[75] Strikingly, the verdict on Kozlov's involvement referred to this alleged criminal plot with Ablyazov as well as the BTA proceedings:

> The accused V. Kozlov, in March of 2010, with the goal of subverting and destroying the socio-political foundations of the constitutional order of the Republic of Kazakhstan, willingly joined an extremist organised criminal group created and financed from abroad by Mukhtar Ablyazov, who is currently sought by investigative organs for the crime of embezzling $7 billion from BTA Bank in 2005, the board of which bank he chaired. The criminal group was founded on the principles of hierarchy and strict division of roles, and V. Kozlov acted as leader of this group in Kazakhstan.[76]

The court's main evidence tying Ablyazov to this plot was a transcript of a Skype call between him, Kozlov and regional leaders of Alga! on 30 April 2011.[77] During the call Ablyazov spoke of the effort to 'topple the government' and the need to unite dissatisfied portions of society into an opposition, including oil workers, but it contained no direct operational details linking the striking workers to Ablyazov.[78]

In a follow-up to the politically charged Kozlov verdict, in November 2012 the public prosecutor's office in Almaty filed a motion to classify as 'extremist' and ban twenty-three internet sites and eight newspapers that operated under the umbrella of the *Respublika* newspaper as well as the news channel KTK-TV.[79] All of these outlets and organisations were, 'in one way or another, connected with Mukhtar Ablyazov'.[80] The international media watchdog Reporters Without Borders commented on the ban thus: 'This unprecedented blow to pluralism is the result of an outrageous misuse of the Kazakh justice system . . . Reduced to a tool of repression, the courts no longer even try to maintain appearances, flouting defence rights, holding summary hearings and violating procedure.'[81] Events at Zhanaozen, which had started as a strike among domestic oil workers in a remote province, had produced an investigation that implicated Kazakh civil society, opposition leaders, major opposition media outlets and Ablyazov himself.

The concerted strategy of blaming 'foreign elements' or externalising the origins of Kazakhstan's political instability was clearly outlined and emphasised by Kazakhstan's foreign minister, Erlan Idrissov, in a speech about the government's campaign against Ablyazov's overseas activities. He justified the government's targeting of Kozlov and crackdown on media outlets as an appropriate response. The foreign minister's comments are worth quoting at length:

Mr. Ablyazov started positioning himself in the West as a democracy champion. He committed a grave economic crime. It was proved in Kazakhstan's courts. Last year there were some court verdicts establishing his guilt in the UK courts. One should be aware that having stolen the money, he is spending a sizable amount to create an empire that would support him in the West; this empire is flexibly carrying out his campaign to create a picture that many now believe in; at the same time he is supporting similar structures in Kazakhstan. So, Mr. Kozlov is not a genuine opposition activist. *Respublika* newspaper is not a truly independent newspaper. K+ isn't a truly independent channel. These are special tools created by Mr. Ablyazov to pinpointedly attack Kazakhstan. We classify the situation around Mr. Ablyazov and the [media and opposition] structures involved as a special campaign orchestrated by Mr. Ablyazov against Kazakhstan. Therefore Kazakhstan does have the right to defend itself against this campaign.[82]

Carrying the full weight and sovereign authority of Kazakhstan's Ministry of Foreign Affairs, Idrissov's comments illustrate how the

Kazakh government not only denied Ablyazov's claim to be acting as a political opponent, but framed Ablyazov's overseas activities as a threat to the Kazakh state itself and a matter of the highest priority in Kazakhstan's foreign relations.

The international hunt for Ablyazov and his associates

On 31 July 2013, Ablyazov was captured and arrested in the village of Mouans-Sartoux near Cannes in southern France. The operation, which involved French police and special forces, ended months of speculation as to the Kazakh fugitive's whereabouts after fleeing the UK. According to one report, Ablyazov had been traced to the property by British private detectives who had tailed his Ukrainian lawyer, Olena Tyshchenko, to France following a High Court hearing.[83] In January 2014, a French court authorised Ablyazov's extradition to Russia and Ukraine on charges of embezzlement. The decision was overturned by an appeals court in April, only to be reinstated in October 2014 and upheld by the nation's highest court in March 2015. With no extradition treaty between Kazakhstan and France, Ablyazov's advocates feared that extradition to Russia or Ukraine would still put the banker in danger of being returned to Kazakhstan, given that these post-Soviet countries are parties to the Minsk Convention, which allows extraditions to member countries of criminal suspects.[84] On 17 September, the French prime minister, Manuel Valls, signed a decree authorising Ablyazov's extradition to Russia; Ablyazov's family appealed to the Council of State which on 9 December 2016 cancelled the extradition order, finding the request from Russia to be politically motivated.[85]

Ablyazov's extradition hearings were part of an array of international proceedings, both legal and extralegal, undertaken by Kazakh authorities and their intermediaries to secure the return of the banker. The most powerful of these had been the issuing of an Interpol Red Notice. Interpol's own guidelines stipulate that such notices should not be abused for political purposes, this deemed contrary to Interpol's rules and regulations – though rights watchdogs have criticised Kazakhstan as one of a number of countries that have abused the Red Notice system by targeting political opponents.[86] Thus, an important subplot in the ongoing international battle between Kazakh authorities and Ablyazov was whether the Kazakh government had improperly used international criminal institutions and procedures to pursue a politically motivated case.

Extraordinary rendition, Italian-style

The most dramatic episode in the Kazakh government's international hunt for Ablyazov could claim no such legal basis. On 29 May 2013, around fifty uniformed and plainclothes Italian agents of the DIGOS police intelligence wing raided Ablyazov's family residence on the outskirts of Rome. Though Ablyazov was absent, the agents proceeded to detain his daughter Madina and his wife Alma Shalabayeva. The two were held on the justification that they had forged identification documents; in fact, Shalabayeva had valid residency permits for the UK and Latvia that automatically granted rights of residency throughout the EU.[87] Just two days later, on 31 May, mother and daughter, accompanied by Kazakh diplomats, were forcibly transported back to Kazakhstan by private jet. The pair were not provided with legal counsel nor was an extradition hearing convened.

The renditions generated an international outcry. International organisations – including the OSCE, the European Parliament and the Council of Europe – and human rights groups such as Human Rights Watch and Amnesty International issued strong condemnatory statements and demanded that the pair be allowed safe passage back to Italy.[88] A subsequent opinion issued by three United Nations human rights experts stated that the 'circumstances of the deportation give rise to the appearance that this was in fact an extraordinary rendition which is of great concern to us'.[89] Italy had thus joined the ranks alongside Russia, China and the United States as external powers that have collaborated with Central Asian governments to perform extraordinary renditions back to the region.[90]

In Italy itself, the episode unleashed a domestic firestorm. President Giorgio Napolitano lashed out against Italian officials for the 'inconceivable case of the precipitous expulsion', stating that the affair had brought 'serious reasons of embarrassment and discredit for the state and so also for the country'.[91] Criticism was heaped on the Interior Ministry and its head, Deputy Prime Minister Angelino Alfano, who putatively arranged the operation on behalf of his close political ally, the former prime minister Silvio Berlusconi, reportedly a close friend of Nazarbayev.[92] A later Italian official inquiry into the events found that the Kazakh ambassador, Andrian Yelemessov, had been intimately involved in the operation's planning and had exerted 'pervasive' and 'massive' pressure on the Interior Ministry and police authorities, without adequate consultation with the Italian Ministry of Foreign Affairs.[93] After severe international criticism, Italian authorities revoked the deportation order and, following efforts by the Italian Foreign Ministry, the pair were eventually allowed to return to Italy from Kazakhstan in December 2013.[94] Ablyazov's daughter subsequently launched a formal complaint against three Kazakh diplomats for their role in the affair.[95]

Casting the wider net

Though Ablyazov's wife and daughter were allowed to return to Italy, Kazakh authorities have continued their relentless effort to arrest and extradite his associates across Europe, making aggressive use of international legal procedures and applying direct diplomatic pressure. As with the case of Ablyazov himself, human rights organisations have sharply criticised these arrests and interventions as politically motivated. Kazakh authorities, in contrast, have sought to tie these figures to Ablyazov's financial crimes, though in some cases they have added additional serious charges via the Interpol Red Notice system, including allegations of 'terrorism'. Figure 2.2 depicts the location of Ablyazov's network of associates across Europe. These included the following individuals.

Aleksandr Pavlov, Ablyazov's former head of security, was detained at a train station in Spain in April 2013 and held in Madrid under an Interpol arrest warrant issued by the Kazakh government on charges of 'expropriation or embezzlement of trusted property'.[96] After

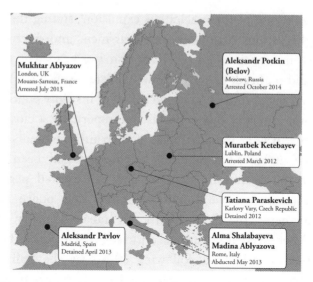

Figure 2.2 European map of detained and arrested Ablyazov associates

challenging the extradition request, Kazakh authorities amended the Interpol notice to include charges of 'plotting a terrorist attack', which led to a second arrest.[97] The Kazakh government's revised extradition request was granted by Spain in July 2013 but was subsequently suspended by a Spanish court when the newspaper *El País* broke a story that the Spanish government, in a manner reminiscent of Italy's Ablyazov operation, had issued a secret decree approving Pavlov's transfer to Kazakhstan after having met with Kazakh officials.[98] Pavlov was released on bail in August with his application for political asylum, as of July 2015, still pending in Spain.[99]

Tatiana Paraskevich, Ablyazov's former accountant, is alleged to have had a managerial role at BTA and was accused of having aided Ablyazov in embezzlement. Paraskevich and her family fled Kazakhstan in 2003 following Ablyazov's first conviction there. She was arrested in Karlovy Vary in the Czech Republic in 2012 on the basis of extradition requests issued by Russia and Ukraine.[100] After being detained in Plzeň's prison for twenty-two months, the Czech high court approved extradition to Ukraine, but the Justice Ministry overturned the decision and Paraskevich was freed in March 2014 after a public NGO campaign claimed that she could face possible torture upon her return to Kazakhstan.[101] She has remained in the Czech Republic and has been promised 'international protection' against international extradition claims.

Aleksandr Potkin (also known as Aleksandr Belov), a Russian citizen, is an alleged Ablyazov associate and former leader of the nationalist Movement Against Illegal Migration in Russia.[102] Accused of having colluded with Ablyazov in a BTA-related real estate financing scheme through the managing and 'legalising' of 2,500 hectares of land in the Moscow Oblast region of Russia, Potkin was arrested in Moscow in October 2014 and accused of money laundering and embezzlement. He was initially held under house arrest, and on 17 October was transferred to state prison, leading to public criticism by Russian opposition figures like Alexei Navalny and a public rally in his support.[103] Kazakh officials launched a follow-up investigation in November 2014 into his 'inciting ethnic hatred' and his allegedly having been hired by Ablyazov to 'study and foment nationalist unrest in Kazakhstan, with the aim of weakening President Nazarbaev's regime'.[104]

Muratbek Ketebayev is a former deputy economy minister under Nazarbayev turned opposition activist. He fled from Kazakhstan to Poland in 2011 and was subsequently accused by Kazakh prosecutors of planning a terrorist attack on Almaty in March 2012 and abetting the incitement of ethnic violence in Zhanaozen.[105] He was detained by police in Lublin in June 2013, but was released after questioning by Polish officials and granted political asylum there in December 2013. On 27 December 2014, following a visit to Aleksandr Pavlov in Madrid, he was arrested by Spanish police on an Interpol warrant issued by the Kazakh government.[106] Tellingly, in the legal proceedings brought against him, the Zhanaozen events that formed the basis of the Red Notice were not mentioned by the Spanish lawyers hired by Kazakh authorities in support of the extradition; instead, the charges emphasised Ketebayev's role in the BTA scandal and his alleged possession of a false passport.[107] Prior to the case being heard, the Spanish Ministry of Justice closed the proceedings and removed Ketebayev's name from the Spanish database. He was allowed to return to Poland in March 2015.

Extending the argument: making sense of Kazakhstan's offshore politics

The case of Mukhtar Ablyazov and his associates is but one instance of a broader pattern of 'offshore politics' involving Kazakh political elites, their new global places of residence and their battles with Kazakh authorities in international courts, civil proceedings and the global media space. Since Kazakhstan's independence a number of the country's senior officials and even presidential relatives have fled the Central Asian state and challenged the regime from abroad. The most prominent among them include a former prime minister (Akezhan Kazhegeldin), a former mayor of Kazakhstan's commercial capital Almaty (Viktor Khrapunov) and even President Nazarbayev's now-deceased former son-in-law, Rakhat Aliyev.

Aliyev's case has attracted the most attention given that, as we saw in Chapter 1, he was once married to Nazarbayev's daughter (their divorce was announced in June 2007). After falling out with the president, he published a sensationalist account of Nazarbayev's alleged corrupt dealings and political manoeuvres, and met a no less sensationalistic end – being found hanged in his jail cell, apparently by suicide, in Vienna in February 2015 while awaiting a murder trial.[108]

As with the case of Ablyazov, this group of exiled officials demonstrate broad similarities in their alleged financial crimes, how they have used their exile to criticise and actively oppose the regime, and how Kazakh authorities have employed the full array of available international tools and foreign relations to target them.

Kompromat goes global: the politics of 'financial crime'

The most important common feature of Kazakhstan's political exiles is that they were all, at one point, powerful elites closely allied with President Nazarbayev. All of them occupied critical positions of power that allowed them to amass fortunes through their access to state assets and networks of influence. They have all been accused of financial crimes including embezzlement and money laundering, thereby triggering a series of anti-money-laundering investigations, asset freezes, Interpol Red Notices and international litigations.

In a seminal case, the former Kazakh prime minister turned opposition leader Akezhan Kazhegeldin was arrested under a Red Notice in Moscow in September 1999 on charges of tax evasion and money laundering. He was eventually released and vowed never to return to Kazakhstan. He was arrested again in Rome airport in July 2000 under the same notice, as Kazakhstan once again sought extradition. Interpol dropped the Red Notice in June 2002, citing lack of evidence against him and Article 3 of the Interpol constitution (which guarantees political neutrality). 'The illegal misuse of Interpol to harass exiled political opponents [of Nazarbayev] cannot be tolerated', Kazhegeldin's lawyer warned in a letter following the rescinding of the notice.[109]

In 2014 the city of Almaty filed a lawsuit in a US district court against former Almaty mayor Viktor Khrapunov, accusing him and his relatives of defrauding the city of at least $300 million and using embezzled funds to purchase real estate in the United States.[110] The claim states that Khrapunov 'abused his position of trust as a public official in order to convert and sell numerous assets belonging to the City of Almaty for his own benefit and the benefit of his co-conspirators',[111] though, as one journalist notes, the timing of the case, which was filed a decade after the alleged acts, raises 'questions about why it took the municipality so long to notice the missing millions'.[112]

Perhaps the most dramatic illustration of allegations of 'financial crime' wielded as a political weapon was actually a case in which an international investigation, ordered by the Kazakh government against a political opponent, spectacularly boomeranged to spark the most publicised corruption scandal since Kazakhstan's independence. The origins of 'Kazakhgate' – the scandal in which James Giffen, a close adviser to Nazarbayev, allegedly structured a series of deals with major Western energy companies in the 1990s through a network of offshore bank accounts tied to Kazakhstan's elite – actually lie in the Kazakh government's attempts to go after estranged former prime minister Akezhan Kazhegeldin.

After Kazhegeldin became critical of Nazarbayev and appeared poised to challenge him for the presidency, he was barred from running for office and in 1998 fled the country. Soon after, Kazakh officials charged Kazhegeldin with financial crimes and prompted Belgian and

Swiss authorities to investigate alleged money laundering and real estate deals. However, as part of that investigation, Swiss authorities identified a number of suspicious transfers between American and European energy companies and Kazakhstan.[113] The resulting investigation identified a number of offshore accounts allegedly tied to Giffen and led to his arrest in 2003 in New York on charges of violating the Foreign Corrupt Practices Act (FCPA) and funnelling over $80 million from Western oil companies into the Swiss bank accounts of senior Kazakh officials.[114] In 2010, after more than seven years of court manoeuvrings, delays and motions regarding the classification status of evidence, the trial came to an end when Giffen pleaded guilty to a single misdemeanour and one bribery count against his company.[115] Giffen had mounted an unusual 'public authority' defence, claiming that he acted on behalf of US governmental entities, which the judge in the case seemed to accept, noting that Giffen 'advanced the strategic interests of the United States and American businesses in Central Asia'.[116]

But the Kazakhgate investigation may never have started were it not for the Kazakh government's own zealous attempt to target a political opponent on accusations of financial crimes. Indeed, the Giffen affair, like that of Ablyazov, reveals that the pursuit of exiles often has inadvertent and unwelcome consequences in the interconnected worlds of global law and finance.

Opposition in exile, politics by proxy

Another characteristic of the exiled Kazakh elite is that they too, soon after fleeing the Central Asian state, presented themselves as democrats opposing Nazarbayev's authoritarianism. Though Ablyazov appears to have been the most active in supporting and funding oppositional movements and media outlets, the others have also publicly denounced the regime and, when faced with extradition hearings and litigations, defended themselves as political targets. Kazhegeldin, Aliyev and Khrapunov all published books that were highly critical of Nazarbayev's rule, with Aliyev's *The Godfather-in-Law* particularly infuriating to Kazakh officials. Soon after its publication in May 2009, the office of the

Kazakh prosecutor general warned citizens not even to touch the book, while media outlets and newspapers were threatened with criminal charges if they printed excerpts or quoted from it.[117] Like Ablyazov, Khrapunov has maintained a detailed website championing himself as an advocate for Kazakh democracy and accusing the Kazakh authorities of targeting him for political purposes.[118]

The exiles have also actively networked with one another, despite some previous rivalries. Ablyazov appears to have maintained close contact with Kazhegeldin in London, while *Respublika* and its affiliates have published in detail many of Aliyev's corruption allegations against Nazarbayev and Kulibayev. Khrapunov, who initially appears to have been allowed to leave for Geneva in 2007 on condition that he stay away from politics, had an Interpol Red Notice issued for him in 2012 shortly after he had publicly pledged allegiance to Ablyazov.

One of the more old-fashioned forms of political alliance, possibly perceived as the core of a strategic political opposition, was cemented in early 2007 when Khrapunov's son Ilyas married Ablyazov's daughter Madina, who also resides in Geneva.[119] In his memoirs, Khrapunov denies that the marriage was politically motivated and alleges that he was approached in Geneva by Kazakh government officials who asked that his son sign a letter pledging loyalty to President Nazarbayev.[120] Like his parents, Ilyas has also been charged by Kazakh authorities with money laundering and heading a criminal group in 1997, though at that time he was fourteen years old and attending a boarding school in Switzerland.[121] Further, as Edward Lemon and Daniel Rosset have noted, these Kazakh exiles in Switzerland hired their own proxies and lobbyists to attempt to influence Swiss institutions, such as parliamentary committees and the Justice Ministry, thereby also embroiling Swiss authorities in the rough and tumble of Kazakh elite politics.[122]

The long arm of Kazakh foreign relations and the politics of image-crafting

A third common feature across these cases is the extent to which the Kazakh government has deployed multiple international tools and efforts to discredit, extradite and pressure exiles. As with Ablyazov, the

Kazakh government convicted all of these figures of serious criminal charges *in absentia*, thereby placing them on the Interpol list and lobbying authorities to freeze their assets. But as with Ablyazov, host countries, especially in Europe, have caught on to the potential political motives behind these listings, making these arrests and extraditions drawn out and complicated.

As in the Ablyazov case, the Kazakh government has also, via its missions, applied direct diplomatic pressure on countries hosting political exiles to arrest them as part of efforts to secure their transfer back to Kazakhstan. And it is here that the personal nature of Kazakhstan's domestic political system is fused with the institutions and practices of foreign relations: Kazakh foreign relations appear increasingly to prioritise the targeting of political exiles abroad.

More broadly, a growing number of commentators and scholars have noted Kazakhstan's extensive international efforts to craft and maintain a favourable image. Whether it is funding major cycling teams and major universities,[123] commissioning studies from Western think tanks,[124] planting stories through non-disclosing proxies in the international media,[125] establishing think tanks in Brussels or hiring lobbyists abroad,[126] Kazakh authorities are pursuing a foreign relations strategy that relies heavily on national branding, communications and soft-power influence. Astana even hired former UK prime minister Tony Blair as a strategic adviser on a contract reportedly worth $25 million a year, a relationship that has drawn fierce criticism from human rights watchdogs who claim that Blair has downplayed incidents like Zhanaozen.[127]

The contested politics of Kazakhstan's international fugitives

Viewed from the perspective of Kazakhstan's externalised politics and forms of global political contestation, these image-crafting efforts also serve a related political purpose: to keep these international political battles out of the scope of discussions of Kazakh domestic politics and foreign policy. By framing and fostering agendas such as improving Central Asia's connectivity, promoting Kazakhstan's role as a political and economic crossroads in Eurasia, or advocating for 'strategic partnership', Kazakhstan's own offshore political operations are actively excluded from Western discussion, analysis and even policymaking consideration. Instead, figures such as Ablyazov, Aliyev, Kazhegeldin and Khrapunov are presented exclusively as international fugitives and criminals, whose stories themselves are not appropriate subjects of political analysis.

What is domestic and what is global? What is onshore and what is offshore? Who is a criminal and who is a democratic champion? What constitutes a legitimate foreign national interest and what is a personal political vendetta? The Ablyazov case reveals just how complicated and blurred the boundaries become when answering these questions. But one characterisation that seems irrefutable is just how globally 'connected' all of these processes, agendas and political frames have become. As our next story demonstrates, even the state itself may be globalised via offshore companies and transnational networks.

3

TAJIKISTAN

THE PRESIDENT OF THE WARLORDS AND HIS OFFSHORE STATE

[The Tajikistan Aluminium Company (Talco)] factory is an impressive sight, but like many of the country's assets, President Rahmon sees it as a means of generating income for himself, his family members, and his inner circle. Although it is a state asset, decisions about the company are not made in the best interests of the country . . . As with other industries, Talco's revenue does not contribute to development of the country; rather much of it disappears for off-budget activities and projects, such as palaces and lavish state entertainments. The people of Tajikistan effectively subsidize Talco, by living without adequate health services, education, or electricity. Hundreds of millions or even billions of dollars have disappeared from the company since 1992, and the huge subsidies Talco receives in the form of cheap electricity are draining enormous resources from the Tajik economy . . . End Comment.

Tracey Ann Jacobson, US ambassador to Tajikistan,
leaked cable, 14 April 2008[1]

In May 2014, the investigative journalist David Trilling received documents from Russia's United Company Rusal, an aggrieved former partner of the state-owned Tajikistan Aluminium Company, detailing some of its offshore dealings on behalf of family members of President Rahmon. These included how Talco's profits had been routed to CDH

Investments Corp. (CDH) and Talco Management Ltd (TML), secretive offshore entities registered in the BVI, at the expense of Rusal. These offshore vehicles in turn financed new Boeing aeroplanes for the private airline, Somon Air, owned by family members, and funded lobbying in the US Congress, apparently circumventing American legislation which requires full disclosure of lobbying on behalf of foreign governments.

In Tajikistan's economy, Talco is a fully state-owned enterprise and the single dominant industrial asset. In 2008, aluminium exports from Talco were reported to constitute 33 per cent of the country's gross domestic product, 48 per cent of its export revenues and 75.3 per cent of its foreign currency reserves.[2] Producing this aluminium consumes approximately half of the total electricity supply of Tajikistan, which is provided by the state electricity utility at rates vastly below market levels.[3] Talco consumes an extraordinary proportion of energy from the national electricity network in a country where power cuts are routine and severe electricity rationing and irregularity of supply are suffered nationwide over the winter. The bloated company employs over 12,000 workers and is characterised by technical processes and management practices which were until recently a model of inefficiency.[4]

This chapter tells the post-Soviet history of Tajikistan through the experience of its aluminium industry, its offshore connections and the astonishing rise of President Emomali Rahmon from farm manager to warlord's placeman to international statesman and deal-maker. The story of Talco tells us a great deal about the secretive world of Tajikistan's family-run state and how it uses an array of offshore jurisdictions, all with the complicity of its foreign partners and intermediaries. Given what the international community knew about Talco and its offshore connections, as illustrated in the US ambassador's striking conclusions, it is remarkable that major Western corporations, lobbyists and governments were happy to do business with Tajikistan while claiming that they were abiding by anti-corruption rules. The story of Rahmon, who rose out of the country's civil war to bring the whole economy under the control of his family and inner circle, suggests otherwise.

Battle for Talco, fight for the state

In the 1990s, Talco emerged as one of the key spoils of Tajikistan's devastating civil war. Its revival and capture by President Rahmon's regime mirrors Tajikistan's own post-conflict story of personalistic state-building. But it is not just a tale of local struggles. Since the late 1990s, Tajikistan's economy has been thoroughly globalised in terms of trade (via connections to multinational corporations and their foreign investments) and labour (with over a million Tajiks – perhaps 20 per cent of its labour force – at work in Russia and elsewhere in the region). In terms of finance, inflows of remittances from Russia rank Tajikistan's economy as the most remittance-dependent in the world, while outflows of capital to offshore accounts demonstrate that national economic development is a chimera. Tajik labour, goods and capital all exist in a transnational market economy, where the state is used to the benefit of a small circle consisting of the president and his key associates.

Soviet beginnings and wartime returns

The story begins more than forty years ago with the creation of Tajikistan's aluminium smelter – the country's single big industrial facility and export-earner. Known by its Russian abbreviation TadAz until 2007, the state company opened in 1975 and is now the world's fourth largest aluminium smelter, based outside the town of Tursunzade near the capital Dushanbe.

The production of aluminium requires the confluence of raw alumina and large amounts of cheap electricity. As Tajikistan does not produce alumina, it is purchased from overseas – from within the Soviet Union until 1991 and on the global market since independence. The nearest sources are Mykolaiv in Ukraine and Pavlodar in Kazakhstan. Since 1991 the smelter has remained state property whilst many other national assets have been privatised. As described by the World Bank, 'the company is not governed by a board of directors or any other type of executive committee' and 'is under the sole command of its director, who reports only to the Tajik President at a monthly meeting'.[5]

Shortly after independence Tajikistan descended into a catastrophic civil war. Upwards of 50,000 lives were lost in a struggle between the country's regional factions. Like many republics of the USSR, Tajikistan had suffered a turbulent period of *perestroika* before the Soviet Union collapsed. By 1991 it was buckling under the pressure of a declining economy and the end of Soviet subsidies, as Islamist, nationalist and regionalist movements from the southern and eastern regions of the country mobilised in protests against a state run largely by the *nomenklatura* of the northern region. Rahmon Nabiyev, a weak president elected in a violent and disputed presidential poll, lost control of the situation. In May 1992, faced with rival demonstrations in the centre of the capital, the increasing involvement of criminal gangs, a weak and divided security apparatus, and the inflow of young men from impoverished villages, Nabiyev distributed arms to his supporters. In return, opposition movements armed themselves from caches provided by allies in the security services. The armed forces, still taking orders from a stricken government in Moscow, were paralysed. The violence began in the capital but quickly spread to the southern regions where peasants had been forcibly settled on collective farms on the basis of their region of origin during the Soviet era. The fighting between these groups was brutal.

By late 1992, order began to be restored as forces from Russia and Uzbekistan intervened to help install a new government composed of leaders from the southern region of Kulob and the erstwhile elites from the northern region of Khujand. Their opponents, largely of Garmi and Pamiri regional origin, fled to Afghanistan or the mountains of the east. Opposition leaders left for Moscow, Tehran and Cairo among other places. But violence continued throughout the 1990s at the border with Afghanistan, around the capital and especially in the mountainous Rasht Valley. By 1997, under pressure from Russia and Iran, and with the coordination of the United Nations, a general peace agreement was achieved. Under the terms of the treaty, 30 per cent of state posts were to be distributed to the opposition factions in return for their demobilisation and disarmament. Although neither side of the agreement was fulfilled by the early 2000s, Tajikistan was largely pacified under an authoritarian president and security structure.

Tajikistan's aluminium smelter was central to the struggles of the war. Talco was one of the key assets over which battles took place, with warlords General Ghaffor Mirzoyev and Colonel Mahmud Khudoiberdiyev fighting for control. Abdukadir Ermatov, the director of Talco from 1994 to 2004, reports of incidents where his life was threatened during the civil war as he struggled to keep the smelter operational.[6] From 1996, he struck a deal with Avaz Nazarov, a friend and businessman from the same region of Tajikistan as him, for investment in the struggling plant.[7] Nazarov was also a business associate of General Mirzoyev, who by this time had established his forces as guardians of the plant at the expense of Colonel Khudoiberdiyev. For the next eight years, Talco's trading activities were facilitated by financing and bartering arrangements with Nazarov and his various companies. Security was provided by Mirzoyev's forces, whose presence deterred rival warlords.

The rise of President Rahmon

As Talco was being rehabilitated, Emomali Rahmon (known by the Russian form of his name, Rahmonov, until 2007) rose meteorically to become president of the republic. Rahmon was merely the head of a Soviet farm during the latter years of the USSR, but as Tajikistan descended into turmoil, he found himself in the right place at the right time. Like Mirzoyev, he was from the southern region of Kulob, an area whose sons had fought to reinstall the government throughout the intense fighting of 1992. At the Supreme Soviet in northern Tajikistan in November 1992, Rahmon was ushered into the premiership by Sangak Safarov – also from Kulob and a former organised crime boss, convicted felon and one of Tajikistan's new warlords. He was a 'puppet president',[8] put in place to represent the interests of the warlords of the south. Rahmon was from the same neighbourhood of the town of Danghara as Safarov and had only succeeded to his position in the Kulob regional assembly after Safarov had murdered the previous incumbent of the post.[9] Within months, a further stroke of luck befell Rahmon as his patron Safarov was killed in a gun battle with another leading warlord, Faizali Saidov. Saidov was also killed. In hindsight, this event was the start of a process whereby Rahmon was able to move skilfully from being a mere puppet to the arbiter, overseer and ultimately repressor of warlord politics. He became president in 1994 and was re-elected in 1999. He changed the constitution in 2003 to allow himself to serve until 2020 and then again in May 2016 to allow him to serve as president for life. He is now officially Tajikistan's 'leader of the nation'.[10]

Rahmon knocked off or incorporated warlord after warlord throughout the 1990s but at the turn of the millennium he still lacked direct control of Talco and, most importantly, its international trading and financial relationships. The Ermatov–Nazarov partnership remained in place with Mirzoyev still on the scene having been incorporated into the state as head of Rahmon's Presidential Guard. From 1998 Talco's principal commercial partner was Nazarov's Ansol Company, registered in the tax shelter of Guernsey in the British Channel Islands. Rahmon accepted these arrangements as, despite the 1997 peace agreement, he remained in a precarious position and faced intermittent rebellions in the region. These arrangements had brought Tajikistan's number one exporter earner back to profitability while providing significant revenues for Nazarov and Ansol.[11] After the civil war Rahmon passed legislation permitting privatisation of state enterprises and regularly suggested to the international community that the smelter would be sold.[12] International bankers and creditors, while surely aware of Talco's violent history, were apparently happy that it was on the right track.

But as they consolidated power, the president and his key associates also decided to keep Talco within the state and bring it under their exclusive control. In the autumn of 2004, government officials and the country's Orienbank, under President Rahmon's brother-in-law Hasan Sadullayev, arranged for the replacement of the management of Nazarov and the Ansol Company. The pretence for this move was allegations of fraud against Ansol based on an investigation and charges brought by Tajikistan's general prosecutor's office. The long-standing deal with Nazarov was ended in favour of new arrangements with offshore companies owned jointly by the Tajik state and private individuals close to the president. Nazarov sued the government of Tajikistan in the London High Court. In response, the Rahmon regime and Talco countersued in an attempt to have the company's previous management and Ansol convicted of fraud.[13] That this conflict over a Tajik state-owned enterprise fell under the jurisdiction of English law was a puzzle for the presiding judges,[14] but indicated the offshore dimension of Tajikistan's national economy and state.

The record-breaking international court case

The London hearings which ran from May 2005 to November 2008 and cost between \$150–\$200 million made the court case one of the most expensive in legal history – costs largely borne directly by the government of Tajikistan and indirectly by its impoverished people. The case became notorious in 2008 as allegation met counter-allegation and ended without conclusion. Talco entered into legal disputes with its partners in the Russian and Norwegian state industrial conglomerates, United Company Rusal (hereafter Rusal) and Hydro Aluminium (hereafter Hydro), which had seen their contracts under the Nazarov arrangement cancelled in 2004. At one point at least eleven proceedings were ongoing; none of these were won by Talco. In several of these, the company, the Tajik state and its key officials were found to have misled the court, while transcripts and judgments from the hearings exposed the details of its secretive trading arrangements and offshore management structures.[15]

The new management would be under the auspices of Rusal, the Russian state company headed by Oleg Deripaska, an oligarch who maintained a working relationship with Vladimir Putin.[16] Court documents present considerable evidence as to how this occurred and, in particular, the role of President Rahmon and his brother-in-law Sadullayev in these events.[17] Sadullayev makes clear in the documents that it was a presidential instruction for his bank to expel Nazarov and Ermatov and take a leading role in managing the smelter's financial and trading affairs. 'In reality,' he testified, 'Orienbank had no option but to accede to the government's request. It was not a "request" at all; the government had rather given Orienbank the task of supplying Talco.'[18] The new management were Sadriddin Sharipov and Sherali Kabirov, close confidants of the presidential family. In his witness testimony Kabirov, then deputy director of Orienbank, declared that he was alarmed that the bank was required by the government to become so deeply involved in the aluminium business. He notes that this was brought about by the debt crisis faced by Talco and the government's desire that in future it 'could contribute its share of the state budget'.[19] Kabirov, who took up a senior management position at Talco in 2005 and became its chief financial officer, would go on to play a key role in the establishment of the offshore company as the secretive cash cow of the Tajik state and a select group of private investors.

Russia's role was also crucial in this hostile takeover. The High Court judge, Justice Blackburne, concluded that Rahmon family members and Deripaska's Rusal conspired to expel Ansol from its partnership with Talco following an August 2004 meeting between Deripaska and Rahmon.[20] An agreement was signed with Rusal in October 2004. Shortly thereafter Ermatov was asked to step down as director and, as a token of compensation, stand as a candidate in the February 2005 parliamentary elections.[21] During the period 2004–05, Rahmon also moved against several former civil war allies and foes to remove them from their positions of power. In particular, General Mirzoyev, the associate of Nazarov who had maintained security at the smelter, was replaced as head of the Presidential Guard in January 2004. Mirzoyev threatened a coup and ironically, as a suspected drugs trafficker and former warlord, was placated with the position of head of the Drugs Control Agency – an anti-trafficking body established a few years before at the request of donors. After several months of tension with the government Mirzoyev was arrested, tried and convicted of numerous offences including murder, embezzlement and the illegal possession of arms. In 2006 he was sentenced to life in prison. It was internal politics which drove these developments but, as we shall see, extraterritorial actions were required to consolidate them.[22] Whilst this process began with the Russian connection, it also entangled Western governments and corporations.

The Norwegian connection

There was an apparent geopolitical context for these moves in 2004. That year was the high point in recent relations between Tajikistan and Russia. The July 2004 agreement between Presidents Rahmon and Putin in the Black Sea city of Sochi addressed issues such as the transfer of Tajikistan's southern border from Russian to Tajik control, the status of Russia's space observation centre in Nurek and Tajikistan's debt to Russia. It also included a number of formal and informal commitments regarding Russian investment into Tajik hydropower and aluminium industries. However, business interests were soon to trump the geopolitical factors to which most analysts look to explain Central Asia's international affairs. As the Tajik state became intertwined with global financial and trading assemblages, the future of Talco clearly revealed the interpersonal dynamics and rent-seeking which occurs across the global economy. Rather than deteriorating political and security relations with Russia causing the breakdown in Rusal–Talco relations, the reverse seems to be true as conflicts between Russian and Tajik elites over a Tajik state company led to a downturn in their international relationship and a shift towards the West.

Norway returns, via the British Virgin Islands

Following the removal of Nazarov and Ansol in December 2004, Talco entered into partnerships with various foreign multinationals via new offshore schemes. CDH and Talco Management Ltd (TML), both registered in the British Virgin Islands, were arranged under the advice of Rusal and became the trading companies for Talco, with TML acceding to the primary role in 2007 (see below).[23] This is a trading arrangement known as a 'tolling scheme' – designed to avoid the companies involved being subject to tax, regulation and scrutiny by any private or public institution – as agreed in the settlement with Hydro.[24] CDH and TML are offshore 'cut-out' companies created to reduce tax burdens. They have no formal obligations to the government of Tajikistan but are owned by various state institutions, businesses and individuals in Tajikistan – reportedly for the profit of the Rahmon family.[25]

The new arrangement was ordered by a presidential decree of 23 December 2004, allowing aluminium to be transferred from Talco to CDH either without payment or merely with very small fees.[26] This new deal intensified many of the features of the old – those that controlled CDH and TML also controlled Talco, creating a greater conflict of interest than the previous arrangement with Ansol (whose owner, Nazarov, did not control but bartered with Talco). In the London court, Justice Blackburne concluded that it is difficult to see how this arrangement could have been for the benefit of Talco which is likely to be operating at a 'significant loss'.[27] As the global price for aluminium remained high over this period, Talco's loss meant someone else's gain.

With high stakes, the battle to control and supply Talco went on. From early 2005 the new arrangement had already begun to sour with the government of Tajikistan's allegation of fraud against their partner Rusal and legal action threatened by Hydro against Talco. Furthermore, according to Kabirov, Rusal had gained control of the supply chain and began 'to make extravagant profits by holding a gun to CDH's head and forcing it to pay a higher price for the alumina supplied by Albaco [a Rusal affiliate]'.[28] More foreign companies became involved, citing the government of Tajikistan's reneging on agreements made under the management of Nazarov and Ermatov, whom it had removed in 2004. This included the American company Gerald Metals which, according to a US embassy cable, was 'pressuring and threatening the Tajik government'.[29] Other foreign multinationals, however, were more effective in pressing their claims.

Financial, legal and political pressure eventually told. In 2006, Talco shifted again, this time with Norway's Hydro Aluminium – part of Norsk Hydro, a conglomerate whose majority shareholder is the government of Norway. This was an interim arrangement that would lead to a final deal and the full reorganisation of Tajikistan's major state industry via offshore vehicles. After a June 2006 settlement between Talco and Hydro, the latter became Talco's principal partner, in place of its rival Rusal. An agreement signed in Dushanbe on 20 December 2006 committed Hydro to longer-term investment and possible tripling of the production capacity of the Soviet-era plant.[30] The Norwegian connection was blossoming. In declaring to his American counterpart a Norwegian interest in investing in Tajik hydropower, Moscow-based Norwegian ambassador Øyvind Nordsletten made comparisons between Tajikistan and Norway a hundred years before.[31] The Americans also saw a glimmer of hope. 'At the risk of seeming overly optimistic,' the US ambassador concluded, 'this could represent a significant shift in Tajikistan's investment climate and geopolitical alliances.'[32] Western officials seemed to genuinely hope that liberalisation might finally take hold.

The final act could now take place. The 2006 agreement provided four years' supply of alumina to Talco, paid Hydro for its losses in four years' supply of processed aluminium, and embroiled Hydro with Talco in its ongoing legal struggles with Rusal's affiliates. In February 2007, the tolling contract was put out to tender once more with, unsurprisingly, the newly formed TML winning ahead of two major international companies, Alaska Metals AG (Switzerland) and Noble Resources Ltd (Hong Kong). The agreement – the fourth trading arrangement in three years – was part of the settlement between the companies and was arranged under the auspices of the European Bank for Reconstruction and Development (EBRD) and the World Bank.[33] Hydro remained the key supplier but was joined subsequently by Alaska Metals and the Fortune 500 companies Noble Resources and Glencore International AG (Switzerland) as minor partners to the deal. It was at this moment that TadAz became known as Talco.

A shift from Russia to the West had seemingly taken place. The 2006–07 moves to push out Rusal came at a time of deteriorating relations between Russia and Tajikistan as Dushanbe pursued an active 'multi-vector' foreign policy of seeking greater cooperation with China, India and Iran among other regional powers. As if to confirm the break with Russia in 2007 Rahmonov changed his surname to Rahmon and his brother-in-law Sadullayev to Asadullozoda, in accordance with Persian naming tradition. For the Rahmon family, de-Russification was personal, financial and political – all at the same time. But for a country hugely dependent on access to the Russian labour market for its vast number of labour migrants, this de-Russification was superficial.

New deal, but same corrupt practices?

In fact, there is little or no reason to believe that either 'de-Russification' or liberalisation governed this period of chaos and uncertainty. Explaining the three shifts in Talco's trading relations – which took place in less than three years from 2004 to 2007 – is impossible without reference to the business interests of its principals and the functioning of Tajikistan's kleptocratic regime. As a leaked US diplomatic cable notes, 'RusAl's development of [the] Rogun [Dam, Tajikistan's other major industrial project,] and a second aluminium smelter was one of the key deliverables during Russian President Putin's October 2004 visit to Tajikistan'.[34] But in early 2005, when Tajik–Russian relations were at a high, the Talco deal had already begun to show signs of strain. As a diplomatic cable of August 2006 notes, 'RusAl wants Rogun for aluminium production, not electricity exports, and without a second smelter or full control of TadAz [Talco], it may not need or want Rogun at all'.[35] This judgement proved correct. Rogun remains unbuilt and the Tajik state has struggled to garner international investment and diplomatic support for its construction. Commercial affairs and personal interests trumped geopolitical dynamics and national interests for all sides. Business simply went on.

It would also be a mistake to view the new tolling arrangement with a Western company, Hydro, and under the auspices of international financial institutions (IFIs) as evidence of openness to liberal reform. These players and their involvement in Talco were not new. Hydro had been involved in Talco for some time, having had its first contract in 1993, and had been in partnership with Rusal from 2000 to 2004.[36] Nor was the involvement of the IFIs new. Hydro's role was discussed in a World Bank-facilitated videoconference in May 2004 involving President Rahmon's adviser on economic issues. The World Bank had been involved in international trading and financing arrangements since the late 1990s. But neither the IFIs nor the major Western multinationals have ascertained what exactly happens to the money that Talco's foreign partners transfer to CDH and TML in payment for its aluminium. From 2006, the tolling arrangement with Hydro meant that

Talco remained in debt while profits were accrued by CDH and TML. Kabirov explained this in terms of outstanding monies owed to Hydro to compensate them for their earlier losses.

Despite the optimism of the diplomats, the December 2006 deal was and remains controversial. Hydro's $150 million losses from being thrown out of the Tajik market in 2004 had been covered (minus a $25 million deductible) by an American political risk reinsurance company, Chubb.[37] In September 2004 Hydro's board was told that 'Tajikistan was challenging politically, environmentally and financially'.[38] Around this time, the post-war government moved to close down media, push out opposition from posts in government (which had been agreed under the 1997 peace agreement) and consolidate the president in power by changing the constitution. Multiple reports by donors and the World Bank observed a high level of corruption in government. But, as the aluminium price remained high in the period 2004–06, the profit motive trumped governance concerns.

It wasn't just the Norwegians who were concerned about the bottom line. Chubb – which understandably wanted to recoup its losses – was apparently lobbying the US State Department, whose embassy in Dushanbe was liaising with Norwegian diplomatic counterparts.[39] A July 2006 diplomatic cable quotes the US ambassador speaking directly to President Rahmon about Chubb and the Americans' other interested party Gerald Metals. 'Whoever was mucking around at TadAz has seriously harmed Tajikistan's interests', he remarked, 'especially because political risk insurers for major investment are a very small club, and the TadAz [Talco] mess is globally known.' The cable reports that 'the President nodded but had no reply'.[40] The new deal signed in December 2006 with 'the blessings of the World Bank and the European Bank for Reconstruction and Development' was a marriage of convenience.[41] It allowed Talco to begin repaying its debt in 2007 and Chubb to get its money back.

Due diligence, or 'don't ask, don't tell'?

The problem for Hydro, the World Bank and EBRD was that they were bound both by Norwegian and international laws against corruption.

Hydro remained embroiled in Talco's legal battles over allegations and counter-allegations of fraud with its other former management and foreign trading partners. In effect, Hydro had simply agreed to switch sides in this complex struggle. The December 2006 agreement allowed Talco to continue its litigation in the London court and continue to make the argument that the previous regime (to which Hydro was a partner) was corrupt. The text of the agreement therefore includes some tortuous explanation. Section 9.6 explains that Talco would continue to be within its right to argue that the previous regime was 'a scheme to defraud' Talco and was 'tainted by corruption'. However, Talco also agreed 'that it shall not suggest that Hydro knew about or ought to have known about any fraud or corruption or that it was guilty of any wrong-doing'.[42] In effect, the deal exonerated Hydro from the charges of corruption while allowing Talco to continue to press the very same charges. The question of whether or not, in fact or in law, fraud or corruption had actually taken place appeared incidental to the new arrangement.

So excused, Hydro was now getting back into bed with a government which was recognised as one of the most corrupt in the world. In the 2006 Transparency International corruption index, released a few months before the Talco–Hydro agreement was reached, Tajikistan ranked 142nd – alongside Angola, Pakistan, Nigeria and Turkmenistan – out of 163 countries.[43] Therefore, for a new relationship with Talco to appear legitimate Hydro needed some distance between CDH/TML and President Rahmon's regime. CDH was wholly owned by Orienbank under the personal control of the president's brother-in-law Hasan Asadullozoda (formerly Sadullayev), via another offshore company called Amatola.[44] TML was owned by different parties but with the same effect of presumed control by the Rahmon family and its close associates. However, Sherali Kabirov, Talco's CFO, describes the ownership of TML 'by and for Tajikistan' in his 2008 testimony:

Talco Management is a BVI incorporated company which is owned by Vostokredmet (35 per cent), the Tajik state uranium producer, Barqi Tojik (35 per cent), the state electricity company and the remaining 30 per cent held by a small group of wealthy Tajik private investors.[45]

This new ownership structure reveals a great deal not only about Talco, but also about how Tajikistan operates as a nation state. The 'wealthy private Tajik investors' were assessed by US diplomats to be a group 'presumably including members of the Rahmon family'.[46]

The identities of the members of the 'small group' remained unknown at the time due to the registration of TML in BVI, an offshore jurisdiction. However, later disclosures via WikiLeaks revealed that there were three individuals who each owned 10 per cent of TML. They were not relatives of the president but included Maruf Orifov, a businessman known to the international community for his joint venture in a supermarket chain with a Dutch investor.[47] The story of Orifov's later downfall is instructive as to how individual businessmen on the fringes of the regime are vulnerable to coercion by state institutions.

Within a year of the deal with Hydro, Orifov was charged with bribery after an apparent sting operation by the national security services.[48] He was refused bail and held in a pre-trial facility – unusual for his offence. Orifov had all his property confiscated – presumably including his 10 per cent stake in TML – and was sentenced to eight and half years in prison – more than double what was requested by the public prosecutor. The specific cause of Orifov's downfall is unknown but diplomats in Dushanbe had a good idea. One of Orifov's supermarkets was located in a building owned by a member of the president's family. US Ambassador Tracey Ann Jacobson reports credibly that Orifov 'ran afoul of President Rahmon's daughter, Tahmina' after he had tried 'to curry favor with the President's "inner circle" by doing business with [her]'. Orifov's fall from grace is, she notes, an 'example of the country's oppressive business environment, and the ruthless manner in which members of President Rahmon's family exert their influence over business owners'. In short, Jacobson concludes, 'it is more important to be close to President Rahmon and his family members than to run a successful business'.[49]

The London court took a similar view with regard to Talco's offshore companies. It recognised that the tolling arrangements were in the interests of the beneficial owners of CDH/TML, which it presumed to be President Rahmon, his family and close associates. The Norwegian company apparently disagreed. In 2007, Hydro's lawyers referred to a forthcoming audit of TML as the basis for transparency in its transactions concerning Tajik Aluminium.[50] But the forthcoming audit would come rather late when a major deal had already been done several months before. As the Carnegie Endowment's Martha Brill Olcott points out, this is ironic given Hydro's 'well-publicized "integrity" program in the area of corruption and human rights'. Olcott argues that the Norwegian company 'must have had some suspicion as to who was really profiting from the new tolling scheme, given the personal roles that President Rahmon and those close to him had played in the negotiations with Hydro'.[51] An IMF report released in 2008 considered Talco's lack of both transparency and financial controls to be 'most worrisome'.[52] Under the provisions of its new agreement with the IMF, following the scandal of the National Bank redirecting IMF credits to the financiers of its cotton industry (cronies of the president), Tajikistan was required to publish an audit of TML (the one mentioned by Hydro's lawyers).[53] However, it would take several more years to reveal the audited accounts of TML, its expenditures on behalf of the president's family and inner circle and the compromises Hydro had made in getting back into bed with Rahmon's regime.

How Talco's offshore connections work

To recap, over the period from 2004 to 2008, by fair means and foul, the Rahmon family and their key associates wrested complete control of Talco from the previous management and Rusal, before coming to a new arrangement with Norway's Hydro as the chief international partner.

While the principal managers and owners shifted over the period from 2004 to 2008, the structure of the tolling agreements has probably changed little since the involvement of Nazarov in 1996 (see Figure 3.1). Although the London High Court hearings did not reach a verdict, they

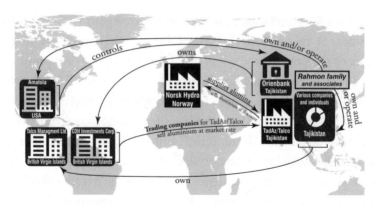

Figure 3.1 Talco tolling arrangements and structures

heard considerable evidence that round-tripping or 'tolling' agreements established under CDH/TML were illegitimate and thus constituted fraud.[54] Justice Blackburne judged in October 2005 that there was 'a seriously arguable case' that, as presented in the evidence by Ansol, 'the new arrangement [from December 2004] was designed to enable the benefit of TadAZ [Talco]'s smelting activities to pass to those who own or control CDH, namely Rusal and/or close associates and relatives of President Rahmonov led [at that time] by Mr [Asadullozoda] Saduloev'.[55] Following the Talco–Hydro agreement of June 2006, the basic structure of the 'tolling agreement' remained in place with CDH, and later TML, accruing profits for the benefits of their owners and to the disadvantage of state-owned Talco. At the very least the IFIs and Hydro were implicated unwittingly in the fraud perpetrated by Talco and its tolling companies.

To the Caribbean and back (twice)

So precisely how did these global economic assemblages work? John Helmer, a Moscow-based journalist who followed the court proceedings, describes the arrangements established by the June 2006 Talco–Hydro agreement:

> The court presentation of the documents shows that, according to a scheme of tolling the raw materials for processing at contrived prices,

Talco receives alumina from Hydro and gives it to CDH. CDH then contracts it for processing by the smelter and receives the metal back in exchange. CDH then sells the same metal back to Talco at the market price, and Talco sells it to Hydro at a loss.[56]

The same basic system was used for TML and is a common means of avoiding tax and ensuring secrecy used by multinational corporations all over the world. The lion's share of profits is transferred to CDH/TML whilst only a portion is returned to Talco in the form of a 'tolling fee' for services rendered. Talco is thus transformed from an aluminium exporter to a processor of aluminium and subcontractor to the offshore trading company CDH/TML. As Talco bears all the costs of production, as well as the legal fees of the court case, it made just $15 million profit over the period from 2005 to 2007, despite an approximately 200 per cent increase in the price of aluminium over this time. Meanwhile, CDH/TML is estimated to have made at least $500 million for its owners.[57]

The revenues lost from the Tajik public purse may have been higher. In 2008, Helmer, drawing on a published IMF report, estimated that Talco earned just 17 per cent of the total value of its exports to foreign buyers in 2006 and 2007. The report lists the value of the 'tolling fees' received as $173 million for 2006 and $183 million for 2007 whilst the total market value of the exported aluminium for each year is calculated at around $1 billion.[58] According to calculations based on the available evidence, this would mean that over the period from 2005 to 2007, Talco, and thus the Tajik state, lost $1.145 billion in revenues due to this trading scheme. If accurate, this would be a massive amount for a country with a GDP of just $3.7 billion in 2007.[59] These profits, according to the trading scheme, were accrued by the owners of CDH/TML and their foreign partners.[60]

The wider political economy in Tajikistan that supports this system is one of kleptocracy and cronyism. Associates and even family members rise or fall and gain or lose pieces of the pie, according to their ability to please the president and act according to his preferences. Some are able to cement these relations by marrying their children into the presidential family. Although in 2004 Hasan Asadullozoda's Orienbank managed the transition following the expulsion of the previous management, in 2007 tensions were emerging in the presidential family over control of business assets in the growing economy. By this time, Talco in particular had paid off various debts to foreign parties and was beginning to turn a greater profit. In particular, Asadullozoda, who was married to Rahmon's younger sister, was said to be in conflict with some of the president's children, particularly Rahmon's eldest daughters Tahmina and Ozoda (the deputy foreign minister). The president's son, Rustam Emomali, was now coming of age and was known for racing his sports car down Dushanbe's main avenue, his unusually successful football team, and his temper.

These matters appear to have come to a head in May 2008, a few weeks after Asadullozoda's final witness statement in the London court case (13 April 2008), when he disappeared from public view for several weeks. Rumours spread around Dushanbe that Asadullozoda had been shot by another family member or associate and subsequently died in intensive care. Most accounts identified 2 May 2008 as the day Hasan Asadullozoda was shot, with some suggesting he may have died several days later. Accounts are sketchy as to who fired at Hasan but regional websites identified Rustam as the shooter.[61] The truth of what precisely happened has never come out and it was not until much later – following a delay in the court proceedings in London – that Asadullozoda's survival was verified.[62] His lawyer told Justice Tomlinson:

> It is regrettable that Mr Saduloev [Asadullozoda] did not sign until last Friday. He did sign. He did not die and then become resurrected and die again. He is alive and well. But, for whatever reasons, for reasons we say of his travel and difficulty with communication and him just being too busy to look at it, too preoccupied, it was not signed until Friday [25 July 2008].[63]

Asadullozoda was dispossessed of some key assets but allowed to remain head of Orienbank. In particular, he would no longer control, formally or informally, Talco's lucrative tolling schemes.

It is easy to see this astonishing but – by Tajikistan's standards – commonplace story of the secret state as being one of local corruption and presidential family infighting. But this framing misses the offshore, international and extraterritorial dimensions of the Talco case. This is not simply state capture by the regime, but the creation of a specific arrangement, with the involvement of the World Bank, EBRD and a Norwegian state enterprise, to defraud the Tajik public and enrich private and global interests. The fraud, its exposure and subsequent demands for reform would not be possible without the dynamics of globalisation to which Tajikistan has been exposed increasingly since the end of the civil war in the late 1990s. What is fascinating is how both the economic arrangements and the political accountability for them both occur in offshore and extraterritorial jurisdictions – in London and Swiss courts, Norwegian state investigations, online press and audits of shell companies.

Details begin to emerge

Such 'transparency' is rare and partial. In the period from 2008 to 2010, IFI pressure mounted on Talco to publish the results of the IMF-ordered audit and revaluation. However, the IFIs themselves are implicated in an arrangement that is perfectly legal and seen as vital for business and thus economic growth. The Tajik political scientist Rustam Samiyev was clear about the reasons for the delay in completion and publication:

> Most likely, Talco is trying to conceal its 'tolling system' of partnerships with raw material suppliers that helps deflect hundreds of millions of dollars into tax-free zones. Nothing is wrong with that practice in the eyes of international business and donors ... Yet it betrays the Tajik people's interests.[64]

On 25 June 2010, the IMF called once again for the publication of the audit and revaluation of Talco and TML on the company's website. On 3 August 2010, Talco announced that it had received these reports from the auditors and provided a rather defensive summary of their findings justifying the legal fees which had been paid.[65] Talco's press release states that the audit showed that the $51 million spent on lawyers in the action against Nazarov and the Ansol Company was 'forced [in order] to uphold the interests of, in the first instance, the country and defence of the company'.[66] Subsequently, TML released audits undertaken by the Yerevan-based auditor Grant Thornton JSC for the years 2009–11 with headline figures but without explanatory notes and detail. They are no longer public but were made available to the authors.[67] They show that by 2011 TML had accumulated consolidated profits of $244 million, had acquired $33 million in property, and made $30 million in what are called 'other expenses'.[68] These profits are considerably less than those estimated by Helmer based on the tolling arrangement and the price of aluminium. This raised the question of what happened to the money, which will be explored below.

In the meantime, Swiss court judgments have established unequivocally that the Rahmon regime's seizure of Talco from its previous management in 2004 was effectively illegal and that tolling arrangements that defraud the Tajik people remain central to the operation of the smelter. In May and October 2013, these courts, operating under the procedures of the International Court of Arbitration, twice found in favour of subsidiaries of Rusal and handed down a total of $345 million in fines, interest and costs to be paid by Talco.[69] What began as a dispute within the Tajik ruling elite was eventually decided via a legal process between several BVI entities, established by a Russian state company, in a Swiss court, according to international law.

The ruling effectively refutes the government of Tajikistan's claims that alumina supply and tolling arrangements established before 2004 were illegal *and* fundamentally different from those it formed after 2004. This claim had been the justification for the government's seizure of Talco from the Nazarov management in 2004 that precipitated the inconclusive London arbitrations from 2004 to 2008. Contrary to the government's claims, the tolling arrangements appear fundamentally similar and have basically the same effect of generating a large slush fund to finance the personal ventures and schemes of the ruling elite.

'Each year,' as *The Economist* stated in 2013, 'Talco produces hundreds of millions of dollars in profits that are routed to a shell company in the British Virgin Islands.'[70] In October 2016, just before we went to press, Tajikistan's own Ministry of Finance released an unprecedented report which stated that $1.1 billion earned by Talco from 2010–16 was unaccounted for and concealed in offshore accounts.[71] The question is what happens next.

The president's slush fund

Talco and the Rahmon regime continue to assert that these tax avoidance arrangements are for the benefit of the country and people of Tajikistan. The aluminium company claims to be currently spending $2.2 billion on two projects to develop production capacity and local raw materials within Tajikistan, but that this can only occur if monies held by TML are transferred back to Talco. These projects are of an extraordinary scale – equivalent to more than one-quarter of the 2013 GDP of the country – and are proposed to occur in a relatively short space of time, with expected completion in three years.[72] This is a vast amount of resources to expend for a state which lacks the impartial bodies and independent legal system to monitor these investments, their contracts and subcontracts. Opportunities for corruption abound and the prospects for successful completion of these ambitious projects are questionable.

A little here, a little there . . .

Indeed, the reappropriation and redirection of state funds to the benefit of private individuals, and vice versa, has been essential to the functioning of Talco in independent Tajikistan. The counter-claim made by Talco in the Swiss court proceeding, which ran from 2008 to 2013, was that the forced takeover of the management and trading affairs of the smelter in 2004 was due to the corruption of Nazarov and Ermatov during the period of their joint control from 1996 to 2004. This was said to include gifts from Nazarov to Ermatov's family members of London and Moscow flats, education fees, sham consultancies and company directorships.[73] However, the two businessmen were managing Talco, a state company, at the time of the growing strength of Rahmon and his regime. Surely any corruption took place under the auspices of President Rahmon. As the Swiss judgment rules:

> Until late 2004, both Mr. Nazarov and Mr. Ermatov were in their positions because of the support of the Government and maintained close relationships with the Government. There is ample evidence that TadAZ [Talco], as the main engine of the Tajik economy, and Mr. Nazarov were used to generate cash for state projects and to fund other expenses, such as official Tajik delegations, schools and security, that would usually be paid for through Government revenue.[74]

Earlier court cases had revealed payments of $1 million per month from Nazarov to the president in 2003, and a total of $1.5 million to purchase jewellery for the president's wife in 2003 and 2004.[75] It was, the court rules in typically understated terms, 'a system lacking in transparency, which created the potential for corruption'.[76]

The potential for corruption was both widespread and widely known at the highest reaches of the state. For example, in 2004, payments of around $8 million were made by Nazarov's company Ansol to a company called Pakhtai Sharitus, a partly privatised cotton business part-owned by the brother of Hasan Sadullayev, the president's brother-in-law.[77] The court concludes that the government must have known about these allegedly corrupt transactions both because the principal beneficiary was a member of the president's extended family and because of the ongoing monitoring of Talco in the period shortly before its takeover by the regime. 'President Rahmon,' the court reports, 'had instructed all ministries to keep close tabs on Talco and its business out of fear that General Mirzoev might attempt a coup d'état financed by Mr. Nazarov and there is no doubt that Orienbank would have acted on the president's instructions.'[78] Once again, family and state, public and private, onshore and offshore, were intertwined as Rahmon sought a stranglehold on the country's economy to the disadvantage of those warlords and businessmen who had done his bidding during the civil war and post-war recovery.

The pattern of using Talco's profits as a national slush fund beholden to the president and his associates continued under the new management. Sherali Kabirov, who remains in place to this day as CFO of Talco, explained in his witness testimony before the London court how, on the instruction of President Rahmon, he would increase the tolling fee paid to Talco by CDH/TML in order to invest in public infrastructure. 'For example,' he testified, 'on one occasion in April 2007 the President asked that [Talco] pay for some local school and social projects.'[79] Since then, Kabirov claims, profits accrued in the BVI by CDH/TML have been directly reinvested back in Tajikistan, again on the instruction of the president. These offshore-routed profits paid for, among other things,

> the purchase of new heavy equipment for [Talco] and the construction of new brick and cable factories. Various further projects designed to facilitate and improve international trade are also underway including the construction of Tajikistan's first 5 star hotel [the Hyatt Regency], the renovation of Dushanbe airport, the establishment of a new airline with modern planes and European-trained pilots, and the purchase of 200 new Peugeot taxis for Dushanbe.[80]

A hotel? An airport? An airline? Taxis? This is quite an extraordinarily long and varied list of items that might be purchased by the state's offshore slush fund. Just as Talco's trading arrangements are a mishmash of domestic and international partners, public and private institutions, so are the profits of the enterprise used to serve an immense variety of purposes that are deemed to be in the 'national interest'.

Buying US planes – and influence

A proportion of the offshore gains were spent in the United States. In January 2014, a BVI-based lawyer operating on behalf of the liquidator of CDH and Rusal subsidiaries who had been victorious over CDH in the Swiss courts in 2013 filed a request to the US district court to open the now defunct company's books and search for its assets. The successful request claimed that 'CDH has been stripped of its assets and CDH's directors and TML colluded in moving CDH's business to TML for little or no consideration'. Furthermore, they alleged that 'Talco's profits have constantly been and are still being moved to TML since 2007 for little or no consideration'.[81]

These documents were made available to the journalist David Trilling who wrote a series of investigative stories.[82] They list wires in excess of $140 million over the period from 2008 to 2014, including around $97 million in 2008–09 which was spent on leasing two Boeing 737 aeroplanes for the new private airline Somon Air, owned by Orienbank and controlled, according to the US ambassador, 'by the President'.[83] These aeroplanes continue to fly commercial flights to and from Dushanbe on behalf of Somon Air. Once again, the line between public and private in the ownership of the airline is so blurred as to disappear from view. The wire transfers suggest that in addition to funding the new airline, CDH funds were also deployed as a maintenance budget for the increasingly degraded Talco plant with over $40 million spent on spare parts, equipment, chemicals and technical consultancy. These appear to be for the aluminium industry but could just as easily be for another private business controlled by the presidential family.

However, the $140 million spent over the period from 2007 to 2014, whilst equivalent to about 2 per cent of Tajikistan's official GDP, is small beer compared with the revenues of TML over this time. Even accounting for the decline in the global price of aluminium, the income of TML in this time can be expected to amount to several billion dollars. The considerable production costs were met by the plant and effectively paid for by the Tajik taxpayer out of the general state budget and subsidised electricity prices. In turn, TML continued to contribute to state projects at the behest of the president. It paid around half of the $5 million cost of the construction of the world's tallest flagpole in Dushanbe – three metres higher than the previous holder of that honour in Azerbaijan – built to mark twenty years of independence in 2011.[84] But this phallocentric act of nation-building is only a small proportion of the money channelled offshore. So what happened to the rest of the TML billions?

The answer to this question is not clear as the TML audits for the years after 2008 are incomplete and lack sufficient detail. We know that much has gone to pay creditors. However, investigations by Helmer and Trilling have revealed where a small proportion of the money is going. Since October 2012, TML has been paying the Washington lobbyists Fabiani & Company $1.2 million per year 'to increase Talco's business opportunities and indirectly, improve the Republic of Tajikistan's investment profile and relationship with the United States'. In an initial blitz of lobbying from January to May 2013, Fabiani staff held over eighty meetings in Congress, largely to promote the Rogun Dam, the flagship state project that would become the highest dam in the world, if built. This included meetings with Republican and Democratic representatives on key committees and some of their senior staff. Part of Fabiani's remit under its contract with TML is 'educating the Administration and Members of Congress, opinion leaders, and representatives of the Government of Tajikistan on issues of importance to Talco Management Ltd'.[85] In order to generate any interest at all, lobbyists tied Tajikistan to the 'Af-Pak narrative' and 'New Silk Road' strategy – Washington's 'inside the beltway' talk for US policy to defeat terrorism and build intra-regional economic ties in Central Asia. By December 2013, this lobbying was apparently gleaning results with a US announcement that it would invest $15 million in the CASA-1000 project to export electricity from Tajikistan.

In January and February 2014, we worked with Helmer and Trilling to get to the bottom of the influence Tajikistan was buying in Washington. It was not difficult to begin to join the dots. It emerged that, having been commissioned by the lobbyists, Hillary Kramer, an investments analyst at Forbes.com, had gone to Dushanbe to record a video interview with President Rahmon and written promotional 'puff pieces' about Tajikistan that were later taken down from the site amid an investigation.[86] The focus of the interview, these articles and the meetings with congressional staffers was the proposed Rogun Dam which, if completed, would provide electricity for both Talco and export to South Asia – but not necessarily to Tajikistan's impoverished domestic consumers.

However, despite the awareness-raising and educational goals of Fabiani on behalf of TML, it soon became clear that our enquiries were unwanted. On 30 January 2014, on the advice of lawyers, Fabiani had filed an amendment notice with the Foreign Agents Registration Act (FARA) stating that its relationship with TML had ended and it was therefore no longer required to report its work for them.[87] But it appears that what was actually terminated was not Fabiani's lobbying on behalf of TML – which may continue to this day – but the reporting requirement.[88] As Helmer describes, following his conversation with Alexander Botting of Fabiani on 26 February 2014:

> According to Botting, the Justice Department has ruled that because the foreign principal isn't a government, and is nothing more than a management company registered in the British Virgin Islands, Fabiani's activities on its behalf, the payments it receives each month, and the meetings it has with US officials, no longer come under the Act and are no longer reportable. Talco Management [TML], the Justice Department was told, is nothing more than a commercial business.[89]

This is a remarkable tale. The offshore vehicle TML is effective not only at hiding the private use of state assets from the weary Tajik people but also at concealing Tajikistan's activities in the US Congress from the Department of Justice. In claiming that the Rogun Dam is a commercial project, both Fabiani and the Justice Department appear to disregard the facts. These pertain to the Rahmon regime's long political struggle to get Rogun built and the statements by Uzbekistan that it would go to war to prevent the construction of a dam which it says would cut its supply of agricultural and drinking water. They also seem ignorant of the publicly available court records that detail how TML is majority-owned by the state and the US State Department's judgment that it is fully controlled by the president of Tajikistan.

Back in the USSR, or neoliberal authoritarianism?

By the summer of 2014, the government of Tajikistan was considering its international trading options once more. Rusal had begun to apply pressure via the opening up of CDH's books, and Talco's CFO Sherali

Kabirov sounded a conciliatory note with the Russian company. Around the same time, as Moscow sought to build its regional bloc against the West, Kyrgyzstan announced its intention to join Russia's Eurasian Union, opening up the possibility of Tajikistan also acceding to Moscow's economic integration project. On the other hand, Tajikistan's lobbying in Washington via the offshore TML appears to have borne fruit with tens of millions of dollars secured to finance the CASA-1000 electricity network and a contract signed with an Italian engineering company to finally build the Rogun Dam.

Tajikistan today

In 2016, ten years after Hydro had signed up to re-enter Tajikistan, the vain (and perhaps insincere) hopes for reform of US and Norwegian officials now look absurd. Chinese investment and soft loans to Tajikistan have eroded the influence of Western aid and the leverage of the IFIs. In 2006, a major north–south highway project was financed by a $296 million loan from the Chinese government.[90] Today, China is by far Tajikistan's largest trading partner, accounting for an enormous 45 per cent of its imports.[91] Many Chinese investments are also made via offshore detours. This use of the unregulated avenues of the international financial system does not imply a commitment to the free market as business in Tajikistan continues to flow through the regime and the country still languishes in the lower reaches of global corruption indices. It is a very different economy from the Soviet one in which Talco was born. Rather than socialism in one country, Tajikistan now practises crony capitalism in the global economy.

Politically, Tajikistan's authoritarian regime has hardened. Since the mid-2000s, the country's secular opposition parties have been dismembered by splits orchestrated by the government while new pro-government 'opposition' parties have been created. Opposition movements such as Group 24 and New Tajikistan have been driven overseas and their exiles pursued relentlessly with the help of the Russian authorities, the abuse of Interpol and the Tajik state's connections to organised crime (see Chapter 7). The last opposition party, the Islamic

Revival Party of Tajikistan (IRPT), whose former leader signed the peace agreement with President Rahmon in 1997, is now banned and declared a terrorist organisation. Lawyers defending the IRPT's leaders have themselves been jailed. According to Freedom House, a leading American human rights group, Tajikistan 'increasingly resembles a one-party state'; it now receives the lowest possible rating of national democratic governance available in the 'Nations in Transit' index which measures 'transition' after the fall of the Soviet Union.[92]

At a cursory glance, Tajikistan appears to be going backwards. But the evidence discussed above suggests that partial liberalisation of the economy and cooperation with new Western actors, including offshore jurisdictions, has enabled the development of Tajikistan's kleptocracy and, by extension, its hardening authoritarianism. Investment from Hydro and other investors, with oversight from the World Bank, provided the resources that allowed the regime to consolidate itself out of the ashes of civil war. Such opportunities were not afforded by the Soviet Union. This is a neoliberal authoritarianism enhanced by the globalisation of finance.

Questions in Oslo

Notwithstanding these rather general conclusions about the culpability of the international financial system, the question for Hydro and the World Bank is whether they should have seen this coming in 2006 when the agreement to re-enter Tajikistan was signed. This debate raised its head in Norway in early 2016 following reporting by the Norwegian business newspaper *Dagens Næringsliv*.[93] This led to the Norwegian government writing to Hydro, in which it has a 50 per cent stake, on 22 February 2016, in order to demand an explanation from the company for its actions in Tajikistan. Hydro's report of 7 March 2016 is revealing, as much for what it does not say as for what it does. The company claims that 'confidentiality obligations' had prevented full disclosure when the matter was raised in the Norwegian press in 2007 but, reading the report, we are left with the impression that much remains hidden from view.[94]

Hydro argues that it has 'zero tolerance of corruption'.[95] In the report, the company argues that it was not party to the fraud and corruption recognised in the High Court's verdict of 2005.[96] However, the parties that were named by the judge as the beneficiaries of the corruption – namely President Rahmon and his allies – were to be Hydro's business partners again from 2007. It is hard to reconcile zero tolerance of corruption with a willingness to re-enter a relationship with a corrupt partner via a creative offshore arrangement. Hydro's proposed solution to this dilemma was that 30 per cent of TML should be 'beneficially owned by parties at arm's length from the Tajik government'.[97] At the same time, the report acknowledges that 'establishing an enterprise in a so-called tax haven generally is associated with a greater risk of corruption and concealment of funds, as a result of lack of transparency'.[98] Hydro therefore commissioned an open source due diligence study. In its summary of the study, Hydro states the following:

> The due diligence revealed nothing that was considered harmful for the reputation of the owners of TML. It was revealed that the private owners were Tajiki businessmen with extensive networks. No information was found to indicate that any of them had been involved in – or investigated for – any improper or unlawful business.[99]

However, in Tajikistan, there is no such thing as 'businessmen with extensive networks' that are 'at arm's length from the Tajik government'. The political economy of the country – as would have been clear from the judgments of the London court and any number of international academic and policy studies at the time – means that all high-level business networks are connected to the regime. Moreover, it goes without saying that such well-connected persons would not be investigated 'for improper or unlawful business'. Only those who fall out of favour with the regime face such investigations, as the case of Maruf Orifov subsequently showed. Hydro had thirteen years of experience working in Tajikistan by this time, and (prior to its legal dispute with Talco) acknowledged it to be 'challenging politically, environmentally and financially'.[100] What was clear to impartial and informed observers in 2006, and remained clear in 2016, is that the boundaries between onshore and offshore and between public and private sectors are, in effect, entirely absent in Tajikistan.

The global character of the family state

One man is the constant in the remarkable story of Talco. That man is Emomali Rahmon. Once a state farm manager, he became the placeman of a brutal warlord and rose, via offshore and international connections, to be the head of a state that he runs in the interests of his family and inner circle. It is commonplace to think of Talco's commercial and legal struggles as a microcosm of Tajik politics. But the reverse may be equally true: Tajik politics is a microcosm of the international and offshore battle to control the country's biggest industry. Amid the drama of thwarted coups d'état, presidential family feuds, the diversion of state resources on a vast scale, secretive foreign lobbying, and one of the most expensive cases in English legal history, Sherali Kabirov used the opportunity of his witness testimony to the London court to defend the honour of the country. 'Tajikistan,' he opined, 'is one of the more successful countries in Central Asia in managing the transition to democracy and it continues to transform and improve itself.'[101]

This picture of the republic is belied by the realities of the family state where the president and his inner circle can act with impunity against their rivals. The list of names of those who have fallen out of favour with President Rahmon and paid a high price – from former Talco manager Nazarov and security chief Mirzoyev in 2004 to the former insiders and latter-day oppositionists Zayd Saidov and Umarali Kuvvatov in 2014 and 2015 (see Chapter 7) – continues to grow.[102] These individuals are, without a hint of irony, portrayed as 'bad apples' and charged with corruption. In March 2015, Rustam Emomali, President Rahmon's son, took on the state Anti-Corruption Agency – a body established ten years before at the behest of Western donors – to ensure that this dividing line between acceptable and unacceptable corruption is maintained.

Corruption is a constant in Tajikistan's family state to the extent that the use of the term with respect to business in the country is something of a misnomer. You can only have corruption if there already exists some alternative state of good governance. This mythic good governance would be based on clear demarcations of the public and private, without conflicts of interest and with the public disclosure of transactions. As the Swiss court ruled, 'charitable support of both Tajik individuals and State projects were not only not secret, but expected in Tajik culture and well-known within Tajikistan'.[103] But the suggestion that this corruption is an entirely cultural and local phenomenon is misleading. Without the financial and international instruments of offshore vehicles and extraterritorial legal processes, corruption on the scale described here would be neither possible nor effective. If major Western companies, American regulators, due diligence researchers and international organisations were not willing to turn a blind eye to the likelihood of corruption via secret jurisdictions, then the capture of the state by the family could not have occurred in the way that it has.

This offshore dimension has been instrumental in the shift of power since the 1990s. The Tajik state used to be distributed across multiple factions of warlords, businessmen and politicians. Now it is in the hands of just one faction: President Rahmon, his family and inner circle. As our next chapter on Uzbekistan discusses, the Tashkent regime and its family members also have their offshore connections, which have led to a corruption scandal of global proportions.

4

UZBEKISTAN'S CLOSED POLITY AND GLOBAL SCANDAL

Uzbekistan is commonly viewed as the contemporary and historical heartland of its region, the only country to border every other Central Asian state. Home to the region's largest population (about 30 million) and the old Silk Road cities of Samarkand and Bukhara, the inheritor of some of the most acute legacies of Russian and Soviet rule, and with a strong sense of national identity, Uzbekistan vies with Kazakhstan for the status of the region's most influential state.

Unlike Kazakhstan, which has embraced a public image as a global crossroads controlled by a cosmopolitan group of influential oligarchs, or Tajikistan with its history of civil war, post-Soviet Uzbekistan is usually portrayed as a self-contained island of repression, stagnation and economic autarky. For twenty-five years since its independence, the country was led by the ruthless Islam Karimov, the former first party secretary of the Soviet Socialist Republic of Uzbekistan, who consolidated his grip on power through a presidential election in 1990 and a number of subsequent uncontested ballots and referenda to extend his term – the latest being in 2015. In a region where repression is the political norm, Karimov, right up until his death in 2016, was perhaps the most brutal of all regional leaders, banning opposition political parties, crushing all forms of dissent and opposition media, condoning and routinising torture, all while using the threat of Islamic radicalism to justify his iron grip.

1 Kazakh oligarch Mukhtar Ablyazov in Almaty, 2006.

2 Kazakhstan President Nursultan Nazarbayev at the Astana Economic Forum, 2013.

3 Tajikistan President Emomali Rahmon and US Secretary of State John Kerry at the Palace of Nations in Dushanbe, Tajikistan, for a bilateral meeting in 2015.

4 The Tajik Aluminium Company (Talco), located in Tursunzade, Tajikistan.

5 President Rahmon's growing family in 2011. Including the in-laws, the family is much larger.

6 Uzbekistan's first president Islam Karimov with John Kerry in Samarkand, 2015.

7 Gulnara Karimova at the World Economic Forum in Jordan, 2009.

8 TeliaSonera's offices in Sweden, 2012.

9 President Kurmanbek Bakiyev of Kyrgyzstan with Donald Rumsfeld in 2005.

10 Maxim Bakiyev and officials from Kyrgyzstan's Central Agency for Development and Investment, 2009.

11 Tajik opposition leader Umarali Kuvvatov, who was assassinated in Istanbul in March 2015.

12 David Nazarov, son of Obidkhon qori Nazarov, at a demonstration following the assassination attempt on his father in Sweden, 2013.

But if we view Uzbekistan's authoritarianism and autarky as a purely internal or local globalised phenomenon, we miss the critical ways in which the country's authoritarian politics, including its elite struggles, rent-seeking and familial infighting, is increasingly taking place within global spaces. Chapter 7 will further explore how the Uzbek government's brutal crackdown in Andijan in 2005, a pivotal moment in the region's post-Soviet history, created a wave of dissidents, refugees and asylum seekers. In response, Uzbek authorities initiated a worldwide manhunt to track down, extradite and even eliminate political opponents and refugees who have fled the Central Asian country.

In this chapter, we explore another critical local–global interaction: how Uzbekistan's closed oligarchic regime and closed economic system have spawned a series of high-profile global corruption scandals and anti-money-laundering investigations involving members of the president's family and their overseas assets. These scandals have attracted the international media spotlight and shed light on the corrupt schemes hatched between international telecoms providers and Uzbek officials to access the lucrative emerging Central Asian market. But they also appear to have exacerbated family rivalries within the president's closest circles, implicating his eldest daughter Gulnara Karimova in an internal power struggle. They demonstrate how, despite Uzbekistan's domestic political and economic closure, its elite and familial politics play out in a global context that includes Swiss bank accounts, New York court hearings and Swedish media investigations.

Charting a course to statehood

Western commentators are often fond of drawing direct connections between Uzbekistan's closed state and the Soviet era. And to be sure, there are several institutional legacies that have endured, including the system of cotton procurement, the primary role of the state and the importance of regional elites in maintaining a stable system of centre–periphery relations. But Soviet Uzbekistan was also the prime example of how Soviet institutions and practices, including the local party structure and system of agricultural production, were co-opted for local and regional purposes.[1] Elites in Soviet Uzbekistan built formidable patronage machines with Soviet resources and took advantage of Soviet federalism in areas like education and labour-market hiring to promote their own social network and political allies.[2] As long as Uzbek elites remained loyal to Moscow and the overall Soviet system, Moscow was willing to tolerate certain amounts of elite embezzlement and autonomy.[3] However, as shown by the infamous Uzbek cotton scandal of the 1980s – where central auditors discovered that the republic had billed Moscow for over a billion rubles of cotton that was never produced – corruption, nepotism and patronage seemed to be the rule rather than the exception as Uzbekistan transitioned to independence.[4]

After a brief flirtation with a democratic political system in the 1990s, political parties were soon eliminated and Karimov quickly moved to consolidate power.[5] He swiftly built a reputation for tight control and was particularly concerned with identifying and crushing all forms of political opposition. The Uzbek regime's propensity for political violence, as Eric McGlinchey has argued, has been particularly targeted at religious organisations and figures, with the government fearful of the political implications of the country's steady Islamic revival.[6] Uzbekistan's elite also promoted new national symbols, myths and cultural events, using the state as an active vehicle for image-crafting and national branding.[7]

The key to Karimov's heavy-handed state-building and political consolidation is the notorious National Security Service of Uzbekistan (SNB), the most powerful of Central Asia's security organs, which plays a critical role in supporting the regime amid the country's system of regional hierarchies and informal networks.[8] These forces were responsible for most of the killings in Andijan in 2005.

Economically too, Uzbekistan has openly bucked calls for liberalisation by consistently protecting its state-dominated economy. Informal patronage networks play a critical role in allocating selective benefits to the bureaucracy and political supporters to retain loyalty to the state,[9] while the economy is still dominated by state monopolies over a number of key commodities and export sectors, including gold and cotton. The latter industry has been fiercely criticised by human rights groups for employing the forced labour of hundreds of thousands of children and civil servants during the annual harvest. Cotton is both a source of revenue for the Uzbek government and an enduring form of social control over rural populations.[10] Children are required to put their education on hold to participate in the annual harvest. Given state pressure, farmers have little other option but to cultivate cotton, with the regime apparently motivated by the massive profits to be had in selling cotton bought at artificially low rates to global buyers.[11] The government's dependence on gold as an export commodity and source of hard currency has frequently led to clashes with international mining companies which have braved the country's dismal investment climate, with Uzbekistan involved in more international arbitrations (most of them involving the gold sector) than any other Central Asian state.[12]

As with Kyrgyzstan and Tajikistan, millions of Uzbeks now live and work overseas as labour migrants, even while Tashkent maintains strict capital controls and trade restrictions. According to the World Bank, in 2011 typical times for the import or export of goods across its borders were over 100 days, higher than even the excessive regional average in Central Asia,[13] while since the 2000s Uzbek customs and security services have moved to restrict border access to neighbours, effectively militarising the country's borders.[14]

In terms of its foreign policy, Uzbekistan has aggressively championed its sovereignty and autonomy. Karimov was intensely distrustful of cooperating with his neighbours, especially upstream Tajikistan which controls access to water sources vital to Uzbekistan's agricultural system. Karimov also mastered the art of pursuing a multi-vector foreign policy, while aggressively playing the region's external powers off against one another in an effort to secure military assistance, preserve his autonomy, and fend off criticism of his repressive practices.[15] Always in the name of privileging the country's sovereignty and autonomy, the Uzbek president balked at deepening regional economic or security cooperation through Russian-led bodies such as the CSTO or the Eurasian Economic Union.[16]

From 2001 to 2005, Tashkent developed very close security relations with the United States, which established a military base known as K2 near the southern city of Khanabad to supply its operations in neighbouring Afghanistan. In return, the United States provided hundreds of millions of dollars in military assistance (both in equipment and training) as a tacit quid pro quo for acquiring basing rights, maintained close intelligence ties, and, according to accounts, regularly cooperated with Uzbek security services in the rendition and even torture of 'terror suspects'.[17] But after the events in Andijan, when Western countries criticised Tashkent's repressive crackdown, Karimov, fearing another 'colour revolution' or challenge to his authority, evicted US forces from their base in K2 and tilted back towards Russia's orbit by joining the CSTO.[18] Beginning in the mid-2000s, the government has closed down the activities of Western NGOs and foundations that it deemed threatening to the regime, as Tashkent has grown increasingly hostile to criticism of its human rights practices by the West.

In the late 2000s, after Western sanctions were imposed following the events in Andijan, the US resumed cooperation with Tashkent to open and maintain the Northern Distribution Network to supply materials to Afghanistan. As the United States began its large-scale withdrawal from Afghanistan, US officials confirmed that they would be transferring 330 military vehicles to Uzbekistan under the Excess Defense Articles programme (EDA), once again igniting debate about the role of US military assistance in the country.[19] But for the United States and certain European countries, especially Germany, the tension between pursuing security cooperation and not condoning the regime's repressive conduct has been acute and difficult to manage in practice.[20]

Uzbekistan's hidden global and extraterritorial connections

This much is familiar to long-time observers of the region and also helps to perpetuate a broader perception among Western policymakers and even scholars that Uzbekistan remains disconnected and closed, impervious to the influence of Western norms, values and media. The lessons of Andijan, in particular, seemed to entrench in the minds of US and European policymakers the assumption that Uzbekistan's isolation makes it impervious to external pressure, even if the West would prioritise the question of political reform above its strategic and security agendas. But these assumptions and the frame of 'closure' have been shaken by a series of international media stories detailing allegations of bribe-taking, offshore schemes and overseas bank accounts involving members of the president's family.

The rise of the president's daughter: global citizen, local monopolist

Perhaps the most well-known member of Central Asia's elite 'transnational uncivil society' is Gulnara Karimova, former president Karimov's eldest daughter, who played a prominent political role domestically as well as serving in a number of high-profile diplomatic posts overseas (see Chapter 1). From an early age, Karimova has lived a cosmopolitan and turbulent life. She was married at nineteen to the Afghan-American businessman Mansur Maqsudi, whom she acrimoniously divorced thirteen years later, in 2001, after a bitter custody row. Karimova took her two children back to Uzbekistan, while the Uzbek government placed Maqsudi's name on an Interpol warrant list for 'import-export fraud', expropriated his Coca-Cola bottling plant in Uzbekistan, and deported twenty-four of his relatives from Uzbekistan.[21] While in the United States, Karimova earned a higher degree at Harvard University's prestigious Kennedy School and styled herself as a pop star, an international fashion designer and head of a flagship charitable organisation. She dabbled in all these pastimes while officially in the service of the Uzbek Ministry of Foreign Affairs, first as counsellor to the United Nations in New York (2000–03), then as counsellor in Moscow (2003–05), then as Uzbekistan's permanent ambassador to the United Nations and international organisations in Geneva (2008–10) and as ambassador to Spain (in 2010).

But it has been Karimova's business dealings that have earned her the reputation of a ruthless predator in the country's relations with overseas investors. For many years, she ran a juggernaut of a business empire and was widely believed by external observers to have controlled the Swiss-registered conglomerate Zeromax, a giant company that seemingly rose out of nowhere in 2001 to control large portions of

Uzbekistan's gold (through a stake in Oxus Gold), cotton, textile, oil and gas industries.[22] US officials characterised the company as the 'middleman' for Uzbekistan's oil and gas contracts and estimated that it siphoned off 80 per cent of the country's natural exports to Russia.[23] Zeromax and Karimova were also reportedly beneficiaries of the logistics contracts that the Pentagon signed with Uzbekistan to transport equipment and supplies as part of the Northern Distribution Network.[24] The company folded in 2010, reportedly owing over $500 million in tax, with Karimova reported to have lost interest in further directing its operations after its overexpansion.[25] A creditors' meeting in Switzerland under the bankruptcy proceeding revealed an outstanding debt of more than $4.6 billion and a number of unfinished large-scale construction projects.[26]

US embassy cables that discussed Karimova's business activities referred to her as a 'robber baron', who gained a slice of almost every lucrative business in a spectacular rise during the 2000s.[27] One now infamous cable observed: 'Most Uzbeks see Karimova as a greedy, power-hungry individual who uses her father to crush businesspeople or anyone else who stands in her way . . . She remains the single most hated person in the country.'[28]

But it was Karimova's suspected involvement, through roles played by her associates, in a number of deals involving foreign telecommunications companies trying to access the rapidly expanding and lucrative Uzbek market, that precipitated the multiple international investigations into alleged money laundering and corruption; these same scandals also appear to have resulted in her fall from grace as the favoured successor to her father. As of summer 2016, Karimova remained under house arrest in Tashkent and did not even attend her father's funeral in Samarkand in September 2016.

Thus, unlike Kazakhstan, home to dozens of oligarchs who have globalised both their individual lifestyles and their economic activities, Karimova's saga reveals a narrower circle of elites in Uzbekistan whom the regime permits to operate in these same transnational circles. Yet, this smaller size, in turn, may have given more political significance to Karimova's exploits within the power circles of Uzbekistan.

The anatomy of a globalised scandal: foreign telecoms and business in Uzbekistan

By reputation, Uzbekistan is known as a tough place for international companies to do business.[29] Perceptions of widespread corruption, insecure property rights and active involvement by state officials in investment decisions should give pause to any prospective international investor. It is also a technological laggard: according to the International Telecommunications Union (ITU), Uzbekistan does not even meet the thresholds for a developing country for its telecommunications equipment and has the lowest level of mobile penetration among the ten CIS countries surveyed in the ITU's 2014 'Measuring the Information Society' report.[30] Thus, from the perspective of international telecoms companies, it is exactly Uzbekistan's relative closure, large population and old technological standards that have made it a potentially lucrative opportunity for international expansion and investment; conversely, from the perspective of Uzbek officials and regulators, the allocation of licences for new standards and spectrums make the modern telecommunications a tempting target for elite predation, especially as technical standards in the industry are regularly upgraded.

In July 2015, US Justice Department officials revealed that they were investigating three foreign telecommunications companies – VimpelCom Ltd (Dutch-registered, Russian-based), Mobile TeleSystems (MTS) (based in Russia) and TeliaSonera (based in Sweden) – for corruption and money-laundering activities in Uzbekistan.[31] These three companies had been the major new international entrants and players since the mid-2000s as the Uzbek market was opened up to international investors. According to a letter written by US Justice Department officials to their Swedish counterparts, the US investigation 'has revealed that VimpelCom, MTS and TeliaSonera paid bribes to Uzbek officials to obtain mobile telecommunications business in Uzbekistan'.[32] In one of the largest enforcement actions ever taken against foreign companies accused of corrupt activities abroad, US officials pressed European counterparts to freeze over $1 billion worth of assets tied to unnamed Uzbek government officials.

On 13 July 2015, the Justice Department won a related hearing when a New York City federal district judge ruled that US authorities could impound $300 million of assets held by Bank of New York Mellon Corp. in Ireland, Luxembourg and Belgium.[33] At the hearing, US officials had argued that the two Russian-based firms – both publicly traded on the US stock market – had used a web of offshore-registered shell companies to funnel more than $500 million in payments to 'a government official and relative of the President of Uzbekistan', identified as 'Government Official A'.[34]

The price of access: all in the family

According to a summary overview of the telecoms scandal undertaken by the Organised Crime and Corruption Reporting Project (OCCRP), Karimova and her associates were involved as gatekeepers in the telecommunications sector and employed three main techniques to extort payments from investors.[35] The first was to require a percentage (26 per cent appears to have been preferred) of the target company or to conceal the payoff as a ghost investment in a local partner or newly formed subsidiary. The outside companies would then be asked to sign agreements to buy back the shares at a later date for a significantly higher price, with the beneficial owner pocketing the difference. Second, Karimova seems to have demanded a premium for her services and lobbying for the allocation of licences, especially new communications standards such as 3G and 4G licences. Third, in cases where executives were reluctant to partake in these payoff schemes, Karimova appears to have directly bullied and threatened companies with expropriation and closure.[36]

Many of the telecoms payments were structured or routed through a company named Takilant, an opaque offshore firm registered in Gibraltar. According to company registry records, it was founded in 2003, originally with three directors, one of whom was 23-year-old Gayane Avakyan; the other two directors, from St Kitts and Nevis, were most likely 'nominee directors' and formally resigned the following year.[37] At the time of the alleged payments, Avakyan was the company's sole registered director, while she was also identified by a BBC report as 'sitting next to Ms Karimova' at a Paris fashion show.[38] A former employee interviewed by the *Financial Times* noted that 'Ms Avakyan worked closely with the first daughter'.[39] The Gibraltar company, according to the OCCRP, has also 'served as a holding company for other Karimova deals including those involving duty-free shops, clothing businesses, and pharmaceuticals'.[40]

Overall, according to an OCCRP table, foreign telecoms companies made a total of $684 million in payments to Takilant, while the offshore company made one $50 million payment to TeliaSonera on 28 December 2007 to purchase its 26 per cent holding of TeliaSonera Uzbek Telecom Holding BV.[41] Figure 4.1, rendered from OCCRP data and the report into the TeliaSonera deals by Swedish law firm Mannheimer Swartling, provides a visualisation of Takilant's transactional role and holdings.

The TeliaSonera case

The unfolding of the TeliaSonera scandal appears to have done the most legal and political damage to Karimova and her associates. The company at the time was a joint Swedish–Finnish venture, 37 per cent owned by the Swedish state, whose leadership team had decided to aggressively expand operations into emerging Eurasian markets including Uzbekistan, Kazakhstan, Tajikistan, Georgia and Azerbaijan.[42] In 2012, Swedish television news programme *Uppdrag Granskning* and a local newspaper alleged that, contrary to initial denials by TeliaSonera, the company had paid a total of $320 million in bribes to the Uzbek regime for licences and access to the Uzbek market, including an initial $250 million deal over licences in spring 2007 which included direct negotiations with the ruling regime and their agents.[43]

The investigation revealed that an initial plan was hatched between TeliaSonera and Bezkhod Akhmedov, at the time CEO of Uzdunrobita (oddly a market competitor), who was widely perceived as head of 'Karimova's Investment Group'. In an interview for a Swedish news programme, one of the two executives from the company confirmed that 'To reach a deal with Gulnara was a prerequisite to the whole deal. And the negotiations with her started in earnest around

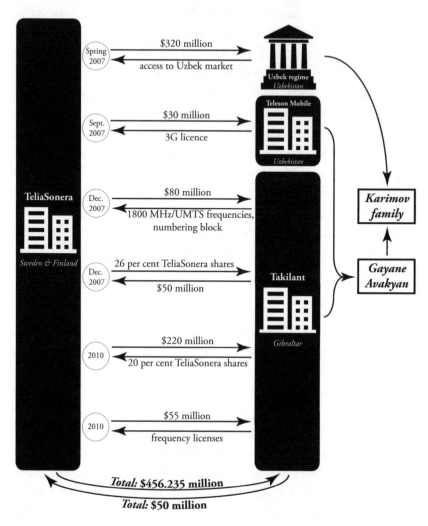

Figure 4.1 Structure of TeliaSonera payments and role of Takilant

February–March 2007.'[44] The executive identified Bekhzod Akhmedov as Karimova's negotiating agent, a point that was corroborated by leaked US embassy cables that commented on a related telecommunications sector negotiation.[45]

TeliaSonera and Akhmedov signed an agreement that detailed a multi-stage sequence of payments, acquisitions and the establishment of new joint ventures over the next few years that would funnel payments to a network of companies and offshore entities: Swedish prosecutors believe that Karimova beneficially owned these ventures. The source quoted by Sweden's public service broadcaster SVT explained that they were 'then informed that Gulnara would receive shares in the new company that TeliaSonera would form ... And that she through a local company would receive around 20 per cent. And that TeliaSonera would buy back the shares two to three years later – at a preset price.'[46] Overall, the OCCRP estimates that over the next three years TeliaSonera paid $456.24 million of documented funds to Takilant and received $50 million in a complex sequence of buybacks and ownership transfers.[47]

Lars Nyberg, then CEO of TeliaSonera, denied all allegations of corruption or improper behaviour.[48] However, as details of the various schemes emerged, including interviews with whistleblowing company executives, the CEO's denials became more difficult to credibly maintain.[49] The company commissioned an external investigative report by the legal firm Mannheimer Swartling that found no direct evidence of corruption or money laundering, but strongly criticised the company for not investigating the legal origins and beneficial owners of its local partners, Teleson and Takilant, and for not looking into how these companies had acquired the licences that they subsequently transferred to TeliaSonera.[50]

Under pressure from the board and intense media scrutiny after the report's release, Nyberg tendered his resignation on the same day, 31 January 2013, stating that: 'Even if this transaction was legal, we should not have gone ahead without learning more about the identity of our counterparty. This is something I regret.'[51] Board chairman Anders Narvinger told a news conference that, 'In hindsight, you can say that we should have scrutinized operations closer', while Swedish financial markets minister Peter Norman stated that the company had failed in the areas of 'general housekeeping, ethics and adhering to its own guidelines'.[52]

The TeliaSonera scandal triggered a wave of international investigations into related allegations of money laundering and corruption, both as part of the TeliaSonera case and in relation to other deals involving MTS and VimpelCom. In summer 2012, Swiss authorities froze the bank accounts of four Uzbek nationals with close ties to Karimova, reportedly worth hundreds of millions of Swiss francs, and a spokeswoman for the Swiss attorney general's office noted that the 'Alleged illegal acts taking place in the telecommunications market in Uzbekistan are considered as the initial money-laundering offenses'.[53] In a statement released in March 2014, Swiss authorities stated that the probe had been expanded in the autumn of 2013 to include Karimova.[54] In addition to the investigations in Sweden and Switzerland, in 2013 the Rue89 website reported that French authorities had opened an investigation 'targeting Gulnara Karimova' which was linked to a money-laundering case involving her associates, while Karimova and her associate Alisher Ergashev,[55] one of the Uzbeks probed for money laundering by Swiss authorities, were found to have signed as owner and director of two companies that were used to purchase luxury properties in France.[56]

Cooperation between Swiss and US authorities appears to have provided a basis for the announcements in summer 2015 by the US Department of Justice and the SEC that it was conducting a global investigation into accusations of money laundering and corruption in the three telecom companies. In September 2016, reports indicated that US and Dutch authorities had proposed a $1.4 billion settlement with Telia (formerly TeliaSonera) to resolve corruption violations relating to its transactions in Uzbekistan.[57]

The VimpelCom case

Though the TeliaSonera case has drawn the most media headlines, the dramatic settlement of the VimpelCom case with US authorities in February 2016 provides even deeper insights into how members of Uzbekistan's ruling elites constructed elaborate 'pay-to-play schemes' in collusion with international telecoms companies. VimpelCom, based in the Netherlands and the sixth largest telecoms company in the world, entered the Uzbek market, like its international competitors, by forming the wholly owned Uzbek subsidiary LLC Unitel or Unitel.

On 16 February 2016, the US Securities and Exchange Commission announced, in coordination with the Public Prosecution Service of the

Netherlands (PPS), a global settlement in which the telecoms provider would pay $798 million to 'resolve its violations of the Foreign Corrupt Services Act (FCPA) to win business in Uzbekistan'.[58] Unitel admitted to one count of violating the FCPA. The announced fine constituted the third largest ever imposed on a company for FCPA violations, making this one of the most significant enforcement actions to date.[59] On 20 July 2016 a Dutch court found Takilant guilty of complicity to bribery and forgery, finding that the firm accepted bribes from VimpelCom Ltd and Telia AB in exchange for mobile spectrum licences in Uzbekistan.[60]

The SEC alleges that VimpelCom bribed an official of the government of Uzbekistan who was related to the president in order to gain access to the Uzbek market and obtain licences, frequencies and channels. Enforcement officials estimate that at least $114 million was funnelled to an entity affiliated with the Uzbek official, while other bribes were 'disguised as charitable donations' and made to charities affiliated with the Uzbek official.[61] According to Andrew Ceresney, director of the SEC Enforcement Division, 'VimpelCom made massive revenues in Uzbekistan by paying over $100 million to an official with significant influence over top leaders of the Uzbek government … These old-fashioned bribes, hidden through sham contracts and charitable contributions, left the company's books and records riddled with inaccuracies.'[62] US attorney Preet Bharara of the Southern District of New York further explained: 'Those payments, falsely recorded in the company's books and records, were then laundered through bank accounts and assets around the world, including through accounts in New York.'[63] A member of the attorney general's office noted that 'These cases combine a landmark FCPA resolution for corporate bribery with one of the largest forfeiture actions we have ever brought to recover bribe proceeds from a corrupt government official.'[64] As with TeliaSonera, the case was truly global in scope, involving a coordinated investigation with authorities in Switzerland, the Netherlands, Latvia and Norway, while the shell companies involved in structuring and concealing the transactions were registered in the BVI and the Cayman Islands, with accounts for laundered proceeds held in Switzerland, Latvia, the UK, Hong Kong, Belgium and Luxembourg.

As was the case with TeliaSonera, the VimpelCom bribery scheme involved the sequenced acquisition of a number of different entities, masked as licence purchases and business transactions. Between 2006 and 2012, representatives of VimpelCom paid bribes 'on multiple occasions over a period of approximately seven years so that VimpelCom could enter the Uzbek market and Unitel could gain valuable telecoms assets and continue operating in Uzbekistan'.[65] Furthermore, the payments were structured through a Gibraltar-based shell company that 'certain VimpelCom and Unitel management knew was beneficially owned by the foreign official'.[66] According to the settlement's 'Statement of Facts',[67] accepted by both US authorities and VimpelCom, VimpelCom and Unitel conspired to provide over $114 million in bribes in exchange for the foreign official's influence on UzACI (the Uzbek Agency for Communications and Information, Uzbekistan's main state regulator of telecommunications) and the use of radio spectrum in the country. These corruption schemes included shell company purchases, a fraudulent buyout, bribes paid for 3G licences, fake consulting contracts, and fake reseller agreements.[68]

Outside-inside politics? Scandal, freezes and house arrest

The fallout of these corruption scandals not only made international headlines, but appeared to set in motion an acute domestic political power struggle and ruling family feud within Uzbekistan itself. Signs of a new concerted campaign targeting Karimova became apparent in autumn 2013 when Karimova was removed from her ambassadorial post in Spain, stripping her of her diplomatic immunity and ability to travel overseas, and returned to Tashkent.[69] In October 2013, Uzbek regulators shut down several television channels controlled by Karimova under the Terra Group holding company, the assets of which were subsequently frozen.[70] The following month, an additional five channels owned by Karimova's associate Firdavs Abdukhalikov were closed, while Karimova tweeted that Terra Group was being investigated for bribe-taking.[71] The week following the Terra Group probe, prosecutors, tax police and police reportedly opened an investigation into possible financial crimes involving Karimova's Fund Forum charity and the organisation ceased operations the following month.[72] And in November 2013, a group of Karimova-owned businesses including record stores, ten boutiques and a cinema complex were also closed down.

In the most dramatic turn of events, on 17 February 2014 Karimova and her teenage daughter were placed under house arrest by Uzbek prosecutors; the search of their home was reportedly supervised by a high-level security official.[73] In a statement later in the year, Uzbek prosecutors asserted that 'Karimova ... may have used administrative levers and provided the "corruption element" for members of an organized [criminal] group'.[74] Karimova's close associates and business partners were also targeted. On 6 February 2014, Uzbek police raided an apartment in Tashkent and detained a group who included Rustam Madumarov, her reported long-term boyfriend, and Takilant-owner Gayane Avakyan; in July 2014 they were sentenced to six and a half and six years, respectively, for economic crimes including tax evasion.[75]

Power struggles with the SNB?

The most dramatic political rift appeared to open up between Karimova and Rustam Inoyatov, the head of the country's powerful National Security Service (SNB). Inoyatov was described in a leaked US embassy cable as a 'key gatekeeper to President Karimov' and 'clearly one of two or three top power brokers in Uzbekistan'.[76] According to one opposition website, Inoyatov allegedly presented Karimov with a dossier detailing Karimova's activities, including the corruption investigations abroad, of which Karimov reportedly had no knowledge.[77] Apparently shocked, the Uzbek president authorised the SNB chief's crackdown on his daughter, though some political analysts in Uzbekistan have speculated that the so-called Khaknazarov Report was publicly leaked in order to bolster the Uzbek president's standing and credibility, and to absolve him of any knowledge or responsibility in his daughter's scandals.[78]

In her public statements and social media accounts, Karimova was quick to point to the domestic political motivations surrounding her detention. In a public comment on her Twitter feed she accused Inoyatov of harbouring aspirations to the presidency and remarked that he was 'scared' of her 'popularity'.[79] Karimova also slammed the accusations of tax evasion levelled at Terra Group, claiming they had been 'pulled out of thin air'. Karimova's Twitter account appears to have been closed down on 6 February 2014, the date of the raid on her associates. But in a letter reportedly authored by Karimova and smuggled to BBC correspondent Natalia Antelava, which was attributed to Karimova with 75 per cent confidence by a handwriting analysis, Karimova wrote that she was 'trying to restore justice'.[80] She lamented 'How naïve I was to think that the rule of law exists in the country', and rued that 'I never thought this could happen in a civilised, developing nation that Uzbekistan portrays itself as'.[81] A few weeks later, another alleged audio recording smuggled out of the country featured Karimova remarking that she and her teenage daughter were being treated 'worse than dogs'.[82]

One of the more bizarre repercussions of the affair was the public spat between Gulnara and her younger sister Lola. In an interview conducted with the BBC, Lola claimed that she had not spoken with Gulnara for twelve years and did not rate her chances of succeeding her father, while Gulnara, according to local media accounts, accused Lola of practising sorcery and using it against their mother.[83] In an interview with a Turkish newspaper in December 2013, Gulnara accused Lola and her husband of being part of the political campaign instigated by the SNB.[84] Whilst the infighting of Tajikistan's presidential family stayed largely under wraps (see Chapter 3), Uzbekistan's court politics had gone public in spectacular fashion.

The problem of recovered assets and political transition

The result of these mounting international investigations and judgments surrounding the telecoms cases has been a worldwide series of asset freezes targeting Uzbek officials implicated in them. In the United States, the most important of these include $300 million worth of assets held in Bank of New York Mellon accounts in Belgium, Luxembourg and Ireland that were frozen by US federal courts as a consequence of the anti-bribery investigations.[85] As part of its action against VimpelCom, the Department of Justice also filed a civil complaint seeking forfeiture of an additional $550 million held in Swiss bank accounts by the Uzbek official involved in the corruption scheme, which it argued represented proceeds of illegal bribes paid or property involved in the laundering of payments.[86] In a letter sent to a US federal court on 21 April 2016, US prosecutors from the Justice Department's Asset Forfeiture asked the court to declare Gulnara Karimova (reportedly named for the first time in US public documents), along with Avakyan and Madumarov, in default of the February forfeiture order.[87]

In Switzerland, a money-laundering investigation was launched against Gulnara Karimova in 2013, just weeks after her diplomatic immunity, from which she had benefited as Uzbekistan's UN representative, had been lifted.[88] The following year, a Swiss federal police report noted that 'the Office of the Attorney General and the Federal Criminal Police continued their investigations on Gulnara Karimova, one of the Uzbek president's two daughters, and on other Uzbek citizens from her entourage who are suspected of laundering illegal profits from the telecommunications sector through Swiss institutions. Since the criminal investigation began, assets worth more than CHF800 million have been confiscated.'[89]

With such global investigations and judgments against international telecoms companies appearing to have impacted upon Uzbekistan's domestic politics and the presidential family, these scattered overseas assets became targets for state reclamation and a priority for Uzbek authorities. In December 2015, Uzbekistan's justice minister, Muzraf Ikramov, reportedly sent a letter to the New York court presiding over the Uzbek telecoms case. The letter reportedly describes how an organised criminal group accepted bribes from telecommunications companies and then transferred these funds to overseas back accounts; Ikramov reportedly notified the court that the Uzbek government intends to retrieve the funds frozen by the US court associated with the government official.[90] According to the same report, the government of

Uzbekistan has retained the services of New York lawyers Holwell Shuster & Goldberg to advocate for the return of the funds.[91] On 4 January 2016 these representatives sent a follow-up letter to the court stating that Uzbekistan 'clearly is an injured party because its officials were the subject of the bribes at issue'.[92]

According to Uzbek and Western media outlets, one of the topics of discussion in the January 2016 annual US–Uzbekistan consultations between Uzbek Minister of Foreign Affairs Abdulaziz Kamilov and Nisha Desai Biswal, US assistant secretary of state for South and Central Asian affairs, was the possible recovery of $300 million in frozen assets from the Bank of Mellon.[93] Just as targeting Mukhtar Ablyazov and his associates appears to be a major, yet unacknowledged, foreign policy priority for the Kazakh government, these displaced sums of money, as well as the underlying international investigations, now appear to be a major target for Uzbekistan's Ministry of Foreign Affairs. Indeed, in April 2016, a court order confirmed that the forfeiture case had moved into settlement negotiations between American and Uzbek authorities, stating that the 'United States of America and the Republic of Uzbekistan … wish to discuss a possible out-of-court resolution and believe that a stay of the litigation would support those discussions while preserving party and court resources'.[94]

Uzbekistan's request gives a new twist to what is an emerging area of global governance: the recovery of overseas assets associated with grand corruption and kleptocracy by a country's nationals. In practice, successful recovery is hampered by different legal standards and burdens of proof in the countries hosting these assets, which often mandate that the requesting party must prove that the assets themselves were the direct fruits of criminal acts.[95] There is some precedent for the tricky policy issue in Central Asia: in 2008, the government of Kazakhstan, as a result of a trilateral agreement with the United States and Switzerland, and in cooperation with the World Bank, established the independent Bota Foundation to dispense about $84 million in funds, which were discovered in Swiss bank accounts in connection with the Kazakhgate investigation, to support social services community groups.[96] Bota could perhaps serve as a model for the return of frozen funds to Uzbekistan, but uncertainty surrounding Uzbekistan's political transition post Karimov, coupled with a growing economic crisis in the country, further complicate the issue politically.

The case also suggests that the issue of asset recovery is itself likely to become a central matter, both in Uzbekistan's foreign relations and internally within the country, as factions compete over these pots of money stranded overseas. Future regime transitions in Uzbekistan may even involve a new government in Tashkent framing asset recovery as an issue of democratisation or 'transitional justice', claiming that these assets, the ill-gotten gains of corrupt activities by members of a previous government, should be reclaimed to redress past political abuses.

Illiberal transnationalism and the autocrat's daughter

Gulnara Karimova's spectacular rise – as international socialite, businesswoman and domestic power broker – and fall challenges many of our assumptions about Uzbekistan's alleged isolation, impenetrability and elite politics. The telecommunications scandals reveal how even an authoritarian and relatively closed society like that of Uzbekistan is enmeshed in transnational networks and global processes. On one level, then, this case echoes other repressive states whose elites and family members have led cosmopolitan lives abroad, while their predatory governments and patrimonial networks extracted rents and personal income streams from their societies at home. What perhaps makes the Uzbek case more unique and intriguing, though, is how the dynamics of political competition and informal alliances within the country's tightly controlled authoritarian system appear to have been shaken to the core by the high-profile overseas Karimova scandal.

The Karimova corruption allegations can be instructively compared with the dynamics explored in the case of Mukhtar Ablyazov in Kazakhstan. In both cases we see glimpses of how high-placed elites, while residing abroad, leveraged their domestic political control, influence and access to enrich themselves. In both cases, the dealings involved were skilfully camouflaged through the use of offshore vehicles, brokers and intermediaries, and in both cases the principals were accused of money laundering via a series of overseas bank accounts and luxury real estate acquisitions. Finally, in both cases, the global and transnational nature of their alleged crimes appears to have strongly impacted politics at home, even in these authoritarian settings with their tightly controlled media environments. In the next chapter we will consider another case of a former insider turned enemy of the state: Kyrgyzstan's Maxim Bakiyev.

5

KYRGYZSTAN'S PRINCE MAXIM AND THE SWITZERLAND OF THE EAST

You're hosting a guy who robbed us . . . I didn't know that behind the beautiful words of democracy are very dirty lies. That's terrible. Britain is one of the founders of democracy and it's impossible to understand its actions against us. I am ashamed for Great Britain and didn't expect politics to be this cynical and corrupt.

Almazbek Atambayev, president of Kyrgyzstan, July 2013[1]

In June 2010, a private jet landed in Hampshire, England. Its passenger, Maxim Bakiyev, was immediately detained, but released after claiming political asylum. Known as 'the Prince' in his home country, Maxim was the son of Kurmanbek Bakiyev, the ousted president of Kyrgyzstan, whose reign lasted less than five years – a period of time sufficient for his family to squeeze the economic life and freedoms out of one of the poorest yet most open countries in the region. Dozens had been killed in Kyrgyzstan by the Bakiyev regime and the organised crime groups linked to it during its increasingly repressive rule. Many died in its violent attempt to hold on to power on 7 April 2010 when the security services were ordered to fire on demonstrating civilians. Hundreds more perished in the chaotic and brutal aftermath as struggles between pro- and anti-Bakiyev factions triggered horrific ethnic violence in the south of the country between Kyrgyz and Uzbeks.

But this was no mere distant local conflict driven by 'ancient ethnic hatreds' and supposedly traditional patterns of nepotism and corruption. The underlying factors were and are global, political and financial. Rather than looking on helplessly as bystanders to a far-off story of corruption and conflict, Western authorities and businesses effectively fuelled this scandal through the weakly regulated global financial system and the ranks of bankers willing to deal with foreign kleptocrats. A bewildering array of companies and service providers became entwined in Kyrgyzstan's offshore banking experiment under the Bakiyevs, led by the upstart Asia Universal Bank (AUB), managed by a small coterie of businesspeople close to the ruling family and particularly the princeling Maxim. In a now infamous leaked cable, the US ambassador herself described Maxim as 'smart, corrupt and a good ally to have'.[2]

'It is so easy to set up a company with hidden ownership in Britain that even a dead man can do it.' So begins Global Witness's 2013 report *Grave Secrecy*, referring to the case of a Russian nominee director who formally 'owned' a company, Velcona Ltd, that sent and received $700 million through AUB. The deceased even travelled to the shareholders' meeting despite having died three years before.[3] Maxim Bakiyev, AUB's chair Mikhail Nadel and their associates exploited loose Western regulations and deployed hidden offshore vehicles to quietly channel many hundreds of millions of dollars, of unknown provenance, through the bank and on to shell companies. Having fled Kyrgyzstan in 2010 via Latvia,[4] Maxim, according to Global Witness, now resides in a £3.5 million Surrey mansion bought via one of the offshore companies set up by AUB.[5] In violation of the principle that an applicant must seek asylum in the first EU country they reach, and despite repeated requests for his extradition by Kyrgyzstan, Prince Maxim became eligible for UK citizenship in June 2016.

Rather than face an international court, or summary justice in Kyrgyzstan, Maxim continues to manage his business interests in secrecy from the comfort of London's hinterland. The UK provided free transit for his riches and safe harbour for him and his family, despite multiple allegations of corruption and his later conviction in Kyrgyzstan for the attempted murder of a UK citizen. Charges of insider trading on the New

York stock market were brought and then suddenly withdrawn without public comment by US Attorney General Loretta Lynch.[6] Other Western banks and companies also enabled his financial dealings. Citibank in New York, the UK's Standard Chartered and Austria's Raiffeisen Bank were all major correspondent banks of AUB which failed to ask enough questions about the source and legitimacy of the money and companies. Meanwhile, AUB retained a veneer of legitimacy through the presence of three former US senators – including former presidential candidate Bob Dole – on its board. Maxim continues to operate beyond borders and through respected Western financial institutions and law firms.

In this chapter we show how the rapid rise of Maxim Bakiyev to become the most powerful businessman in Kyrgyzstan was a product of authoritarian politics, liberal banking laws and global financial connections. Britain, its City of London and its overseas territories are at the centre of this story. To build and maintain these connections, the Bakiyevs' opponents were silenced or eliminated and the state itself was looted while a British businessman, Sean Daley, was shot on the streets of the capital Bishkek and subsequently sued Maxim Bakiyev in the London high court. Much of the wealth Bakiyev accrued has been retained, enabling him to fund his defence from his English mansion. However, although he used the global financial system while in power, the new and apparently less corrupt Kyrgyz government has been unable, unlike the Kazakh and Uzbek regimes, to deploy the global criminal justice system to successfully track him down. The impression remains that, for the wealthy, global finance enables corruption via secretive Western jurisdictions whilst the law simply cannot catch up.

Liberal reform and its illiberal consequences

In the 1990s the academic John Anderson asked whether Kyrgyzstan was both an 'Island of Democracy' and the 'Switzerland of the East'.[7] But unlike Switzerland, Kyrgyzstan lacks the institutions to protect its national political life from being infected by the money laundering that its combination of openness and secrecy enable. It was the free flow of money from onshore to offshore that was instrumental in making

Kyrgyzstan's politics a dirty, violent and repressive business. Anderson lamented that 'the capitalist experiment has brought with it both the technical difficulties that arise in trying to impose Western models of development on a state with very little tradition of capitalism or free market economics, and corruption and criminality on a hitherto unseen scale'.[8] Well-meaning attempts at liberal reform produced the economic conditions for the evisceration of infant hopes for democratisation. The AUB case should not be seen as a surprise, but as a direct consequence of the liberalisation of finance promoted by Western government, donor agencies, banks and consultants.

Kyrgyz politicians and Western officials disagreed on many things in the aftermath of the Bakiyev regime and its scandals, meeting each other with mutual incomprehension. However, they largely agree that Maxim Bakiyev, his father and uncles were the principal architects of the 'dark years' from 2007 to 2010 when the state was thoroughly criminalised and its assets were stolen by its leaders. But to truly understand Maxim's astonishing rise one needs to recognise the combination of corrupt family politics (a feature common to all states in the region), economic and political liberalisation (to a much greater degree than found among its neighbours) and enduring donor dependency that marks out Kyrgyzstan's specific place in Central Asia.

The rise and fall of a post-Soviet reformer

Kyrgyzstan is the exceptional state of Central Asia. In the 1990s, it carried the hope for political reform in the region and, even today, remains more open to international cooperation, more free in its financial regulations, and more competitive in its politics than any other country in the region. It has hosted an American university since 1997 and a US air base during NATO operations in Afghanistan from 2001 to 2014. Authoritarian regimes elsewhere in the region quickly consolidated power after the early 1990s. Kyrgyzstan alone was able to proceed with some political liberalisation, while its constitution is, on paper and in practice, the most democratic in Central Asia – although this is a very low bar indeed.

Kyrgyzstan's first president, Askar Akayev, was the only one of the Central Asian Soviet leaders to speak out against the August 1991 coup against Mikhail Gorbachev. An accomplished physicist at the Academy of Sciences, Akayev was part of the nuclear scientist Andrei Sakharov's group of reformers in the 1989 Congress of People's Deputies. Returning to Kyrgyzstan, he was elected first secretary in 1990 and later president – the only successful case of a reformer from outside the governing elite making it to power in a Central Asian state. In January 1992, following Russia's model, Akayev's government removed price controls from the vast majority of goods and began the privatisation of state enterprises and the downsizing of their staff. Inflation was at 900 per cent in 1992 and 1,300 per cent in 1993. Undeterred by these price rises, which were deemed inevitable by international experts, Akayev introduced the national currency, the Kyrgyz som, in May 1993, and allowed it to float freely in international markets with a minimum of currency manipulation. The new and independent National Bank's goal was doctrinally monetarist: 'to achieve and maintain price stability through the pursuit of the appropriate monetary policy'.[9]

Foreign direct investment was also championed, particularly in mining. Akayev's first act of emulating Switzerland came in 1992 with a $14 million line of credit from a Swiss bank in return for a 1.6-ton Kyrgyz-gold collateral. This deal was arranged by the émigré businessman Boris Birshtein – who acquired an office in the White House, Kyrgyzstan's executive building – and his Swiss-based company Seabeco. Akayev later conceded that $4 million was left unaccounted for in a deal which had been struck before any system of accountability and oversight had been established.[10] By 1996 a new agency for FDI was in place and Canada's mining giant Cameco had entered a long-term joint venture with the state gold company Kyrgyzaltyn to develop the large Kumtor deposit. As a trailblazer in the region, Kyrgyzstan was enthusiastically supported by the IMF, EBRD and Asian Development Bank (ADB), which provided credits and grants to fund this rapid marketisation. It was these loans and grants that were crucial to Kyrgyzstan's capitalist development. Over the period from 1994 to 2005, Kyrgyzstan received far more development assistance per capita than any other

Central Asian state and quickly became aid-dependent. Much of this was granted to achieve political and economic reform. But it was financial deregulation (including with regard to foreign aid, credits and loans) that had sped ahead of political and economic liberalisation.

By the mid-2000s, Kyrgyzstan retained a high regulatory burden (with an average of 168.8 procedures required to open a business in the period from 2004 to 2010 reported by the World Bank's 'Doing Business' reports[11]) but had attained relatively low inflation and comparatively few controls on the movement of capital in and out of the country. The country has accurately been described as 'crony capitalist' – a form of market-based economy that is more widespread than reformers assume.[12]

The state became, in the words of Swedish academic Johan Engvall, 'an investment market'.[13] Families with connections bought positions in the state via payments to senior incumbents who enabled them to generate personal income from the state's regulatory functions: permits, inspections, licences, etc. Akayev family members, including Askar's son Aidar Akayev and son-in-law Adil Toiganbayev, were at the head of this structure. They controlled a huge range of businesses by the end of Askar's tenure – from a ski resort to a mobile telephone provider – but few of them were purely domestic.[14] Many of these businesses benefited from foreign financing or joint ventures with companies from the West, Asia or the post-Soviet region. Others were subcontractors to foreign donor agencies. Most infamously, three Akayev-linked companies were contractors to the Americans' Manas air base, netting the family an average of $40 million per annum between 2002 and 2005. These revenues were embezzled through a network of offshore and US accounts (see Chapter 6).[15]

But relative political freedom and aid dependency in Kyrgyzstan meant that, unlike in the other countries of Central Asia, the system was never fully controlled by the Akayev family. The considerable power bases and business interests still held by those who had left government meant that Akayev's regime could not last. In short, Akayev was caught between two stools. On the one hand, his family stole too much and shared too little to maintain their standing among the several hundred families who wanted a share of the pie. On the other hand, Akayev was simply not harsh enough in dispossessing and imprisoning his erstwhile allies and new opponents to establish an efficient and effective authoritarian regime.

The impoverished masses in the regions were the foot soldiers of the new rebels. In the period after 2002, elite-led protests emerged as a form of mobilisation strong enough to challenge and remove central government. When the Akayev regime used guns to silence the protests in the southern district of Aksy in 2002,[16] subsequent protests remained largely localised. But the cat was out of the bag and, following successful popular uprisings in Georgia's Rose Revolution of 2003 and Ukraine's Orange Revolution of 2004, the Kyrgyz opposition began planning its own 'colour revolution'.

The Tulip Revolution of 2005

Following fraudulent parliamentary election results in March 2005, mass political upheaval forced Akayev to flee the country. The 'Tulip Revolution' was so named and planned by a coalition of oppositional elites and announced in advance by former foreign minister Roza Otunbayeva in a speech to the Carnegie Center in Moscow on 11 February 2005. Her scheme identified her fellow opposition leaders who would take down the government.[17] Apparently according to plan, the Akayev regime fell on 23 March, six weeks after Otunbayeva's speech. However, while Otunbayeva and colleagues anticipated and instigated the uprising, they were never in control of a process which was only ever partially organised. Like one of the authors, who was then a professor at the American University of Central Asia in Bishkek, anyone who witnessed the chaos across the country in March 2005 – the bickering and barracking between the leaders, and the looting and disorder which followed the fall of Akayev – can bear witness to the delusion that the uprising was ever properly controlled or managed.

The Tulip Revolution revealed the instability that may occur in semi-authoritarian capitalist regimes where coalitions of politician-businessmen are allowed the space to challenge an increasingly kleptocratic elite. As the political scientist Scott Radnitz argues in his book

Weapons of the Wealthy, the events of March 2005, 'ushered in a new phase of Kyrgyz politics in which intimidation trumped negotiation as a means of resolving conflict'.[18] Civil society, as funded and supported by foreign donor organisations, played a minimal role in these events. Corrupt political leaders and the global financial services industry played ever-increasing roles.

It was not supposed to be this way. Edil Baisalov, the charismatic leader of the Coalition for Civil Society who, courtesy of international donors, had been in Kiev for the December 2004 Orange Revolution, had expected long-term occupation of Bishkek's Ala-Too ('Heavenly Mountains') square. Here, he imagined, the revolutionaries would spend days discussing the new constitution and the nation's future.[19] Following Akayev's dramatic flight from power on 23 March, some of Heathershaw's national colleagues at the university stood guard in a vain hope of protecting the presidential White House from looters as teenagers ran amok inside. The youth movement, KelKel, composed of students and young professionals, stood back when youths stormed the seat of government; its members organised the monitoring of government buildings to try and protect state property.

But these activists and students, who themselves actually grasped the value of democratic politics and an open society, did not lead the Tulip Revolution and had no authority in the eyes of those whose anger had fuelled the uprising. It was thus of little surprise that some of the first targets after the White House fell were the private businesses of foreign and local investors who had benefited most from the Akayev period. Just hours after the revolution, the large and iconic Turkish-owned Beta Stores supermarket was looted and set alight by persons of all backgrounds and ethnicities. Finally, and briefly, business in Kyrgyzstan was open to all.

Maxim and the new regime set up shop

Despite this unpromising start, some in the disunited coalition that pushed Akayev from power held genuine hopes of reform. Otunbayeva saw the revolution as a second chance following the disappointment of the post-1991 transition under Akayev. Her colleagues in the new regime had been specifically mentioned in her February Moscow speech. Like her, they were all former Soviet and post-Soviet apparatchiks, including Felix Kulov (a former Soviet security official and vice-president to Akayev imprisoned in 1999 and released from jail in the early hours of the Tulip Revolution), Kurmanbek Bakiyev (a former prime minister from southern Kyrgyzstan), Azimbek Beknazarov (a southern MP whose arrest had triggered protests that were violently suppressed in 2002) and Almazbek Atambayev (a former presidential candidate and head of the Social Democratic Party).

The rise of the Bakiyevs

Bakiyev, Beknazarov and Atambayev had all been crucial in mobilising their local supporters in the protests; all had independent wealth to fund their political campaigns and business interests that needed political protection. After weeks of internal wrangling, Bakiyev, from the southern region of Jalal-Abad, emerged as the figurehead of the 'revolutionary' movement and was easily and peacefully elected president just three months after the March 2005 uprising. Kulov, from the capital Bishkek, was to serve as his PM in a so-called tandem of the north and south of the country. With remarkable speed, quiet was restored to the capital.

But it was the calm before the storm to come. It was not long before the revolutionaries' unity and national agenda for reform disappeared from view. Between 2005 and 2007, Bakiyev's former allies were gradually sidelined. Otunbayeva was the first to go. Lacking a regional power base, her nomination for foreign minister did not pass the divided parliament in summer 2005. Kulov was PM from 2005 until December 2006 before finally jumping before he was shoved. Beknazarov was appointed prosecutor general from which post he continued to wage war against his archenemy Akayev and family before leaving government. Atambayev served brief periods as minister of industry, trade and tourism and then as prime minister in 2005 and 2007 before returning to opposition and beginning to plan the next 'revolution'. Just as Akayev, the northerner, had faced southern and northern opposition, so Bakiyev, the southerner, would, eventually, be targeted by opponents from all regions of the country.

From 2007 to 2010, however, Bakiyev realised a period of domestic repression far greater than that of his predecessor. As he usurped his former allies at home, the regime dismissed the directives of Kyrgyzstan's donors and allies in the West. In 2007, Bakiyev rejected the option of joining the World Bank's Heavily Indebted Poor Countries Initiative, which would have written off some debts in return for greater deregulation. In so doing, he signalled that his government was no longer willing to dance to the tune of economic reform as Akayev's had done during the period of 'transition'. Moreover, Bakiyev and his many close male relatives, including six brothers and two sons, began to take total control of the economy. Janish, a brother, became a key security official who was deemed responsible for violence against protestors when the regime collapsed. Several other brothers held lucrative roles. Marat, an elder son by Bakiyev's Russian wife, became ambassador to Germany. But it was Maxim, the younger son, who was the heir apparent. In a few years, he had sufficient political control and financial freedom to run the state's economic affairs for his family and associates despite only holding an official post for the last few months before the regime's demise.

Despite Kyrgyzstan's refusal to the World Bank, the country had already undertaken significant financial deregulation which provided fertile ground for the entrepreneurial young Bakiyev. Maxim was in his late twenties when his father won the presidency. Up until that point he had been unknown in Kyrgyz politics and business. Maxim graduated from the Kyrgyz-Russian Slavic University with a degree in law in 1999 and is understood to have begun his career at the Russian Interpravo law firm, but he quickly developed associations with Western institutions. He became a member of the advisory council of the UK-based consulting firm BCB Solutions Ltd and developed its portfolio in the Middle East. Later, he became a member of the board of the Latvian company Maval Aktivi, where he was purportedly in charge of strategic development, and began his association with the Latvian banker Valeri Belokon – a man who would become a key figure in the AUB affair and Maxim's most direct link to the UK. Maxim also bought a stake in Blackpool FC, the English football club of which Belokon was president.[20]

Maxim's own rapid rise as an international businessman was mirrored by Kyrgyzstan's rise to become, for a brief period, a key node in the offshore financial system, an unlikely 'Switzerland of the East'. Maxim's power base, of course, lay in his father's regime and provides a study of the ease with which new predatory regimes can emerge in the contemporary global economy. This process involved three phases, none of which was purely local or domestic. They included, first, muscling out rivals and seizing companies; second, centralising control in the state; and third, laundering the proceeds of Maxim's seizures through an internationally recognised bank. These steps, engineered through offshore vehicles and the international financial system, were taken under the passive oversight of the international community, its diplomats and financial regulators.

Step one: Maxim gets the gold

Not long after arriving in power, the Bakiyev family began to muscle its way into controlling most of the country's businesses and key assets. The mobile phone provider Magacom, owned by a British-based, offshore-registered firm, representing Russian investors, was allowed to continue to operate only by selling a 49 per cent stake to a Hong Kong-registered company that acted as a front for Maxim, according to a Kyrgyz investigation.[21] Later, Maxim and allies pushed the Russians out via a Bishkek court judgment which awarded them 100 per cent of Megacom. Companies linked to Maxim's associates also took over the lucrative contracts to refuel NATO planes operating out of Kyrgyzstan – a deal done via offshore vehicles nominally but legally located in Western jurisdictions and havens (see Chapter 6). Soon enough, the list of businesses that had changed hands in favour of the Bakiyev family was almost equal to the list of the most prominent companies in Kyrgyzstan.

This seizure of control was both financial and physical. A Kyrgyz state commission credibly claimed in November 2011 that there was a total of thirty contracted killings during Bakiyev's five-year tenure in power.[22] An independent journalist, Gennady Pavlyuk, was apparently thrown from a building in Kazakhstan. President Bakiyev's former chief of staff, Medet Sadyrkulov, was killed in suspicious circumstances in a remote mountainous region, having broken from the Bakiyev family and entered opposition politics.[23] But it was not just the locals that suffered. Instability and violence around the commodities sector grew in the Bakiyev period with foreign investors targeted by aggrieved local residents on the one side and predatory elites on the other. Western investors in Kyrgyz mining – including Oxus and Aurum Mining – report meeting with Maxim and facing demands of many millions of dollars to retain their licences and avoid trouble. On refusing to pay, trouble duly followed.

In Oxus's case the alleged attempt at extortion came after the company had spent five years building a gold mine which was soon to become operational. In late 2005, according to witness testimony heard in both Kyrgyzstan and the UK, President Kurmanbek and his son Maxim had offered to help Oxus retain its position in the country over the interests of a new investor, Global Gold, allegedly financed by the now-deceased Russian oligarch Boris Berezovsky and supported by the regime, if the company paid a sizeable bribe.[24] Following a meeting with the president in New York, the company's CEO Bill Trew went to Bishkek to meet with Maxim and discuss the return of the licence to mine to Oxus. More than ten years later he recalled the conversation in the London court:

> I was told Boris [Berezovsky] had actually paid Maxim USD 5 Million. He said to me, he said, 'There's absolutely no way we can return the licence without paying Boris his USD 5 million back, plus something else, all right?' So he said, 'Are you prepared to pay me USD 15 Million?' and I said, 'Look, we're a public company, we're not prepared to pay any.'[25]

Following this reported act of corruption, Oxus lost its multi-million dollar investment in Kyrgyzstan once and for all, and without compensation. More seriously, its chief in Kyrgyzstan was the victim of an apparent assassination attempt.

Muscling out Oxus Gold

On 7 July 2006, Sean Daley, Oxus's representative in Bishkek, was shot and wounded by gunmen near his home in the capital following a visit by the British MP Sir Tony Baldry to lobby on behalf of Oxus.[26] Four shots were fired, with one bullet hitting Daley and damaging his internal organs. He received life-saving treatment in Bishkek but continues to suffer from the psychiatric and physical effects of the attack. The story remains shrouded in a great deal of mystery. However, certain facts are apparent.

In the first half of 2006, Oxus had launched a concerted campaign to retain their stake in the mine. On 10 January 2006, British Prime Minister Tony Blair wrote to President Bakiyev 'expressing his hope that there would be restitution of the licence to Oxus Gold'.[27] The president flatly refused to consider Blair's request and, on 16 March 2006, instructed Prime Minister Kulov to proceed with 'unconditional refusal from further co-operation with Oxus Gold'.[28] Informally, however, the lobbying of Daley and Baldry seemed to be having an effect on the media and parliamentary opinion, and on some voices within the government at a time when the Bakiyev regime had yet to achieve complete control of the state. When Baldry left Kyrgyzstan on 6 July it was in expectation that a deal to return the licence to Oxus would soon be completed. As he later told the London court:

> I had two or three days of perfectly constructive, sensible negotiations, culminating in some perfectly sensible bilateral meetings with the President's adviser, and, as I say, when I got on the plane at Bishkek to come back to the UK, I certainly anticipated returning to Kyrgyz[stan] within a comparatively short period of time to finalise an agreement with the President.[29]

It was not to be. Were the Oxus executives deluded or had their progress merely created powerful enemies? After having invested approximately $55 million for exploration purposes, Oxus was finally and irrevocably pushed out of Kyrgyzstan following the attack on Daley. This has been described as an 'effective expropriation of the Oxus Gold stake in the Jerooy gold mine'.[30] The suspension of its licence by the Bakiyev regime was quickly challenged in Kyrgyzstan's courts by Daley, Oxus's general manager. The prominent commodities reporter Mineweb notes that Oxus's alleged failure to meet its production schedule, which has apparently caused a loss of around $145 million in taxes to the Kyrgyz government, was nothing other than an 'excuse the Kyrgyz government used for the termination of the company's licence'.[31]

Court documents from Bishkek link Maxim to Daley's shooting and were the basis for a subsequent civil action against Maxim in the London court. The key figure is a man called 'Ivanov', a long-standing business associate of the Bakiyevs, who knew Daley and is now living in a third country. 'Ivanov' was later revealed to be Mr Bertii Sin Beti (known to the Bakiyevs as 'Benny'). Sin Beti's testimony before the court in Bishkek, which he would withdraw from the later London hearing, was the vital evidence used to demonstrate Maxim's guilt. The Kyrgyz court records describe a meeting between Maxim and Sin Beti, following the assassination attempt on Daley, which was interrupted by his brother Marat and uncle Janish, in which the three Bakiyevs began to argue:

> The quarrel proceeded for about 10 minutes, during which Sin Beti had heard the name of Sean Daley ... Maxim was telling them off for not sorting out Sean Daley. When they left, Sin Beti asked Maxim Bakiev what happened with Sean Daley, to which M. Bakiev answered that 'these idiots have shot only 2 times, instead of 10 to kill him'. To his [Sin Beti's] question, 'what was Sean Daley to be killed for?', Maxim Bakiev replied 'Sean Daley is a representative of Oxus that bypassed [me] on the matter of Jerooy, addressed parliament and resolved the matter in favour of Oxus'. He also added that Sean Daley was hospitalised and would never leave Kyrgyzstan.[32]

According to Sin Beti, at this point he decided to step in to save Daley's life and requested a meeting with President Bakiyev in which he suggested there would be an 'international scandal' if Daley did die. Convinced, President Bakiyev ordered his family to allow Daley to recover and leave Kyrgyzstan.[33] But the immediate objective of Maxim and partners was achieved. Twelve days later, the State Geological Agency of the Kyrgyz Republic granted the licences previously held by Oxus to the Austrian-registered company Global Gold Holding (hereafter Global Gold).[34]

By October 2006, Oxus was expelled from the site and its involvement in Kyrgyzstan effectively ended. The company itself defined the incident as 'the government-sponsored illegal occupation last Thursday [19 October 2006] of premises owned by Talas Gold Mining Company, Oxus' joint venture company at Jerooy'.[35] The official website of state company Kyrgyzaltyn opaquely noted that Global Gold was represented by a 'certain Russian business' without naming investors.[36] Others were much more open about Global Gold's origins. Mineweb, for example, states that Global Gold was 'put in place in late 2005 to deal with the Kyrgyz government over the effective expropriation of the Oxus stake in the Jerooy gold mining'.[37] As a Western investor was pushed out, a well-connected Russian investor moved in to take control of their state-of-the-art facility, despite lacking a track record in gold mining and without payment to Oxus.

In addition to revealing something about onshore politics in Kyrgyzstan, the Jerooy case highlights that these actors used complex financial schemes to hide final beneficiaries via the structuring of their shareholding companies. Caution is advised, however, as there are very few public resources to shed light on Global Gold's finances and the evidence presented to the London court was partial due in part to the secrecy afforded to companies registered in offshore jurisdictions. Moreover, according to Oxus CEO Trew's testimony in London, not only did lawyers representing Berezovsky block attempts to access offshore company documents in BVI, but the British intelligence service MI5 encouraged the company to back off in its investigations.[38] However, according to the Russian website Compromat.ru, whose findings seem to concur with those of Oxus's investigation, Global Gold was registered on 17 March 2006, in Austria, just months before it was awarded the licence in Kyrgyzstan. From Austria, one can follow a long list of offshore jurisdictions that effectively conceal the share-holding beneficiaries. Compromat.ru states that the company was wholly owned by another company, Vitiano Holding Ltd, registered in Cyprus, formally owned by investment manager Alexander Turkot, and beneficially owned by Berezovsky.[39] Further detail on the company's ownership came from a *Forbes* investigation. According to this information, Global Gold was registered in Austria in the name of Rafael Filinov, president of Triumph Fund and representative of Berezovsky and his partner Badri Patarkatsishvili. Rafael Filinov arrived and stayed in the Kyrgyz Republic for one and a half years with the objective of arranging the Jerooy deal. In an interview with *Forbes*, Filinov observed, 'I made it nice, invested $12 million for it. Found good buyers and since I did it all "in white" [clean], they gave a good price. In 2007, the stake in Jerooy was sold – and $130 million was transferred on Patarkatsishvili's account, as Berezovsky's manager.'[40]

The Kyrgyz opposition also criticised the Bakiyev regime for alleged connections with Berezovsky. According to Kyrgyz opposition MPs, on 26 July 2006 Berezovsky paid an unofficial visit to Kyrgyzstan and was introduced to President Bakiyev via Maxim.[41] The opposition claimed at that time that Berezovsky's visit was specifically linked to Kyrgyz gold-mining. Later, during a raid of Berezovsky's offices, Russian police alleged they had found documents that contained information about preparations for a forceful capture of the Ak-Tuz gold deposit and the funds allocation necessary for that capture.[42] After Berezovsky's death, the *Forbes* investigation into his business further claimed that he supported the Tulip Revolution, after being involved in the Orange Revolution, for which the Bakiyevs 'rewarded' him with the Jerooy project.[43]

Whether or not Berezovsky was directly involved in the deal, Global Gold proved not to have invested for the long term, but apparently for the money they could make from a quick sale. In 2007, Jerooy changed hands again, as reported by Filinov (above), and Maxim was once again instrumental. Aidan Karibzhanov of the Kazakh private equity company Visor Holding made a deal in 2007 'through a relationship with' President Bakiyev. Maxim, Karibzhanov told Bloomberg

News, 'pitched the deal'.[44] In May 2008, Visor paid Oxus to compensate them for their losses in an out-of-court deal.[45] Eight years later, the Jerooy mine was still not fully operational.

There is now a great deal of evidence that the Jerooy deals were made via Maxim Bakiyev. The case of Oxus's exit and Global Gold's entry shows how transnational networks connect the states of the former Soviet region to one another *and also* to offshore jurisdictions beyond. This chain of offshore connections is illustrative of a complex multilayered and multi-structured scheme; yet that is typical of transnational business networks.[46] These chains also demonstrate that simply muscling control of business interests is ineffective in Central Asia without *both* the organising control of the state *and* the international connections provided by offshore vehicles, correspondent banks and financial ingenuity. These arrangements are depicted graphically in Figure 5.1. This brings us to steps two and three of the Bakiyevs' expropriation of the Kyrgyz economy.

Step two: centralising control

After using state power and financial connections to muscle in on businesses like Oxus in the lucrative gold sector, the second step in the Bakiyevs' money laundering was to centralise control through the state. By 2008, it was clear that a pattern of control with Maxim at the centre of affairs was emerging. Foreign investors were just as much subject to these informal rules as local business, as a revealing summary of the visit to Kyrgyzstan by a real prince revealed. In a leaked US embassy cable, Tatiana Gfoeller, US ambassador to the Kyrgyz Republic, describes assisting UK business representatives and diplomats in briefing Prince Andrew, the Duke of York, brother of Charles and second son of Her Majesty the Queen, on his October 2008 mission as UK trade emissary:

> While claiming that all of them never participated in it and never gave out bribes, one representative of a middle-sized company stated that 'It is sometimes an awful temptation.' In an astonishing display of candor in a public hotel where the brunch was taking place, all of

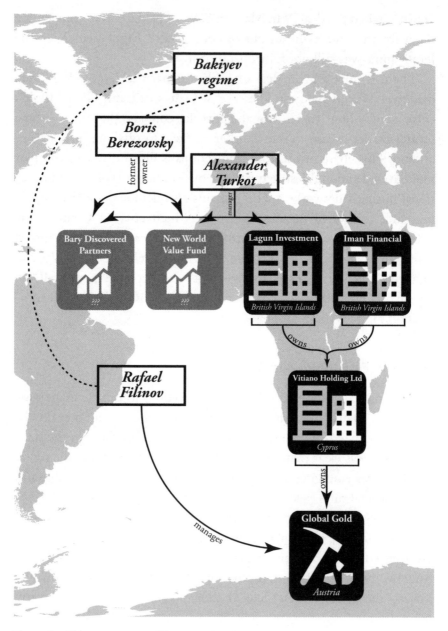

Figure 5.1 The organisation of Kyrgyzstan's gold sector

150

the businessmen then chorused that nothing gets done in Kyrgyzstan if President Bakiyev's son Maxim does not get 'his cut.' Prince Andrew took up the topic with gusto, saying that he keeps hearing Maxim's name 'over and over again' whenever he discusses doing business in this country. Emboldened, one businessman said that doing business here is 'like doing business in the Yukon' in the nineteenth century, i.e. only those willing to participate in local corrupt practices are able to make any money. His colleagues all heartily agreed, with one pointing out that 'nothing ever changes here. Before all you heard was Akayev's son's name. Now it's Bakiyev's son's name.' At this point the Duke of York laughed uproariously, saying that: 'All of this sounds exactly like France.'[47]

The sheer normality of this corruption, and British business's implied connivance in it, is as striking here as the imperial manner of Prince Andrew's own prejudices.

The Prince and TsARS

As the Bakiyevs' power grew, they decided to formalise the gatekeeping aspect of 'Prince' Maxim's informal system. On 29 October 2009, President Bakiyev made his son head of the new Central Agency on Development, Investments and Innovations (CADII, known as TsARS, its Russian acronym). With the National Development Fund (NDF) handed over to the agency, the disposal of all foreign credits, including Russia's $300 million, as well as the state's share in the biggest state-owned companies, was passed to TsARS. Maxim claimed that the Russian loan would be used for a low-interest credit system to alleviate poverty. With his connections to the West and evident financial and business acumen, the jury was still out on Maxim in the Western diplomatic community while anger was building in Kyrgyzstan itself. As one US diplomat commented following the creation of TsARS, 'now that he is officially in charge of the Kyrgyz government's economic development policies and programs, it may become clear whether he will use his position for the good of Kyrgyzstan, for the enrichment of himself and his friends and associates, or for a little of each'.[48] The 'little of each' would prove an elusive balance to strike.

By 2009, Maxim had arrived at the height of his powers, courted by everyone from ministers to senior apparatchiks, and increasingly coming to the attention of the United States. The US chargé d'affaires Lee Litzenberger described the effect of Maxim's combination of ruthless politics and financial acumen in an entertaining diplomatic telegram from the summer of 2009 describing the opening party of a new resort hotel, owned by Maxim, at Issyk-Kul, Kyrgyzstan's beautiful mountain lake. Maxim arrived at a nearby airport in his private plane, travelled to the hotel in a large motorcade with police escort, and moved around the party itself with eight bodyguards. He mingled among the guests with his official wife Aijana (he was well known to keep a mistress) on one side and Prime Minister Igor Chudinov on the other. Neither Aijana nor Chudinov looked happy to be there but each demurred to the man of the moment who, by that time, was perhaps even more powerful than his father.[49] Although holding no government position at this time, he was courted by all of Kyrgyzstan's business and political community.

Despite this same lack of official status, it was Maxim who worked behind the scenes to get a new agreement for the United States air transit centre in Bishkek to be renewed over Russian objections. On 13 July 2009, less than two weeks after unexpectedly being invited to Maxim's party at Issyk-Kul, Litzenberger had dinner with Maxim at one of his Bishkek restaurants. The US chargé d'affaires heard Maxim's claims to have arranged the deal over the base and his obvious attempts to ingratiate himself with the US government. The base politics of Afghanistan, when President Obama was considering a reinforcement of US forces there, appear to have encouraged American diplomats to reciprocate Maxim's overtures at a time when the warning signs of the corruption, brutality and ultimate fragility of the regime were becoming apparent. Litzenberger concludes in his summary of dinner, 'in the wake of the new Transit Center agreements, Maxim's favourable disposition towards the United States could be of benefit to our interests'.[50]

The telegram alluded to the fact that Maxim had already been deeply involved in discussions over the future of the air base with the

Department of Defense. Maxim had a stake in the continuation of the refuelling facility through his relationship with its main fuel subcontractor, Mina Corp. In June 2009, Kyrgyzstan publicly announced that it had reversed its decision regarding the closure of the air transit centre. In the preceding months, Erkin Bekbolotov, the CEO of Mina, played the role of intermediary between Maxim and the US Department of Defense for back-channel negotiations, as revealed in a US congressional report, *Mystery at Manas*.[51] But the report, lacking direct evidence of inducements being offered to Maxim, pulls its punches. 'While Mina had a huge financial incentive to save the base,' it notes, 'it is unknown what motivated Maxim Bakiyev to intervene.'[52]

Step three: banking the profits

Maxim's standing, and that of the regime, was dependent on a third element which was crucial for the Bakiyevs' corruption. Seizing assets and centralising control mean little without being able to bank them in a reputable institution, thus laundering your monies and moving them offshore. All this dirty money was all very well but without a sophisticated cleaning service it would be stuck denominated in Kyrgyz som. Corruption, at the grand scale, never exists without money laundering, and therefore only exists through the international financial system headquartered in London and New York. So for the regime, the most important thing was not making money (an easy thing for a ruling family in Central Asia) but transferring it offshore in order to clean it up and keep it safe. Tellingly, the next most important person at Maxim's summer 2009 party was a man who was central to his business operations: Mikhail Nadel, head of Asia Universal Bank (AUB). According to Litzenberger's account, Nadel 'acted like the second host of the party, loudly toasting with the men and making advances at the women'.[53]

Asia Universal Bank

Asia Universal Bank was registered on 22 August 1997 in Kyrgyzstan as the subsidiary company of International Business Bank, Western

Samoa. Nadel owned 66 per cent of the shares and saw the value of the bank increase sharply after 2005, following his partnership with Maxim. On 7 April 2010, the bank's assets totalled 24 billion som ($533.3 million). The genius of Maxim, Nadel and their financial magician, the Moscow-born US citizen Eugene Gourevitch, was that they used the opportunity of Kyrgyzstan's open financial system and the Bakiyev family's control of its politics to set up a vast offshore network flowing through Bishkek. That network was centred on AUB. At the same time, many of the country's assets, including TsARS itself, were managed by the new MGN Group, under Eugene Gourevitch.

It was not just Kyrgyzstan's major businesses and government that banked with AUB, but organisations from all over the world that demanded safety and secrecy. Temir Sariyev, the finance minister who later investigated AUB's operations, describes its business as such:

> A lot of money came in from companies overseas, money that needed to be sterilised, several billion dollars every month. There were all sorts of suspicious transactions. AUB was off-limits to regulators; in fact, the bank told its clients, 'We control the state so no-one can interfere with us.' The clients needed guarantees that their cash wouldn't be seized or arrested. So their money would arrive in AUB, spend the night, and then get transferred out via six or seven shell companies overseas. AUB earned commissions on these transactions, hundreds of millions of dollars.[54]

As Sariyev describes, AUB's remit was by no means limited to companies in Kyrgyzstan, but extended across and beyond the post-Soviet space. It was an integrated part of the global financial system.

It is in these terms – the sheer normality of AUB – that its owners and operators have defended the bank. Mikhail Nadel argues that the new government of Kyrgyzstan 'savagely looted and destroyed' AUB in May 2010 while defending AUB's extensive use of offshore shell companies:

> Offshore companies aren't a carte blanche for stealing. These companies are used worldwide to minimise the taxation of [beneficial owners]. Look at the ownership structure of the ten largest banks in

the world: their principal owners are offshore funds. Opening an account of an offshore company, a bank should check the client's business. Offshore is not a business itself. The geographical location of Kyrgyzstan and its liberal banking laws allowed AUB to attract international business into the country.[55]

To this extent, Nadel is correct to point to the quite routine nature of the use of offshore companies. When the Swiss arm of the UK's largest bank, HSBC, is fined more than a billion dollars for laundering the money of Mexican drug cartels in the United States, cases like AUB should not surprise us.[56]

But the specific use of international frameworks and Western institutions to enable and enrich AUB's international transactions, and the means by which this is covered up, ought nevertheless to cause us some concern. The scale of AUB's operations was vast. Kyrgyz investigators claimed that a staggering $1 trillion flowed through Kyrgyzstan during the Bakiyev years – around 200 times the GDP of this small country. After 7 April 2010, all this came tumbling down. In the days prior to the fall of the Bakiyev regime, the bank had transferred hundreds of millions of dollars in assets offshore and out of reach of any future investigation. It was able to do this because of AUB's business model of being a conduit for the rapid, safe and secret transfer of assets from one jurisdiction to another. In February 2011, an audit by the accountancy firm BDO commissioned by the European Bank for Reconstruction and Development noted that AUB was used for money laundering and that its computer system was designed to conceal its payments, more than 80 per cent of which were not validated by SWIFT, the international financial transfer system.[57] In the Kyrgyz prosecutor's words, 'the maintenance of accounts of suspicious companies and the manipulation of the bank's balance sheet involving large sums served as an instrument for the illegal extraction of revenue'.[58]

Kyrgyzstan goes offshore

Three ingredients are required to maintain such a system: anonymous companies, major international correspondent banks and a veneer of respectability.

First, shell companies are the vehicles for the transfer of funds. Anonymous shell companies are either unlisted, having no more than an address in an offshore jurisdiction, or listed under a nominee shareholder or director, a person who signs a paper to represent and conceal the company's real beneficial owners. The UK, particularly at that time, offered little oversight of company registration and the use of nominees. Global Witness, which has campaigned for the declaration of beneficial ownership for many years, uncovered in the AUB case that:

> the shareholder of one UK company was a Russian man who had actually died some years before the company was registered. His identity had been used to hide the real owner of a company that appeared to have $700 million flowing through its account at AUB while doing no business in the UK and failing to file accounts with the UK corporate registry as required.[59]

Most of AUB's clients were such shell companies. *Grave Secrecy* details many of their cases. Most were registered in the UK, New Zealand and Belize – some of the world's safest and most secretive jurisdictions. They were inactive in the real economy. All were registered after President Bakiyev came to power in 2005, were set up by a small group of company service providers, and many were linked to Maxim.[60] Some of these uses of shell companies may simply be to avoid tax. But, as Global Witness researcher Tom Mayne argues, the secrecy of the shell companies and lack of regulation means that more nefarious purposes are both possible and undetectable.[61]

Second, AUB's required correspondent relationships with some of the world's biggest banks were established. The Swiss bank UBS was eventually suspicious enough about AUB to close its account. But Citibank, Raiffeisen and Standard Chartered all kept their accounts with AUB open and refused to answer questions about their anti-money-laundering checks when asked by Global Witness researchers.

Third, these hidden transactions also needed a respectable international public face. This was provided by a board which included former US senators Bob Dole, the 1996 Republican presidential candidate, and

J. Bennett Johnston, a Democrat from Louisiana. For this service, the two American statesmen were paid $175,000 each.[62] Given this relatively small sum, it seems implausible – 'absurd' in Johnston's words – that such wealthy and influential individuals would have taken on the risk of being found out had they any reason to doubt that Nadel's bank was anything less than legitimate. They were by no means the only respected Western individuals and institutions to, wilfully or naïvely, withhold judgement. Many regulators, correspondent banks and company service providers were also left with egg on their faces.

The aftermath

On 7 April 2010, this cronyist political and financial system, based in Kyrgyzstan but extending across the world, came crashing down. Hundreds of lives were lost in the 7 April 'revolution' and the violence that followed in the south of the country. Stability has slowly re-emerged in Kyrgyzstan, but the aftermath of the Bakiyev reign and the financial operations of AUB are ongoing in Kyrgyzstan and across the global financial system. Maxim was on his way to the United States on the day the regime fell and diverted to Latvia before arrival in the UK, never to return to Kyrgyzstan. Onshore and offshore jurisdictions tell two quite different tales. The new interim government of the Kyrgyz Republic rapidly pressed charges against the Bakiyevs and their allies. In March 2011, the Leninski district court sentenced Gourevitch, *in absentia*, to fifteen years in a reinforced penal colony on corruption charges. Two years later, Maxim was sentenced *in absentia* to a twenty-five-year prison sentence for corruption. A Bishkek court found him guilty of signing deals that lost Kyrgyzstan hundreds of millions of dollars via illegal privatisation of state assets. Specifically, he was convicted for the illicit sale of state energy firms and public land near a popular tourist resort.[63]

But the new government under Roza Otunbayeva and, later, Almazbek Atambayev, has been as unsuccessful in processing these cases abroad as they have been successful at home. An Interpol arrest warrant has remained outstanding against Maxim since 2010,[64] with little prospect of delivering his return to Kyrgyzstan to face trial on corruption charges. Two months after his sentencing in Bishkek in 2013, a federal court in New York dropped an extradition case against Maxim, days before a scheduled 13 May hearing in London which would have brought him to the United States to face charges of securities fraud on the New York Stock Exchange (see below). Foreign minister Erlan Abdyldayev expressed profound disappointment with the American justice system. 'US authorities at all levels have noted the severity of the crimes committed by Bakiyev. But, unfortunately, one of the main principles of democracy – the rule of law and the certainty of punishment – has failed.'[65]

Why justice has been swift and severe in Kyrgyzstan and non-existent in the Western world where Maxim now resides cannot simply be explained by the lower burden of proof required by the court system in the country of Maxim's political enemies. There simply is not the system in place or support offered by foreign governments and international institutions to governments like that of Kyrgyzstan that seek to investigate money laundering. International regulators do not look into transnational laundering and do not fund initiatives to tackle *this kind* of corruption. Whilst the World Bank has demanded audits of state assets across Central Asia, and donors have funded anti-corruption agencies in more than one state, they seemingly ignore the international banks and corporate practices that allow money laundering to happen, to be covered up, and make it incredibly hard to investigate. Moreover, by 2015, the government of Kyrgyzstan faced a total of eleven international arbitrations arising from the business dealings of the Bakiyev regime and its aftermath, with claims against the state totalling around $1 billion.[66] Lacking the resources and experience to pursue these cases, it was yet to secure victory in a single one of them, losing the Manas Bank arbitration to Belokon and his company for about $16 million. Kyrgyzstan, if it loses each of these arbitrations, faces a bill equivalent to 15 per cent of its GDP.

At the heart of this story is a failure in the international financial system to effectively identify money laundering when it occurs – therefore, ineffectively implementing anti-money-laundering rules. It is not that there is a lack of knowledge of money laundering but that well-founded suspicions lead not to legal investigation but, at best, to withdrawal and neglect. In 2006, the Central Bank of Russia, of all places, led the way and was the first national bank to cancel correspondent relations with AUB.[67] Around forty Russian banks were affected. In 2008, the US embassy in Bishkek advised against extending $10 million of America's Overseas Private Investment Corporation (OPIC) support to AUB due to its 'troubled past and limited AML track record' and reputation for 'tax evasion and other questionable activities'.[68] But despite these warning signs other audits passed AUB with no concerns.

When we met Baktygul Jeenbaeva, deputy director of the National Bank of Kyrgyzstan, she was visibly frustrated by the government's lack of progress and the limited support they have received. She noted that all the international regulatory entities signed off on AUB's books – including the IMF and Deloitte. These clean bills of health granted by international regulators are shocking given that an estimated $1 trillion flowed through the bank during this time with little or no checking. Just as auditors failed to uncover misdeeds, foreign courts have insisted they provide proof of criminality in specific cases. Jeenbaeva expressed frustration about overseas legal requirements for having to prove that money was acquired due to criminal activities, a prerequisite for asset recovery in most jurisdictions. She noted that they have received no cooperation from New Zealand, Switzerland and Latvia on inquires. Very little assistance has been forthcoming with the exception of the US Department of Justice and the pro bono advice offered by US law firm Akin Gump Strauss Hauer & Feld. 'There was great disappointment for us that, for a long time, no one was able to help', she remarked. 'On the international level they have created the infrastructure for money laundering and expect us at a national level to investigate it!'[69]

Maxim in Londongrad

In the summer of 2010, after the violent but unsuccessful attempt of the Bakiyev regime to retain power, Maxim was in London and Blackpool FC, in the north of England, was preparing for its first season in the

Premier League.[70] The starry life of a UK-based oligarch-businessman apparently beckoned for the fallen prince. But Maxim faced multiple international struggles to re-establish his business after the sudden ousting of his family from Kyrgyzstan. The London that Maxim has made home has been called 'Londongrad', a name pointing to the cosy confines offered to Russian and post-Soviet oligarchs, their assets and families. It is also arguably one of the most significant sources of instability in Central Asia. 'You're hosting a guy who robbed us', complained Kyrgyzstan's new president Almazbek Atambayev to the *Guardian* newspaper in 2013. 'I didn't know that behind the beautiful words of democracy are very dirty lies.'[71]

The London(grad) hosting affords Maxim and other former elites individual legal protections and secrecy that they routinely violated when ruling back home. When asked in July 2010 about whether Maxim would be given the right to remain in the UK, Damian Green, the minister of state for immigration, replied that 'it is not Home Office policy to comment on individual cases'.[72] This policy has remained in place. Whilst such discretion is a matter of responsible data protection for the UK government, it is effectively assured for the wealthy by UK lawyers, accountants and reputation managers. Therefore, what we know about Maxim since his arrival in the UK comes from criminal investigations, court cases and investigative reporting which have teased some of the details out from under the cloak of secrecy.

Insider trading on the New York Stock Exchange

Philip Shishkin's investigations have revealed that Maxim did not rest on his laurels but tried to recreate his financial dealings from London with the help of Eugene Gourevitch, the Bakiyevs' financial adviser. 'Through a shell company registered in New Zealand,' Shishkin writes based on court documents that he has seen, '[Maxim] set up a Latvian bank account stuffed with $45 million worth of securities.'[73] Gourevitch, a New Zealand shell company and a Latvian bank are three elements also present in the AUB system. Maxim and Gourevitch began using the bank account for trading deals on the stock exchanges of the US, the

UK and elsewhere, making several million dollars investing in a Louisiana oil services company.[74]

Unfortunately for Maxim, Gourevitch, under the pressure of being wanted in three countries, was cooperating with the FBI and feeding them information on his boss's activities. Taiyyib Ali Munir, the London broker supplying Maxim with information, was charged and pleaded guilty in 2012.[75] On 12 October 2012, Maxim was arrested in Belgravia, the London district beloved of Londongrad's residents. The US Department of Justice had brought charges against the 34-year-old for 'conspiracy to commit securities fraud and obstruction of justice'.[76] Maxim faced 'two counts of conspiracy to defraud and conspiracy to pervert the course of justice in the USA between April 2010 and April 2012'.[77] Whilst the extradition request was dropped in May 2013, and the charges dismissed, there is no indication from the US authorities as to whether the file on Maxim has been closed.

One possible explanation for why the insider-trading case against Maxim broke down in 2013 is apparently related to the corruption of evidence by the key informant. Shishkin argues that Gourevitch, the unprincipled dealer-turned-informant, had apparently compromised the evidence against Maxim.[78] While facing charges in the US, Italy and Kyrgyzstan, Gourevitch's Twitter profile smacked of a juvenile bravado: 'Former banker. Trader. Atheist. Family man. Born to spread misery vicariously and viscerally. Kyrgyzstan's Most Wanted. Not even remotely gangsta.'[79]

In June 2014 Gourevitch was sentenced to more than five years in prison on charges of fraud against Maxim – a fraud which was carried out while Gourevitch was cooperating with US litigators in the insider-trading case against Maxim. Gourevitch's lawyer, Marc Agnifilo, argued that 'this case [against him] is essentially about him screwing up as a cooperator', but asked for leniency on the grounds of the 'bizarre' series of events which since 2010 had led Gourevitch to fear for his life. While working for Maxim Bakiyev, Gourevitch had access to 'real, juicy, immediate, tangible' insider information, Agnifilo argued in court.[80] Maxim escaped prosecution, it seems, due to the greed and incompetence of his one-time adviser.

Maxim faces the High Court

Other skeletons also refused to remain in the closet. Sean Daley, the British businessman and representative of Oxus Gold who had almost been killed in the street in Bishkek in 2006, visited Kyrgyzstan after the 2010 ousting of the Bakiyev regime to enquire of the prosecutor's office whether they would re-open the case into his attempted murder. Four years later, on 4 April 2014, a district court in the capital sentenced Maxim to lifelong imprisonment *in absentia* for his part in organising the assassination attempt.[81] The irony of this judgment was that Maxim was absent from Kyrgyzstan but present in Daley's home country, the UK, and living little more than 50 miles from the businessman, given that the UK Home Office, then under Secretary of State Theresa May, had already refused a Kyrgyz request for Bakiyev's extradition to face trial.[82] Such was the Kyrgyz government's anger that senior Home Office lawyer Busola Johnson visited Kyrgyzstan in 2014 in an effort to assuage the Kyrgyz sense of injustice. As the British embassy in Bishkek reported, she described her visit thus:

> My aims in coming to Kyrgyzstan were two-fold. First to gain a deeper understanding of the Kyrgyz perspective and second, to offer Kyrgyz legal colleagues a clear account of the UK Mutual Legal Assistance regime, and the legal framework in which we work.[83]

Despite little help from the UK authorities, Maxim was not out of the woods – Daley brought a personal injury claim against him based on the evidence presented to the Bishkek court. If an English court would confirm the Bishkek court's evidence, it appeared that there was a chance that the UK would be forced to approve the extradition of Maxim back to Kyrgyzstan to serve his sentence, despite the lack of an extradition treaty between the UK and Kyrgyzstan. Once again – as was the case in Tajikistan's battles over its aluminium industry – the dictators and former dictators of Central Asia play out their power struggles both at home and abroad.

On 22 June 2016, the trial began at the High Court in London. Maxim was defended by the solicitors Hickman & Rose, a law firm which describes itself as 'renowned for the work we do in holding governments and their police forces to account'.[84] In a tiny but packed courtroom there was barely enough room for Maxim's considerable legal team, up to seven of whom appeared to be in attendance. For the seven days of proceedings Maxim sat just feet away from the man whose killing he was alleged to have ordered ten years before. Witnesses included the executives of Oxus and Global Gold, former president Kurmanbek Bakiyev (via video link from Belarus), former PM Felix Kulov (from Kyrgyzstan) and the defendant himself. Under questioning by Joel Donovan QC, Maxim denied everything, including the attempted murder of Daley, involvement in the Jerooy mine's licensing, and even the allegation that he had gained any advantage at all from his father's time as president.

> *Donovan:* By the time your father was forced from office in 2010, you were a very rich man, weren't you?
> *Maxim, with a smirk:* Well, depends what you consider as a rich man.
> *Donovan:* Well, rich enough to fly your private plane into Britain when your father was deposed?
> *Maxim:* Yes, I've had money to pay for this.[85]

Maxim had good reason to feel confident in his position. The star witness in support of the claim – former family friend 'Benny' Sin Beti – had not only refused to turn up in court but had written to the defence asking to withdraw his testimony, alleging he had been pressured by Daley to give evidence against Maxim.

The judgment handed down on 29 July 2016 was categorical. Mr Justice Supperstone, the presiding judge, agreed with the defence that Maxim's conviction in Kyrgyzstan was inadmissible and that Sin Beti's original evidence constituted mere 'hearsay'. 'For many reasons', Justice Supperstone concluded, 'I do not find that evidence [of the involvement of the defendant in the shooting of Daley] to be reliable'.[86] However, the judge was far less certain regarding Maxim's denials of involvement in the Jerooy mine, his erstwhile association with Boris

Berezovsky, and the struggle over the licence. Whilst he concluded that there was 'no hard evidence' regarding Berezovsky's involvement, Justice Supperstone remarked that 'I do not accept the Defendant's evidence that he had no dealings in relation to the Jerooy gold mine'.[87] Maxim walked away from a trial that had found in his favour but which had concluded that he had effectively deceived the court under oath.

Maxim continues to deny any involvement in both the shooting of Sean Daley and the struggle over the Jerooy mine in Kyrgyzstan. The Bakiyev family insist that theirs was a progressive government for Kyrgyzstan which was ousted due to the ambitions of their rivals and with the support of Russia. Maxim Bakiyev's trial and conviction in the Bishkek court was, he insists, entirely politically motivated. But another conclusion can also be drawn. The judgment in London demonstrates that the law, either at home or abroad, has once again been proven ineffective in uncovering the whole truth of the shady events of business in Central Asia and bringing justice for the people of Kyrgyzstan. The wider reality of the brutal control of Kyrgyzstan by the Bakiyev family and their regime remained out of view. One exchange between Maxim's counsel Angus McCullough QC and Oxus's Bill Trew hinted at both the difficulty of finding the truth and the political reality of life in Kyrgyzstan during the Bakiyev era:

> *McCullough:* The reality of the position is that the shooting of Mr Daley was not going to have any impact at all on Global Gold's securing of the licence, was it?
> *Trew:* I don't think it was. I just think it was total spite from the kind of corrupt, nasty people that you're defending, sir.[88]

Maxim – who has gained the right to remain in the UK – has, thus far, navigated British financial, legal and asylum systems successfully. He may now be eligible to apply for full British citizenship.

Sovereign power and its offshore links

For a few years, under the regency of Maxim Bakiyev, Kyrgyzstan finally achieved the status of 'Switzerland of the East'. But rather than being a source of pride for the country's elite it is a great source of embarrassment that Kyrgyzstan is being cast as a pariah by the elite banks and lawyers of the global financial system in which AUB had thrived. Whilst the AUB scandal has tarnished the reputation of Kyrgyzstan's banking sector, it is the international system itself that lacks the oversight and regulation to prevent further spates of money laundering and extortion from and through Central Asia.[89] The country, through which billions of dollars once secretly flowed, now faces $1 billion in international arbitration claims from major multinational corporations who had their contracts cancelled and their assets dispossessed under the Bakiyevs' reign and in the chaos of its aftermath.

The case of Maxim Bakiyev is a remarkable example of how local control and brute force are not enough for dictators without borders. Contemporary authoritarian governance works through the sovereign power to act as gatekeeper to the multinational corporations and foreign states that want to do business. It also requires global connections to bank the profits of rule in offshore accounts far from rival factions at home and hapless regulators abroad. Whilst the Bakiyev regime lost power its members have stayed one step ahead of the new government that seeks to bring them to justice. None of the owners and directors of AUB have been convicted or even faced the legal pressure which forced the cooperation of Eugene Gourevitch with US prosecutors. The new government of Kyrgyzstan has found that pro bono support is not enough to successfully track down those who stole from the state and took full advantage of the rights and protections of a new adopted home.

But the Bakiyev regime did not merely seek to use the offshore financial system. It briefly but lucratively became part of it. AUB's success was based on Kyrgyzstan becoming a new offshore jurisdiction – free from regulation, free from public disclosure. How rapidly and relatively easily this could be done is a salutatory lesson for those who maintain that self-regulation is adequate for the offshore world. Financial jurisdictions are never independent of the political systems that enable them. State legislatures in Delaware and Nevada, and British governors of the overseas territories such as BVI, have taken decisions to allow tax avoidance and financial secrecy. Just as the absence of effective global governance has enabled dictators without borders, so too can those same dictators assure their relatives and clients that they remain out of the reach of regulatory power.

6

THE NEW OFFSHORE SILK ROADS

At an international ministerial meeting in New York in September 2011, US Secretary of State Hillary Clinton announced: 'Let's set our sights on a new Silk Road – a web of economic and transit connections that will bind together a region too long torn apart by conflict and division.'[1] The following day, Clinton explained that 'An Afghanistan firmly embedded in the economic life of a thriving South and Central Asia would be better able to attract new sources of foreign investment, connect to markets abroad and provide people with credible alternatives to insurgency', stressing that regional trade could also 'open up new sources of raw material, energy and agriculture products for every nation in the region'.[2] The New Silk Road (NSR) strategy continues to be a centrepiece of US policy in Central Asia and Afghanistan, building directly on a fifteen-year legacy of Central Asia serving as a logistics hub to supply the war effort in Afghanistan.[3]

Just two years later, in a speech given at Nazarbayev University in Astana in September 2013, Chinese premier Xi Jinping announced that China would promote a 'Silk Road Economic Belt' across neighbouring Eurasian states.[4] Over the next months, Chinese policymakers and analysts further outlined ambitious plans to promote regional cooperation, economic integration and new transit corridors by funding large-scale infrastructure and development projects designed to connect East

Asia with Asia, Europe and the Middle East. The proposals consisted of both the land-based Silk Road Economic Belt – which includes building transportation (high-speed rail, airports and roads) and energy infrastructure (power generation and energy pipelines) – and an accompanying '21st Century Maritime Silk Road' belt, supported by upgrades to ports and logistics hubs, intended to link China to the Indian Ocean, Persian Gulf and Mediterranean Sea. Collectively these two belts have been termed One Belt, One Road (OBOR). According to the *South China Morning Post*, OBOR represents the 'most significant and far-reaching project the nation has ever put forward'.[5]

The contemporary US and Chinese visions of New Silk Roads as networks promoting regional 'connectivity' are just the latest in a long-standing set of attempts to unlock, transform and integrate the Central Asian heartland with the rest of the world. Empires that originated in the wider Central Asian region and spread to the world include the ancient Turks and the Persians, the more recent Mongols and their successor khanates.[6] The famed original Silk Road – actually a complex network of routes and centres of trade which spread from China to Europe and the Middle East – is usually viewed as one of the first examples of 'globalisation', of which Central Asia was front and centre. More recently, at the turn of the twentieth century, Halford Mackinder himself warned that Russia's construction of new railways in Eurasia, building on the Trans-Siberian Railway, could tip the balance from oceanic power to land power, unleash regional economic development, and extend Moscow's influence across a 'clear run of 6,000 miles'.[7] From this perspective, the seventy years of Soviet rule and its experimentation in economic autarky seem like an interlude in these various efforts to connect Central Asia economically and politically to the rest of the globe, an imperative that once again is on the agendas of the great powers.

Yet, if we dig more deeply, the almost obsessive emphasis of US and Chinese officials on the virtues of 'connectivity' both misdiagnoses the origins of Central Asia's developmental problems and dangerously obscures the actual networks of local, regional and offshore actors that have already allowed Central Asia's crony capitalism to flourish in this new era of globalisation. Contra Mackinder, US and Chinese officials publicly go out of their way to tone down the political implications of advocating for greater regional 'connectivity', claiming that geopolitics should remain a less pressing priority than addressing the region's development and transport needs.

However, the current US and Chinese Silk Road visions both have their origins in their respective strategic policies and security concerns in the region as they were formulated in the 2000s. For the United States, the current agenda of promoting connections between Afghanistan and Central Asia was born out of the post-2001 effort to supply the American military campaign in Afghanistan. For China, the 2000s saw the intensification of Chinese security and economic engagement in Central Asia, with the driving priority of modernising and stabilising the restive western province of Xinjiang and the surrounding Central Asian region. Thus, the most current New Silk Road plans have their origins in the strategic priorities and domestic actors that have emphasised the importance of regional 'connectivity' for their own purposes.

As this chapter will show, the transnational networks that link outside private and security actors, local elites and offshore centres have been as critical for both US and Chinese regional actors and interests. In the US case, Washington's enormous logistical effort to support and supply its military campaign in Afghanistan encouraged elite rent-seeking and moneymaking schemes designed to profit from the large logistical contracts that the Pentagon doled out in the region. Similarly, the acquisition of Central Asian energy assets by Chinese state-owned energy companies in the 2000s, while on the surface readily explained by rapidly growing Chinese domestic energy demand, was undergirded by a series of political and legal arrangements founded on similar elaborate transnational schemes and offshore networks.

In both cases, the Pentagon and Chinese energy companies evoked their respective national interests to justify these arrangements, encouraging opaque deals conducted through shell company intermediaries. These cases serve as a cautionary tale: the large inflow of infrastructure spending, development projects and transportation corridors promised by the New Silk Roads may in fact further exacerbate the region's severe governance problems and informal networks, rather than promote sustained growth, development and new enduring global connections. The New Silk Road may actually terminate not at new flourishing trading or transit hubs across Eurasia, but in offshore bank accounts and holding companies controlled by regional elites and their international brokers and global intermediaries.

Washington's Central Asian bases and logistical networks: the business of supplying the Afghan War

For the United States, the NSR is a direct legacy and outgrowth of the Central Asia-hosted logistical hubs and resupply routes that supported US and ISAF military operations in Afghanistan. Following 9/11, the issue of 'connectivity' emerged with the challenge of supplying US and ISAF forces in landlocked Afghanistan for Operation Enduring Freedom (OEF). The United States established military bases in southern Uzbekistan (Karshi-Khanabad, or K2) and at the Manas airport, near Bishkek, in Kyrgyzstan. Washington also concluded a series of overflight agreements with the other Central Asian states and refuelling agreements with Turkmenistan and Tajikistan.[8] From resting on the margins of the former Soviet Union, the region, almost overnight, had transformed into this critical beachhead in the new American-led Global War on Terrorism.

Throughout the 2000s, then, Central Asia played a critical logistical role in the Afghanistan campaign. At the same time, however, these facilities and supply lines became the subject of scrutiny and contentious politics and bargaining, as US policymakers tangled with questions of politically and financially supporting their Central Asian hosts' authoritarian politics, security agendas and opaque prone companies. In the cases of the bases in Uzbekistan, US concern about placating the regime to maintain basing rights and access led to Washington's acquiescence to the repressive crackdown by Uzbek authorities on political opponents, while US security assistance to Uzbekistan was widely viewed as a tacit quid pro quo for securing Tashkent's consent.[9] After the Uzbek government's crackdown in Andijan in May 2005, US officials were divided between backing an international condemnation of the government's actions, including calling for an international investigation, and toning down criticism in order to preserve base access.[10] In late July 2005, the US was formally evicted from K2, though the two countries would resume security cooperation a few years later on the Northern Distribution Network. In Kyrgyzstan, similarly, the US presence at Manas was associated with US support for the corrupt rule of two Kyrgyz presidents, while their overthrow by organised protests made the status of the base the overriding political issue on the agenda.[11]

Then, in 2007 and 2008, following attacks by insurgents on supply lines in southern Afghanistan and disputes with Pakistan, US defence planners launched the Northern Distribution Network (NDN), a set of logistical supply routes designed to bring supplies into Afghanistan from the north. Traversing the Eurasian heartland, NDN routes, operated by large commercial logistics companies, originated in the ports of the Baltic states before crossing Russia, Kazakhstan and Uzbekistan by rail, with most containers entering Afghanistan via the Uzbek border city of Termez.[12] A related but less used route, the NDN South, originated in the Georgian port of Poti and traversed Azerbaijan by rail, with cargo then being ferried over the Caspian Sea and brought down through Kazakhstan by truck. Despite the enormous distances, cost and complexity of negotiations involving commercial cargo companies and state-owned railway and trucking carriers, by 2010–11 the NDN carried about 75 per cent of non-lethal ground sustainment cargo to US forces in Afghanistan.[13]

A number of investigative stories on the underlying logistical arrangements themselves revealed how Central Asian elites were systematically profiting from the US-led war effort – from the government of Turkmenistan depositing landing and access fees collected from US operations at the Ashgabat airport into a personal presidential overseas bank account, to widespread allegations that the NDN had emboldened state-owned companies and contractors in Uzbekistan to raise transit fees and levy informal payments in order to squeeze out maximum profit from the US resupply effort.[14] Even after the post-K2 rapprochement with the United States, according to leaked US embassy cables, President Karimov of Uzbekistan threatened to cut off access to

NDN supply lines if the United States persisted in criticising the country's domestic affairs, including its dismal governance and human rights record.[15] Reports of similar systematic corruption along supply routes in Afghanistan, including the institutionalisation of extensive pay-offs to warlords, seemed to emphasise that the Afghanistan resupply effort had generated rental income for a wide variety of local actors.[16] Despite these political and governance challenges, policymakers and defence planners mostly viewed the NDN as a success, having delivered goods and materiel, in difficult circumstances, to Afghanistan.

For a group of US analysts and policymakers, the NDN itself also presented a potential opportunity to expand the US strategic footprint in the region and permanently connect Central Asia to Afghanistan. At around the time of the NDN's ramp-up, US defence planners and their allies in Washington's policy community publicly floated the idea that the NDN itself could serve as a basis to promote trade, regional cooperation and economic development in the region. Ideas for a 'New Silk Road' had already been floated as part of the US strategy to reorient Central Asia away from Russia, but the NDN's establishment gave the NSR new momentum.[17] The influential Washington-based think tank the Center for Strategic and International Studies even published a series of public reports that examined the potential transformative economic benefits of NDN and framed 'connectivity' as the main challenge confronting the region after the US drawdown.[18]

These accounts not only dramatically overestimated the potential customs revenues to Afghanistan from such trade, but – crucially – failed to acknowledge that the NDN itself was not based on private entrepreneurship or independent local companies vying for new markets, but rather enriched a small group of state-owned transportation monopolists who benefited from the steady hard-currency payments made by a dedicated and captive client – the US military.

This analytical conflation was also criticised in a hard-hitting report by investigative journalist Graham Lee, who set out to evaluate whether NDN-related truck routes and shipments were indeed facilitating greater commerce and efficiency; instead he found that regional cross-border economic cooperation had significantly deteriorated during the period of the NDN.[19] Lee's research revealed that road and rail freights had been hiked several times by Uzbekistan, Tajikistan and Kyrgyzstan and that many of these ad hoc hikes appeared to specifically target cargo bound for ISAF forces in Afghanistan.[20] Overall, Lee calculated that 93 per cent of revenues – $905.41 million of the $977.75 million in annual NDN transit fees in Central Asia – actually went to the coffers of regional governments, as opposed to private or market entities.[21] In his own research, academic Alexander Diener similarly found that border officials continued to exact unofficial fees from NDN operators and refused to adopt, or even wilfully sabotaged, new cargo-tracking technologies designed to expedite cross-border shipments.[22]

In political-economy terms, the NDN promoted and sustained local rent-seeking, not local private entrepreneurship. Without US troops at the end of the supply chain, the 'private' demand for such services and goods was very low indeed, while the informal barriers to trade within the Central Asian region remained among the highest in the world.[23]

Fuelling the Afghan War through offshore companies and informal networks: the case of the Manas air base

The procurement of fuel to support operations at the Manas air base, near Bishkek in Kyrgyzstan, illustrates how the war effort spawned complex transnational networks linking fuel suppliers, predatory elites, subcontractors and mysterious offshore companies.

Across two successive Kyrgyz presidencies – those of Askar Akayev (2001–05) and Kurmanbek Bakiyev (2005–10) – base-related fuel contracts were implicated in accusations of insider deals and corruption, while both presidents themselves were overthrown by popular protests amid broad perceptions of corruption and nepotism. Soon after the 9/11 attacks, US defence planners secured approval from the regime of President Askar Akayev to use the civilian international airport in Kyrgyzstan as a key air base for operations in Afghanistan. The airport's runway had just been repaved and the facility could accommodate heavy aircraft such as cargo planes and refuellers. Soon after securing final approvals in December 2001, Manas became a critical logistical hub, first (from 2001 to 2002) as a base for a wide array of multinational coalition forces and then, after 2002, as a staging area for almost all US personnel going in and out of Afghanistan, and as a hub for refuelling operations carried out by KC-135 refuelling aircraft. The base operated until June 2014, when the Kyrgyz government chose not to extend the five-year lease agreement from 2009.

All of these operations required the consumption of vast quantities of military-grade jet fuel – 3.6 million gallons of fuel (the equivalent of about five Olympic swimming pools) per day.[24] Kyrgyzstan itself is land-locked and with no natural local supplier, so from the very outset finding a reliable source of fuel was an urgent priority for the Pentagon. In fact, its first refuelling contract was signed in November 2001, preceding even the formal agreement with the Kyrgyz government over use of the base.[25] The Pentagon's Defense Logistics Agency (DLA) awarded the sole-source contract to Avcard, a Maryland-based logistics company, which was subsequently extended without competitive bids. In 2003, a new company, Red Star, registered in Gibraltar with opaque beneficiaries, took over the main fuel contract.[26]

Both Avcard and Red Star were principally supplied by two main local subcontractors, each owned by a member of the president's family. The first, Manas International Services Ltd (MIS), was owned and controlled by Aidar Akayev, the president's son. The second, Aalam Services Ltd, was owned by Adil Toiganbayev, President Akayev's son-in-law. According to a *New York Times* investigative report, from 2003 to 2005, MIS received $87 million and Aalam $32 million in subcontracts, out of a total of $207 million spent by the US Department of Defense on fuel.[27] Further, a subsequent FBI investigation, now classi-fied, found that Akayev and his associates had embezzled hundreds of millions of dollars from base-related schemes through a vast network of thousands of offshore companies and US-based accounts.[28] After the ousting of Akayev in the 2005 Tulip Revolution, internal Kyrgyz inves-tigations revealed that both MIS and Aalam were among a list of forty-two Kyrgyz companies affiliated with Akayev, while investigators also found that the tender for the Manas refuelling complex was only published after the deal had already been agreed.[29]

Following Akayev's fall, the fuel complexes would once again stir up controversy under the presidency of Kurmanbek Bakiyev. In 2007, after the Pentagon had awarded eight consecutive contracts (including five no-bid extensions) to Red Star, a mysterious new entity, Mina Corp., took over the main jet fuel contract. Even though their managements insisted that they were distinct corporate entities, Mina and Red Star shared some remarkable similarities: both were registered at the same overseas address in Gibraltar, both maintained offices in the same complex in London, and both shared local offices in Kyrgyzstan in the Bishkek Hyatt.[30] A *Washington Post* investigative story on Red Star and Mina stated that 'the companies themselves ... are largely invisible. In dealings with the Pentagon they have used addresses in Toronto, London and Gibraltar, each apparently little more than a mail drop.'[31] The three beneficial owners of Mina were subsequently revealed as Douglas Edelman, a Californian businessman who had opened a popular American-style restaurant in Bishkek, Erkin Bekbolotov, a Kyrgyz businessman, and a retired US lieutenant colonel, Chuck Squires, who had actually served as US defence attaché to Kyrgyzstan until 2000 and ended his career as an adviser to US Central Command.[32] Over the next four years, Mina would receive about $1.29 billion in fuel contracts, including four separate no-bid extensions.[33] The DLA invoked reasons of national security to waive 'full and open competition' procedures, while potential competitors complained that their lower bids were ignored due to Pentagon favouritism and secrecy.[34]

Mina's fuel deals were scrutinised following the fall of Bakiyev in April 2010. Edil Baisalov, the chief of staff to Acting Interim Premier Roza Otunbayeva, characterised the fuel companies as an 'indirect way for the Pentagon to bribe the ruling families of Kyrgyzstan'.[35] After the company could not secure a meeting with Otunbayeva herself, its representatives arranged a meeting with her 28-year-old son in Istanbul in July 2010 in order 'to explain the business'.[36] A subsequent investigation by the US House of Representatives found no smoking gun of corruption or direct financial payments made by Mina to the Bakiyevs.[37] However, the report admonished DLA-Energy, observing that 'When red flags of potentially corrupt or anti-competitive behaviour did arise, the agency took no steps to address them', and that 'DLA-Energy conducted only superficial due diligence on Mina and Red Star, and turned a blind eye to allegations of corruption'.[38]

The *Mystery at Manas* report also uncovered a complex web of Mina subcontractors and airport-related businesses and agencies, with indirect ties to the Bakiyevs, which appear to have been designated as preferred contractors by Kyrgyz authorities. One letter, written by the Joint Stock Company Manas International Airport, the airport's governing authority, to DLA-Energy and dated 17 April 2006, warned Pentagon officials that any companies participating in the main fuel contract tender would require a pre-approval letter from the Kyrgyz authorities. The letter then listed a detailed number of criteria that any contracting party would have to fulfil, including using only three officially licensed Kyrgyz jet fuel operators and demonstrating a 'Past history and track record of jet fuel supplies into the Kyrgyz Republic in the quantities required'.[39] These criteria, according to the report, 'distinctly favored the incumbent contractor, Red Star Enterprises'.[40]

The report's most revealing finding was uncovering an informal transnational fuel-smuggling network.[41] Mina had sourced fuel from Siberian refineries that, in turn, was designated for 'civilian-use only', thereby circumventing Russian export controls. Both Russian and Kyrgyz officials sent false certificates describing these fuel exports/imports as intended for civilian use, even though the quantity and destination of these shipments should clearly have alerted authorities in the Russian Federation and the Kyrgyz Republic of the fuel's actual military purpose. Thus, the collusion of this transnational fuel-smuggling network – which involved a Gibraltar-registered fuel vendor to the Pentagon and its local suppliers, a Russian refinery, and Russian and Kyrgyz bureaucrats – can be contrasted with the public story of intense geopolitical competition between Washington and Moscow over the future of the Kyrgyz base.

Perhaps most tellingly, US Defence Secretary Robert Gates refers in his memoir to Bakiyev's 'amazingly corrupt' government, which 'saw our continued need for the airfield as a rich source of revenue or, as I called it, extortion'.[42] Considered over its thirteen years of operations, the fuel contracts at Manas also serve as a warning of the type of insider arrangements, opaque networks and offshore structures that can come to link private and government interests under a geopolitical imperative. Rather than promote economic development and private sector competition, the DLA contracting process fed into the rent-seeking, politically run monopolies and patronage structures of consecutive governments, while the clever use of shell companies and foreign bank accounts helped to conceal the actual beneficiaries of these schemes. Far from lacking 'connectivity', such schemes point to the very complex configurations of local, regional and global actors that were established in the region to supply the US-led war effort in Afghanistan.

China's response: 'One Belt, One Road' and the 'March West'

China's 'One Belt, One Road' initiative is considerably more ambitious than the American New Silk Road project, involving potentially unprecedented sums of overseas investment and the establishment of new regional institutions and international financial vehicles. The total value of OBOR-related projects, estimated by *The Economist* to be worth $1 trillion 'in government money',[43] will be funded by China's existing sovereign wealth fund, Import-Export Bank, Chinese Development Bank and the New Silk Road Fund (controlled by the People's Bank), as well as by newly created Chinese-led regional financial institutions, including the BRICS-led New Development Bank (NDB) and the Asian Infrastructure Investment Bank (AIIB). The Silk Road Fund, NDB and AIIB were created as recently as 2014, with the purpose of providing new vehicles for funding overseas infrastructure projects.

Chinese officials themselves now openly suggest that OBOR, supported by these new regional economic architectures, will encourage 'new models of international cooperation and global governance' that will align development priorities and foster deeper all-round integration.[44] The contrasts with the US-backed NSR here are striking, for the US version offers no new regional institutions and very little financial support; instead it repackages existing projects such as the proposed Turkmenistan–Afghanistan–Pakistan–India (TAPI) natural gas pipeline into what is already a thin project portfolio. Indeed, while the NSR appears to be intended to signal that US withdrawal from Afghanistan is leaving behind some sort of blueprint for economic development, OBOR signals China's arrival as an alternative source of international development finance and even Chinese-led international order.

Internationally, Chinese officials see OBOR as a way of expanding China's economic engagement and political ties with its neighbouring states and shaping a political community that is increasingly responsive, if not completely friendly, to China's foreign policy interests and domestic priorities. For some, this is a blueprint that has emerged from the influential 'March West' doctrine articulated by noted analyst Wang Jisi. In a much-cited series of policy papers, Wang advocated that China expand its westward footprint in order to stabilise its restive regions, strengthen its political community and find ways to cooperate with the United States, in contrast to the competitive relations Beijing and Washington were experiencing in the East Asian theatre at the time.[45] At the same time, investing in these new regional banks and development initiatives offers a potentially more productive use for accumulated foreign exchange reserves than maintaining them in US treasuries, while these new projects could also potentially be used as part of the broader effort to internationalise the use of the yuan.[46] Given the Eurasian corridors of OBOR, China must also try and deal with a Russia that is already wary of Chinese economic inroads and which has launched a competing, and fundamentally different, alternative regional architecture – the Eurasian Economic Union (EEU), comprised of Russia, Belarus, Kazakhstan, Armenia and Kyrgyzstan, and which is designed as an economic protection block, dominated by Russia, to codify a sphere of economic and political influence.[47]

But, as with the US case, geopolitics is only one driver of the aggressive 'connectivity' quest. Domestically, the development and stabilisation of the restive western province of Xinjiang continues to inform discussion and justification of the OBOR;[48] indeed, the cities of Ürümqi, Korgas and Kashgar remain at the centre of various proposed OBOR routes (west, north and south). In addition, slowing growth rates within China (from 10–12 per cent to 5–7 per cent in 2015) mean that domestic suppliers of the decades-long Chinese construction boom now require new overseas outlets to continue their operations. Without new external markets and large-scale projects, Chinese cement and steel manufacturers – the latter of which currently account for over 50 per cent of global overcapacity – will face huge adjustment costs: they view Central Asia as a desperately needed new market. For example, the giant machine-building company XCMG announced plans to invest $490 million in Xinjiang to create a base to produce cranes, bulldozers and excavators to target Central Asia.[49] Financial services also have a stake, with companies like UnionPay, issuer of China's largest domestic payment card, strongly supporting OBOR in order to expand its circulation and broader use at Central Asian ATMs and point-of-sale machines.[50] Thus, OBOR is partly strategic and partly an umbrella framework for accommodating the regional agendas of a number of Chinese companies, regions and local actors, many of which lack effective oversight from Beijing and/or pursue their own narrow interests.

Roadblocks to Chinese connectivity

Beijing also faces a number of regional political and economic impediments to its connectivity vision. Not least, the underlying Chinese (and US) assumption that building transportation infrastructure will necessarily spur economic development and formal trade is publicly appealing, but remains analytically questionable. Certainly, the work itself will support Chinese construction companies and materials manufacturers. However, merely building infrastructure (the hardware) within an environment as prone to rent-seeking and poor governance as Central Asia is unlikely to reform entrenched crony capitalism – quite the opposite in fact, as these upgraded networks may provide additional opportunities for cronyism and the distribution of informal payments.[51] For example, comparative research on road-building and development in sub-Saharan Africa has underscored that new roads tend to exacerbate local governance problems and can generate unforeseen costs in the form of maintenance obligations that states already ill-equipped to build infrastructure are not in a position to meet.[52]

In fact, there is evidence to suggest that despite recent upgrades to the Central Asian transport corridors, in terms of both rail and road, regional transit times and informal barriers are actually getting worse, not better. According to the Asian Development Bank CAREC's annual survey of transit times and trade barriers, from 2013 to 2014, the time required for cargo (which is overwhelmingly from China) to cross a border point significantly increased: from 5.6/4.2 days to 9.9/4.8 days (average/median) by road and from 29.9/24.0 days to 32.6/24.0 by rail.[53] The report made note of the cumbersome procedures on the Central Asian side of the border, such as at the Korgas–Altyn-Kol crossing where the Kazakh side lacks the same reloading capacity as its Chinese counterpart and thus takes significantly longer to inspect and clear shipments. Reloading and processing times in the border warehouses appear to be a major cause of rail-related delays (compared with customs clearance on roads).[54] On the roads, customs procedures and clearances are the most cumbersome, including unofficial payments for technical issues and larger 'rent-seeking' bribes from customs officials.[55]

Consistent with our account of how global structures actually feed local interests and corruption, major externally funded infrastructure projects also risk being diverted for private benefit, especially when, as in the case of Chinese assistance, external disbursements lack monitoring and conditionality. A recent case of the Chinese funding of a major highway project in Tajikistan offers a cautionary tale.[56] Shortly after the Dushanbe–Chanak highway was opened in 2010, built with about 80 per cent Chinese funding, tollbooths appeared on the road. The company operating the toll was identified as Innovative Road Solutions, registered in the BVI, with no previous corporate history or record of bidding on or operating highway projects. Subsequent local investigative stories tied the offshore company to associates of the ruling family, estimating that it was opaquely funnelling a private annual revenue stream of between $25 million and $30 million to the government's inner circle.[57]

In this way, much as in the case of the Manas fuel contracts, legal and financial globalisation allows Central Asian elites to create layers of hidden networks and informal arrangements that may actually obscure the exact contracting parties that have pioneered these new routes of 'connectivity'.

'Go West – and offshore!' Chinese energy companies in Central Asia

China's new energy pipelines in Central Asia have transformed the region's export infrastructure. They include an oil pipeline that traverses Kazakhstan and a network of gas connectors, known as the Central Asia–China pipeline, that originates in Turkmenistan's gas fields and runs through Uzbekistan and Kazakhstan before crossing into Xinjiang to flow into the Chinese east–west pipeline.[58] This new energy infrastructure has been accompanied by a set of major loans-for-energy deals that have made China an important regional investor and creditor.[59] The gas pipeline, in particular, has turned Turkmenistan into a critical exporter for Beijing and has vaulted the state-owned oil company CNPC over the Russian giant Gazprom, formerly the regional monopolist, as Central Asia's main gas producer and distributor.

But much like the Manas fuel schemes involving the Pentagon, China's state-sponsored energy deals in Central Asia have woven together a number of local, corporate and private interests through complicated offshore schemes and intermediaries in the name of official bilateral energy cooperation. These networks constitute an equally powerful, yet hidden, form of 'connectivity' that undergirds the more visible markers of pipelines and refineries.

Since 2013, allegations of corruption have dominated domestic headlines and rattled China's energy sector. Chinese authorities launched an unprecedented crackdown and investigation of corruption in CNPC, the country's largest energy company (with revenues totalling $432 billion in 2013), whose subsidiary PetroChina is the world's fourth largest oil producer.[60] Investigators examined a host of overseas transactions involving the company's groups, including offshore spending accounts, equipment supply deals, oil service contracts and oilfield acquisition.[61] The investigation had touched upon the company's overseas activities in Turkmenistan (among other overseas locations), and had implicated two major executives who had previously headed major subsidiaries in Central Asia. These allegations and subsequent investigations also revealed complex webs of offshore vehicles involved in acquisition deals, as well as shell companies associated with individual executives working for the energy giant.

Internationally, state committee investigations have revealed lax oversight and uncovered a number of corruption-related scandals. Between 2002 and 2012, Chinese oil companies went on a spending spree overseas, making more than 150 deals and over $120 billion worth of investments to acquire a variety of overseas holdings.[62] The great financial crisis of 2008–09 was an important marker, as it ushered in a raft of new overseas purchases, mergers and acquisitions, and loans-for-energy agreements between China and cash-strapped Eurasian and Latin American governments.[63] On the Chinese side, these deals were structured and financed by the Chinese Development Bank (CDB), which funnelled state development funds to assist in the acquisition of overseas energy assets.[64] Loans from the CDB were used to structure deals worth $8 billion and $10 billion (to become $13 billion in 2013, when CNPC also acquired a stake in the large Kashagan international consortium) in Kazakhstan and Turkmenistan, respectively, guaranteeing Chinese oil companies access to Turkmen gas supplies and shares in Kazakh energy companies in return.[65]

But the oversight of these deals was poor. A report issued by the Chinese government's Central Commission for Discipline Inspection in 2014 found that the overseas investment projects of CNPC were at risk of corruption given that they 'did not go through standardized decision-making processes'.[66] During this time China lacked a Ministry of Energy to comprehensively oversee or regulate these overseas activities carried out by the new networks of government officials, oil companies, diplomatic actors and the trading sector.[67] Though formally state-owned, these companies behaved competitively with each other and also appeared to have facilitated interpersonal networks of access and influence.

The use of offshore vehicles figured prominently in these efforts, by both the energy companies themselves and a host of officials involved in the deals. An international investigation into offshore documents surrounding Chinese energy dealings conducted by the International Consortium of Investigative Journalists found that these 'oil companies and their executives set up dozens of companies in the British Virgin Islands (BVI), Cook Islands and other offshore jurisdictions between 1995 and 2008'.[68] The report stated that 'there was no evidence that oil companies or their executives were engaged in illegal conduct', but noted that it was 'unclear in some cases whether the overseas entities controlled by oil executives were established on behalf of their employers or as personal holdings'.[69] All three major Chinese energy companies had set up offshore subsidiaries in the BVI, while BVI officials themselves reported that 40 per cent of their business had come from China and other Asian countries.[70] As the report further noted:

> Some of the offshore companies have been disclosed in the annual reports of the listed arms of the three oil giants. But many do not appear to have been publicly reported. It's not clear whether they were reported internally to the Chinese government, a requirement for state-owned firms.[71]

For example, the report discovered a number of BVI-registered shell companies of which China National Offshore Oil Corporation (CNOOC) and CNPC senior officials were the sole directors and shareholders.[72]

CNPC's Central Asian dealings

Not surprisingly, Chinese oil operations in Central Asian countries have been connected to accusations of corruption and the use of shell companies to camouflage ownership structures and underhanded deals made with Central Asian elites. Perhaps the most well known of these scandals surrounded a CNPC deal to acquire one of Kazakhstan's largest energy companies, Aktobe MunaiGas. A *Wall Street Journal* investigation, based on the allegations and materials originally supplied by exiled political dissident Mukhtar Ablyazov (see Chapter 2) and published in Kazakh independent newspapers, found that the 2003 acquisition of Aktobe by CNPC had been mediated by a mysterious BVI-registered holding company, CNPC International Caspian Ltd (CICL).[73] CICL's start-up capital was reportedly just $100, and it proceeded to sell at a later date a 49 per cent stake (for $49) to yet another BVI-registered company, Darley Investment Services. Over the next two years, CNPC bought back Darley's stakes in the company for $165.90 million, netting the beneficial owners of the company an enormous profit from their initial $49 outlay. According to the report, the structured deal yielded a $150 million payoff to a business partner of presidential son-in-law Timur Kulibayev.[74]

In Turkmenistan, the terms of the very strong energy cooperation between CNPC and Turkmen authorities is shrouded in secrecy. Whatever the long-term benefits of sustained piped gas from Turkmenistan, energy analysts estimate that, in the short term, CNPC as a company appears to have suffered significant losses in the deal, mainly due to domestic gas prices not being able to cover the high costs of importing through Turkmenistan.[75] Yet unofficial payments appear to have been a key part of the deal. One CNPC official working in Turkmenistan, when interviewed by journalists, explained that 'We plan these payments into our budgets. We know about it here in Ashgabat and they know about it in Beijing. They know that's how things work here, and so we include the bribes in our balance sheets. We don't have any other choice.'[76] The same study, after surveying Russian, Western and Turkish firms operating in the country, found that foreign companies working in energy or construction typically had to inflate project budgets by 20 to 30 per cent to cover the costs of these domestic 'commissions'.[77]

Reports from Chinese authorities identified the Turkmenistan deals among those being investigated for corrupt schemes, while Zhang Benquan, who headed CNPC's subsidiary in Turkmenistan before becoming CNPC's subsidiary manager in Iran, was among those subsequently detained in 2014.[78] Perhaps the most colourful report detailing CNPC's global efforts to maintain access in Turkmenistan, as recounted in a *Wall Street Journal* story, involved the Chinese energy giant paying for the US pop star Jennifer Lopez to hold a concert in Ashgabat in 2013.[79] According to Lopez's publicist, the energy company 'made a last-minute "birthday greeting" request prior to Jennifer taking the stage' for her to sing 'Happy Birthday, Mr President' to Turkmenistan's premier.[80]

Thus, offshore and personal networks appear to have been integral to the development of this new energy infrastructure connecting Central Asia to China: as more information emerges about these scandals and networks of influence, we are observing how some of these Chinese state companies can also be arenas for personal profit and political gain.[81] As one academic analysis observed, China's increasing use of offshore vehicles to structure and mediate outward and inward investments 'suggests that Chinese actors will emulate the practices of developed state multinational corporations and high-net-worth individuals'.[82]

Central Asian connectivity revisited

In Washington and Beijing policy circles, the buzzword of 'connectivity' is regularly posited as the key to promoting economic development in Central Asia. Both US and Chinese policymakers even go out of their way to deny that promoting transportation and energy infrastructure is in any way geopolitical or tied to regional strategic agendas. But a closer look at the recent networks of outside economic actors, local elites, offshore entities and transnational intermediaries reveals a complex web of regional collusion across the supposedly 'disconnected' regions of Central Asia that now lie at the very core of China's OBOR strategy and the US New Silk Road concept.

Similarly, as the Pentagon serviced and supported its military efforts in Afghanistan, US officials oversaw, or at the very least acquiesced to, a number of transnational rent-seeking schemes, smuggling networks and murky contracting arrangements involving opaque contractors and shell companies. The red flags and corruption discovered in the Manas fuel contracts suggests that the Northern Distribution Network could provide a very different precursor to the New Silk Road than its proponents advocate or even envisage. Connected Central Asian elites, their intermediaries and subcontractors constructed elaborate schemes for allowing external actors to build infrastructure and manage logistics across the region. Consistent with this book's theme, these connections built upon official bilateral deals and foreign policy objectives, but beneath the surface actually benefited a range of private interests through opaque transnational schemes and global shell companies. Accordingly, the phrase often used by US officials – that the United States is interested in 'great gains', not geopolitical 'great games' – reveals an unintended yet important twist: in Central Asia, the plans of Beijing and Washington to build New Silk Roads are likely to continue to involve playing many offshore games, whilst the touted gains will be afforded to the region's kleptocrats, not their impoverished citizens.

7

POLITICAL EXILES AND EXTRATERRITORIAL REPRESSION

On 16 June 2014, Alexander Sodiqov, a Tajikistani researcher ordi-
narily based in Canada, was arrested while conducting an interview
with a member of a political party in the Pamir Mountains region of
eastern Tajikistan. Sodiqov, a colleague working with one of us on a
UK-funded research project on conflict management in Central Asia,
was charged with espionage and held for thirty-six days in a high security detention facility where he was interrogated and maltreated by
officers of Tajikistan's national security services. After a global campaign
by academics, international media coverage and concerted diplomatic
pressure, Sodiqov was eventually released to return to his family in
Canada.

It was unprecedented for an academic researcher in Tajikistan to be
identified as a threat and treated in this way. However, Sodiqov's case
showed that Central Asian autocrats operate beyond boundaries, in all
senses. Those who challenge their reputation and control of information risk being treated like former regime insiders – as a genuine threat
to the regime. Opposition figures and security officials alike wrongly
associated Sodiqov with exiled activists and politicians. Dictators
without borders treat all of their diaspora – from human rights activists
to former regime insiders – as dangerous, and such suspicions are
infectious.

As we have seen, Central Asia's dictators have successfully integrated themselves into the global financial system to achieve an economic and political presence beyond their borders. This final chapter explores how they have employed legal and illegal means to practise security overseas and export their repression abroad. Building on our work on Kazakhstan (Chapter 2), we have constructed an original database – the Central Asian Political Exiles (CAPE) database – in collaboration with colleagues and student researchers at the University of Exeter, detailing the pursuit of political exiles by Central Asian governments.[1] As of 2016, it includes 126 entries of exiles (comprising 163 persons) who have been subject to measures of repression overseas. All but two of them have been targeted since the year 2000. We look here at the two countries – Tajikistan (with forty-seven entries) and Uzbekistan (with forty-eight) – who are the keenest employers of extraterritorial security practices against their exiles. Kyrgyzstan (with ten entries) pursued exiles under the Bakiyev regime or in association with the ethnic violence of 2010. Kazakhstan (with ten entries) and Turkmenistan (with eleven) have tended to target former regime insiders. However, these figures probably represent the tip of the iceberg.

Our research suggests that there are patterns of extraterritorial repression whether practised against human rights activists or Islamists. While dictators are often without scruples, they pursue their opponents with an eye to efficiency across three phases, from warning and intimidation (stage one), to arrest and confiscation of property (stage two), to rendition, disappearance and attack, including assassination (stage three). Remarkably, all this takes place, as outlined in Chapter 1, with the assistance of international institutions and cooperative arrangements – not just within the former Soviet region, but beyond. While Central Asians subject to politically motivated charges in the West will usually escape extradition, they may find their lives blighted by fear of arrest and the inability to travel for years. The long arm of Central Asian dictators has even led to the coercive extradition of the wife and daughter of a Kazakh oligarch from Italy (see Chapter 2) and suspicious deaths in Austria, Sweden and Turkey.

Migrants, exiles and the export of repression

Central Asian states have generated diaspora communities since their birth. While the region's governments have obsessed about *national* ideologies, histories and development strategies, their peoples have, by choice or by force, adopted *transnational* lives in ever-increasing numbers. To Central Asian presidents this is an aberration. 'I call "lazy" those who go to Moscow and sweep its streets', remarked Uzbekistan's autocrat Islam Karimov in June 2013. 'One feels disgusted with the fact that Uzbeks have to travel there for a piece of bread. Nobody is starving to death in Uzbekistan.'[2]

However, labour migration is indeed a lifeline for many ordinary Central Asians. These people sit at the opposite end of the social scale to the likes of Ablyazov, Bakiyev, Karimova and others who have appeared in the preceding chapters. But their lives are indirectly connected in that the corruption these elites practise while in power is one of the biggest reasons for the lack of economic opportunity for their poorer countrymen. Beginning in the 1990s, economic stagnation in Tajikistan, Kyrgyzstan and Uzbekistan generated a dramatically increasing outflow of labour migrants, mostly to Russia and Kazakhstan. By World Bank estimates, the remittances of these migrants account for around 40 per cent and 25 per cent of Tajikistan's and Kyrgyzstan's GDPs respectively, making these countries officially the two most migration-dependent economies in the world.[3]

Around a million people each from Kyrgyzstan and Tajikistan are working in Russia at any one time. In absolute terms, however, Uzbeks are the largest Central Asian diaspora population in Russia. Recent figures from Russia's Federal Migration Service (dissolved in April 2016) suggest there are 2.3 million Uzbek migrants in Russia, but the real number is thought to be higher.[4] This inflow of hard-currency remittances has helped to offset domestic capital flight and to shield communities in these countries from the worst of the global financial crisis, even as it has plunged millions of migrants into a chronic state of personal and legal uncertainty, exploited by middlemen and corrupt local officials in their host countries.[5]

Given the vital role migration plays in tackling poverty in Central Asia, and the safety valve it apparently provides by mitigating resentment towards corrupt governments, one wonders why migrants are so pilloried by their home governments. Of course, large flows of migrants do indeed lay bare poor governance and weak economies back home, embarrassing Central Asia's dictators. But there is also a more immediate concern for these autocrats. The very limited political space that exists throughout the region has prompted political opponents to seek refuge and political asylum abroad. They often do so in the same countries where ordinary Central Asian labour migrants are found: firstly Russia, and secondly elsewhere in the former Soviet Union, Turkey and the Gulf countries. Inevitably, paranoid officials fear political exiles will organise labour migrants to rebel against their homeland. Whilst sustained diaspora mobilisation by Central Asian groups remains uncommon, there are examples of online campaigns and external funding of independent media and opposition movements in states such as Kazakhstan, as we have seen. In short, as politics moves beyond borders, so too does repression.

These exile communities are now quite well established, although constantly under threat. Three main centres for political exiles have emerged in Moscow, Istanbul and Dubai – but all of these states have cooperative relations to a greater or lesser degree with the Central Asian states. Beyond these centres there are peripheries in the West, with notable refugee communities in Europe and North America. In our CAPE database, we have identified four main categories of exile. First, and of the greatest concern for Central Asian governments, are former regime insiders (such as those covered in Chapters 2–5 of this book). Second, and overlapping with the first category, we have secular opposition movements, often founded by former MPs and senior officials. A third and distinct category is that of banned clerics and alleged religious extremists, often accused of belonging to forbidden groups such as Hizb ut-Tahrir, the Islamic Movement of Uzbekistan or others listed as terrorist organisations. Finally, and often overlapping with the second and sometimes the third categories, are independent journalists and rights activists who are a threat to the extent that they continue to work on investigations into state corruption, repression and malpractice.

In response, the Central Asian states have adopted a number of aggressive extraterritorial tactics to target dissidents residing abroad. Extraterritorial security can be understood as *the practice of internal security within the territory of a foreign state*. Such measures are nothing new in the region, with the Russian tsar's secret police chasing opponents overseas in the nineteenth century and the well-known foreign assassinations by Stalin's NKVD security operatives, including the killing of Trotsky in Mexico in 1940. More recently, former KGB officer Alexander Litvinenko was assassinated in London in 2006, poisoned with radioactive polonium-210, 'probably', an official British report concluded, under the orders of President Putin.[6] These acts typically target political rivals of regime members. In Central Asia, too, extraterritorial security takes the form of acts overseas to protect the security of the regime at home. Apparently an oxymoron, extraterritorial *internal* security pertains to the protection of regimes of power from their political opponents in exile – be they former regime members, secular opposition movements, religious groups or independent activists and journalists.

Such repression beyond borders requires elaborate networks between states, as well as ties between state security services and organised criminal groups. The region's national security services have maintained professional ties with their former Soviet counterparts, demanded extradition of political opponents under new regional security frameworks, and even kidnapped and assassinated political opponents and dissidents both within the wider region and abroad. For example, the 'Uzbek File', written by Litvinenko, alleges that Uzbek and Russian security services conspired to provide protection for mafia groups for a price.[7] Indeed, many security services across the region have maintained links with one another and organised criminals operating across the region.[8] This evidence leads some to talk of the nexus between the state and crime. As David Lewis argues, these policies 'produce the sense of an extraterritorial state, reproducing its repressive mechanisms in a range of foreign jurisdictions'.[9]

What is relatively new in this extraterritorial security system is the use and abuse of international legal and policing agreements, including

Interpol, to pursue political opponents abroad. Just as international financial liberalisation and the 'offshore system' enable dictators to operate beyond borders, so too do international and regional agreements on law enforcement cooperation. Once again, the liberal order is subverted by authoritarian regimes while its supposed guardians in major Western states stand by or are complicit themselves in these systems of extraterritorial security.

The infrastructure of extraterritorial internal security

As Chapter 1 discussed, the first and foremost context of extraterritorial security in Central Asia is the existence of a common and enduring cultural, economic and political post-Soviet region, a full twenty-five years after the collapse of the USSR. The boundaries of the 'region' here are ambiguous. Russia and Belarus are arguably part of a common space with Uzbekistan and Tajikistan, something formally recognised in their membership of the Commonwealth of Independent States (CIS), the international arrangement that succeeded the Soviet Union. This arrangement allows for extensive international cooperation on criminal justice and intelligence, and provides the visa-free travel that enables very high levels of migration between the countries. By contrast, Afghanistan, a territorial neighbour of three Central Asian states, is arguably not part of the region due to its lack of a recent shared history, political culture, economic space and security environment.

The evident and ongoing tensions between former Soviet states on matters of high-level security and geopolitics sometimes cause analysts to underestimate the continued importance of shared laws, norms and practices. The Minsk Convention ensures that members assume each other's domestic legal systems are robust and effective guarantors of the rights of their citizens. Arrests and extradition requests can therefore be routine processes, with little more than diplomatic assurances that the case is not political and the subject will not be subject to torture. The CIS Customs Union and Eurasian Economic Union promise further cooperation between members on these matters. More important, perhaps, than these formal instruments are the customary ties between security professionals in the former Soviet states, with evidence that targets may be arrested even before a formal international warrant is issued.

Rather than this common space shrinking for extraterritorial security in the face of the rise of nationalism, the transnational space has widened alongside increasing attention to national sovereignty. A 'league of authoritarian gentleman' – and they are almost all men – is emerging, extending from Eurasia into East and South Asia, and to the Middle East and North Africa.[10] The rise of the Shanghai Cooperation Organisation (SCO) is a case in point. The SCO presents itself as a new-style international organisation that champions the principle of non-interference in the sovereign affairs of its member states – a not-too-subtle jibe at the political and economic conditions imposed by other Western-led groups. It includes a further five observer states (Mongolia, Iran, Afghanistan, India and Pakistan[11]) and three dialogue partners (Sri Lanka, Turkey and Belarus), bringing together established autocracies and fragile democracies, whose relationships with the SCO bear witness to the new impetus of 'emerging markets' and 'rising powers'.

Originally, the SCO's precursor, the Shanghai Five, resolved lingering Soviet-era border disputes among its members, but the group has now expanded its activities to include security, economic initiatives, infrastructure development and education. In 2001 it agreed to a new Shanghai Convention on Combatting Terrorism, Separatism and Extremism. Though the organisation's formal headquarters is in Beijing, cooperation among the SCO's internal security services is conducted through the poetically named Regional Anti-Terrorist Structure (RATS), located in Tashkent. Under the mantra of combating the 'three evils' of terrorism, extremism and separatism, RATS maintains a consolidated watchlist of regional 'extremist' individuals and organisations. The list has expanded dramatically, initially from 15 organisations and individuals in 2006 to 42 organisations and over 1,100 individuals in 2010. Human rights groups fear that this expansion is the result of authoritarian 'logrolling', as each country lists its own regime threats in exchange for agreeing to other countries' designations, which may include political opponents in addition to bona fide terrorists.[12]

The United Nations special rapporteur on counter-terrorism and human rights has expressed 'serious concerns' about SCO data-sharing and listing procedures, noting that they are 'not subject to any meaningful form of oversight and there are no human rights safeguards attached to data and information sharing'.[13] RATS may even be sharing surveillance technologies under new cybersecurity initiatives launched in response to the political mobilisation facilitated by social networks during the Arab Spring. In 2009, SCO member states signed a new Anti-Terrorism Treaty that allows for suspects to be transferred among member states with minimal evidence of their crimes, and even permits member states to 'dispatch their agents to the territory' of another SCO member state when conducting a criminal investigation.[14]

Of course, many exiles live beyond the territories of SCO members, knowing full well that they are at risk within these borders. Unfortunately for these exiles, it is now clear that Central Asian states are able to employ extraterritorial security powers well beyond this regional treaty area, and even on a global scale. The tracking of Mukhtar Ablyazov and associates (see Chapter 2) was done via the combination of Interpol arrest warrants, high-level lawyers and private investigators who traced the assets and members of the Ablyazov group across Western Europe, from the UK to Spain, France and Italy. The issuing of Interpol Red Notices has been an increasingly important tactic in the armoury of extraterritorial security for Central Asian regimes. Whilst the pursuit of political opponents through Interpol is expressly forbidden, it is now well documented that the region's dictators have circumvented these restrictions via diplomatic assurances and the restriction of the warrants to economic crimes (which are falsely portrayed as being 'nonpolitical'). Moreover, some evidence suggests that Interpol is not able to adequately oversee the many thousands of warrants submitted to it every year.[15]

This infrastructure of extraterritorial security works not simply via these institutions and legal provisions, but by the interplay of legal, extralegal and flat-out criminal practices. The legal and illegal dimensions are arguably dependent on one another and effectively work together to overcome any international legal and political barriers to extraterritorial internal security measures. The intertwining of legal and extralegal with internal and external, in David Lewis's words, 'force us to reconsider the spatial nature of the authoritarian state, which at once asserts hard boundaries and closed borders against external influence, while attempting to reproduce its own repressive discourses and practices in external jurisdictions'.[16]

Here we identify a three-stage extraterritorial security process. Individuals are, first, put on notice; second, arrested and/or detained; and third, rendered, disappeared, attacked and/or assassinated. This three-stage process is identified from the extraterritorial measures deployed against political exiles as detailed in the CAPE database. Each stage contains both legal and extralegal practices and both internal and external measures. Within territories governed by the Minsk Convention the three stages appear to follow in order – an extraterritorial process that has become habitual and institutionalised. In certain cases there can be a fairly rapid acceleration through the stages to extradition, where in other cases the process can take years or be halted at stage one or two. Outside the Minsk area, this process can take much longer, may not get past stage one, or, in the most troubling cases, passes rapidly to an assassination attempt (stage three). Our research with human rights organisations and exiles suggests that there is a high level of awareness of these stages by both sides – the state security agents and the targets – with both recognising that they are part of a brutal, high-stakes game.

Stage one: on notice – warnings, threats and defamation

The first stage of the extraterritorial security process is being placed 'on notice'. In an informal sense, being on notice is a permanent state of affairs for all political exiles. Having left their home countries, almost all have relatives, associates or business interests remaining there. It is routine for these to be visited by security officials, asked for information about the exile, told to pass on a message, and be subject to direct or indirect threats about what will happen to them, their jobs or their business if the exile does not return to face whatever punishment the state wishes to administer. In the mildest cases this can simply involve moral pressure and muckraking. In one case known to the authors, an exile's in-laws were convinced by security services that he had abandoned his wife and children too quickly and was an irresponsible father. Under pressure from the family he returned home, was questioned frequently and struggled to find a job. In another low-profile case, the exile's father-in-law lost his job as a middle-ranking bureaucrat and his mother was also placed under pressure in her position working for a state agency, constantly being reminded that the situation with her son made her situation tenuous.

More serious cases of being 'on notice' often involve public defamation and often move on to actual violence against associates and dispossession of property. Muhiddin Kabiri, the leader of the Islamic Revival Party of Tajikistan, left the country in March 2015 after his party lost its seats in parliament in the elections of that month and state clerics called for it to be banned. In exile, he was subject to a public campaign against him in the official press. The state-owned newspaper *Jumhuriyat* accused him of corruption and announced that a criminal investigation was being prepared against him for an allegedly illegal privatisation: in 1999 he had purchased a hospital and transferred it to a fellow party member at the request of Said Abdullo Nuri, then the party's leader. Kabiri reported that, by June 2015, when he was residing temporarily in Moscow, 'the majority of facilities and buildings my family owns have been either seized or pressured in such a way that speaking of business in its true meaning is simply impossible'.[17]

These informal threats are often accompanied or succeeded by the formal laying of charges in national courts followed rapidly by an international arrest warrant being issued. This is a very straightforward process within the Minsk area, where cooperation between security services is so institutionalised and unquestioning that, in some cases, warrants are issued in Russia or another foreign jurisdiction before they have even been heard by the particular Central Asian state's court. The issuing of Interpol Red Notices is a little more bureaucratic and, theoretically, involves thorough checking to ensure the person is not a political target. However, such controls are routinely circumvented. Dozens of Red Notices can be found on the Interpol website against persons who were once regime insiders or representatives of opposition parties and movements. While the requesting nation's security services may possess evidence that such persons have committed crimes, there is no guarantee of its veracity. The choice to pursue prosecution is typically political and therefore in violation of Articles 2 and 3 of Interpol's constitution, which presents it as a body that respects human rights and forbids it to enable state actions of a 'political, military, religious or racial character'.[18]

In a report published in November 2013, Fair Trials International, a British legal reform group, documented multiple cases of a political character.[19] Moreover, they demonstrated that even where political requests are denied, two other means are available to foreign security services seeking arrest and extradition. They identify 'draft Red Notices' to denote the temporary record stored on Interpol's database prior to approval by the secretariat. Although such notices are supposed to be approved or removed within twenty-four hours, they often stay on for much longer and are downloaded onto the national security databases of police and port authorities all over the world. A second common practice is that of diffusion, where national agencies contact other national agencies directly to issue 'a request for international cooperation, including the arrest, detention or restriction of movement of a convicted or accused person'.[20] Foreign countries are not required to treat any of these requests, even approved Red Notices, as international arrest warrants. However, many members, including Western European countries, do consider them de facto arrest warrants.[21]

Stage two: arrest, detention, dispossession

The formal issuing of an arrest warrant overseas, sometimes following an Interpol Red Notice, effectively initiates stage two of the extraterritorial security process: arrest and detention. As the arrested exiles are by definition foreign citizens, often in a precarious state of residence (awaiting asylum requests or notification of a temporary right-to-remain), they are typically detained, often for a considerable period of time, following arrest. As we have seen, several Kazakh former officials have found themselves in this position.

Such formal measures of arrest and detention are often accompanied by intensified physical pressure and targeting of relatives. Alnur Musayev was a former senior Kazakh official and head of the national security services whose old staff were turned against him by the Kazakh government.[22] As an ally of the erstwhile son-in-law of President Nazarbayev, Rakhat Aliyev, Musayev rapidly fell out of favour after Aliyev's own fall from grace and fled into exile. He was declared wanted in August 2007 for alleged participation in the so-called Nurbank murders (believed to be kidnappings at the time) and convicted *in absentia* in 2008 alongside Aliyev for charges including running a criminal racket, plotting a coup, kidnapping and theft of state property. In September 2008 in Vienna he survived an attack by four armed Russian speakers who alleged they were sent by Nazarbayev to kidnap him.[23] Later, in February 2014, he was found guilty in Kazakhstan of orchestrating the 2006 murder of opposition leader Altynbek Sarsenbayev, after the men who were originally convicted in 2006 were given a retrial and blamed Musayev and Aliyev for plotting the murder. One of the original convicts was released on bail months later in November 2014. Such internal moves against Musayev were accompanied by increased pressure against him in exile, where he lived alongside Aliyev in Austria. He was arrested by Austrian authorities and charged in June 2014 but was acquitted by a court in Vienna in July 2015.

Cases such as that of Musayev are fascinating for what they tell us about the regime of which he was once a central part. At that time, he might have murdered and racketeered with impunity, as his former commander-in-chief now, conveniently, alleges. The fact that he has been targeted for political reasons does not mean that he did not commit crimes. However, in other cases there is not nearly enough evidence to support charges against the accused, even in a flawed legal jurisdiction such as Russia. Many other exiles subject to stage two of the extraterritorial security process therefore find themselves in a prolonged state of legal limbo. One aspect of this limbo is the uncertain legal status which sees applicants refused asylum despite receiving recognition from the UN High Commissioner for Refugees (UNHCR) and non-extradition orders from the European Court of Human Rights (ECHR).[24]

This limbo has been endured by a number of members of political religious movements. Rustam Zokhidov, for example, was arrested in St Petersburg on 14 July 2010, accused of being a member of Hizb ut-Tahrir, an organisation banned in Uzbekistan but legal and active in many democratic states. His arrest record of the same date stated that he had been arrested in accordance with the Minsk Convention as a person who was on an international wanted list. The initial detention order did 'not set any time-limits for the detention and referred only to the Minsk Convention'.[25] On 19 November 2010, the president of the First Section of the ECHR indicated to the respondent government that the applicant should not be extradited to Uzbekistan until further notice. But Zokhidov had his request for asylum and refugee status dismissed in March 2011. This was challenged by his lawyers and dismissed once again by Russia's Federal Migration Service (FMS) in July 2011. The FMS cited the Russian Ministry of Foreign Affairs judgement that the human rights situation in Uzbekistan was 'ambiguous'. Moreover, it argued,

> with a view to securing internal stability, the leadership of Uzbekistan is conducting a strict policy of control over attitudes and mind frames in all segments of Uzbek society, and of suppression of all terrorist and fundamentalist religious threats, backed up by the security forces and the judicial system.[26]

Stage three: rendition, disappearance, attack and assassination

Such states of uncertainty hamper exiles in their fight against moving on to stage three of the extraterritorial security process, that of extradition or deportation, often to face torture and conviction at home, or extralegal measures to assassinate, disappear or unlawfully render the person back to their home country. We use 'rendition' to refer to all modes of illegal transfer to a home or third country and summary extraditions which violate due process and/or transfer the person to a country in which they are likely to face torture and/or politically motivated prosecution. Such stage-three actions are significant in number with respect to Tajik and Uzbek exiles.

Rustam Zokhidov, already detained, provides one such case. Court documents from the ECHR describe what happened next:

> At 7 a.m. on 21 December 2011 several individuals who introduced themselves as police officers and officials of the St Petersburg branch of the FMS burst into the flat occupied by the applicant and his family on the pretext of an identity check. The applicant immediately called his lawyer, K., and switched his mobile to conference call mode so as to enable her to participate in the conversation. The applicant and K. informed the intruders that proceedings concerning his application for refugee status were pending before the appellate court and the applicant showed them a stamped copy of his appeal statement. They also informed them that he could not be returned to Uzbekistan because the Court had applied Rule 39 in his case, which was pending before it. The applicant showed the officers a copy of the Court's letter. The applicant's lawyer also informed the officers that she was on her way to the flat, but at that moment the connection was cut. Despite these explanations, the applicant was handcuffed, placed in a car and taken to an unknown destination.[27]

His relatives were not allowed to follow him. Zokhidov made two anguished phone calls to family members later that day from an FMS holding centre. He was deported to Uzbekistan on an evening flight without being checked in or registered for the flight, in a practice which bears the hallmarks of an illegal rendition. However, the subsequent justification for this measure by the Russian FMS was framed in the legal terms of Zokhidov not being qualified to stay, having violated the terms of Russia's Refugees Act.

On arrival in Uzbekistan, Zokhidov was taken from Samarkand to Tashkent by officers of the national security services. He was held in detention and in April 2012 the Samarkand city court convicted him of the offences for which his extradition had been sought, and sentenced him to eight years' imprisonment. Zokhidov was represented by a court-appointed lawyer, having been 'advised' to tell his relatives to discontinue their communication with his lawyer in Russia 'in order to avoid any problems'. During a brief meeting with him in the presence of the prison escort officers, Zokhidov's wife noticed signs of exhaustion and ill treatment on his face. Neither he nor his relatives were provided with copies of the trial judgment. Defence lawyers in Uzbekistan refused to take on the case, saying that it 'was political and that becoming involved in the case could lead to their losing their lawyers' licences'.[28]

Our database and the judgments of ECHR record a growing number of incidents like that of Zokhidov. These are examples of the use of national legal means of deportation and extradition to return a political exile despite this being expressly forbidden under an ECHR Rule 39 judgment and disallowed under international law.[29] Despite claiming they are upholding the rule of law, both Kyrgyzstan and Kazakhstan have deported or extradited Uzbek citizens en masse.[30] Often this is done purely on the basis of diplomatic assurances, despite a long track record of torture and lack of due process. It is in this third stage where the overlap between legal and extralegal measures is most obvious. In fact, all returns to home countries where a reasonable chance of torture is present counts as 'refoulement', forbidden under treaties signed by all states in question, both the places of exile and places of torture. It should therefore be of no surprise to find that the endgame of the extraterritorial security process includes not only formal legal measures of extradition and deportation, but also illegal rendition (kidnapping by security personnel), disappearance and even assassination. If exiles reach this third stage, they live in constant fear of such an attack and have little or no opportunity to negotiate a solution short of their killing or return to long-term imprisonment.

Uzbekistan: hunting the Andijan exiles

One situation where such extreme measures have been used to their fullest extent is in the case of the exiles from the Andijan uprising of 13 May 2005.[31] The Tashkent government was itself shocked by these events and sought to shift the blame wholly onto the alleged terrorists. Accused by human rights groups, the European Union and the United States of having used excessive force, it reacted with recalcitrance, asking

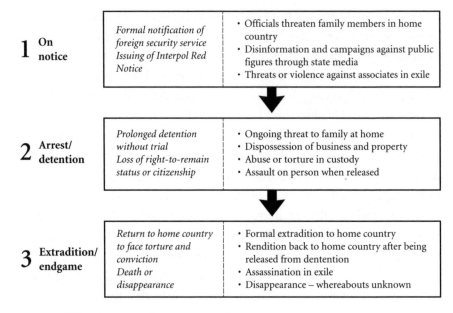

1	On notice	*Formal notification of foreign security service* *Issuing of Interpol Red Notice*	• Officials threaten family members in home country • Disinformation and campaigns against public figures through state media • Threats or violence against associates in exile
2	Arrest/ detention	*Prolonged detention without trial* *Loss of right-to-remain status or citizenship*	• Ongoing threat to family at home • Dispossession of business and property • Abuse or torture in custody • Assault on person when released
3	Extradition/ endgame	*Return to home country to face torture and conviction* *Death or disappearance*	• Formal extradition to home country • Rendition back to home country after being released from dentention • Assassination in exile • Disappearance – whereabouts unknown

Figure 7.1 The extraterritorial security process

the US to leave its air base in the country and withdrawing cooperation on development. The Uzbek activist and scholar Alisher Ilkhamov, exiled in London since 2004, counts some 245 demonstrators who were arrested and sentenced to long prison terms, and says at least eleven died as a result of torture.[32] The leader of the Association for Human Rights in Central Asia, Nadejda Atayeva, another Uzbek exile and a refugee in France, estimates that in the ten years between 2005 and 2015, 1,000 refugees from Uzbekistan applied to her for assistance. Many of these Andijan exiles were accused by Tashkent of being religious extremists and were often identified as being part of a group known as Akramiya, a term used to refer to the supposed followers of Akram Yuldashev, an Andijan native and cleric, who had been jailed in 1999 by the Uzbek authorities on grounds of extremism. The state-employed Uzbek scholar Bakhtiyar Babadjanov presented 'evidence' to his colleagues at the Carnegie Endowment of a Quranic commentary supposedly written by Yuldashev in which he apparently justifies violent jihad against secular governments, alongside video footage of demonstrators in Andijan shouting *Allahu Akbar* ('God is greater').[33] But whether Akramiya exists at all as an organisation is disputed by other experts on Uzbekistan.[34]

As it has sought, unsuccessfully, to control the international discourse on Andijan, the Karimov regime has been more successful in harassing the exiles who escaped to Russia or further afield. Human Rights Watch found that the majority of persons who fled Uzbekistan after Andijan had relatives back home who had subsequently been harassed, threatened or imprisoned; often such people were required to merely pay a bribe to avoid the matter being taken further.[35] Of the large group of refugees that crossed into Kyrgyzstan, many were granted asylum in third countries while others were returned to Uzbekistan under a great deal of international protest. A little over a month after the uprising and massacre in Andijan, on 18 June 2005, Russian police arrested on international warrant twelve Uzbek men in the town of Ivanovo. These men were charged in Uzbekistan over the period 17–19 June 2005 for offences including membership of Akramiya, Hizb ut-Tahrir and the Islamic Movement of Turkestan, financing terrorist activities, attempting a violent overthrow of the constitutional order of Uzbekistan, aggravated murder and organising mass disorder on 13 May 2005 in Andijan. In an indication of the close level of cooperation between Russian and Uzbek security services, some of these men were arrested in Russia *before* charges were even filed in Uzbekistan.

The twelve defendants included a man named Ismoilov, in whose name a case would be brought against Russia in the ECHR. The defendants were not informed of the reasons for their arrest and were puzzled by their apparent connection to the Andijan events, given that only one of them had been in the region at the time and most of them had been living in Russia for several months or years. On 20 June 2005 they were questioned by security agents from Uzbekistan who beat them, threatened them with torture in Uzbekistan and told them they would be forced to confess to various crimes and be sentenced to long prison terms or death. They were held for a year and their extradition was approved in 2006. However, on 5 March 2007, after repeated appeals to the ECHR and Russian courts, the applicants were released. The case of *Ismoilov and Others v the Russian Federation* appeared to have set a precedent against extradition and was a victory for the Uzbek and Russian human rights communities.[36] Unfortunately, it only upped the stakes for the Uzbek security services, which would now move to extralegal measures to return or eradicate its Andijan-linked exiles.

The rendition of Azamat Ermakov

The case of Azamat Ermakov is one which demonstrates the effective collusion between Russian and Uzbek security services for the rendering of Andijan exiles back to their home country. Ermakov believes he came to the attention of the Andijan authorities due to his performance of *salat* (the ritualised daily prayers undertaken by Muslims across the world). He fled the country in March 2009 when he heard his neighbour had been arrested for praying and feared his own arrest and torture during detention. The Tashkent regime sees things differently. In September 2009, following his departure, the regional prosecutor's office brought charges against Ermakov for setting up a criminal group to overthrow the constitutional order of the state. The statement of charges refers to the events as an armed attempt by Akramiya to seize power with the assistance of international terrorist forces and, it comments darkly, 'under the influence of certain States acting on the basis of double standards and seeking to achieve their own geopolitical aims'.[37] Ermakov was placed on the Interpol Red Notice list. He was arrested in November 2009, held for a period, and ordered for extradition in April 2010. However, he was released on 22 September 2010 following the application of Rule 39 by the ECHR. On 4 October 2010 the government of Russia submitted that it had taken steps to ensure that the applicant would not be extradited to Uzbekistan until further notice.[38]

If Azamat Ermakov thought he was now safe from harm, he was wrong. He remained on the cusp of stage three of the extraterritorial security process, under house arrest in Russia. He was arrested again in July 2011 on charges of possession of a hand grenade, which he claims was planted by police, and sentenced to sixteen months in a high-security prison. As of the beginning of 2012, Ermakov was one of twenty-five named persons detained in Russia under threat of extradition or rendition to former Soviet states. Such was the ECHR's concern about these cases that it wrote to the Russian government in January 2012, in connection with another case, expressing 'profound concern at the repeated allegations concerning the secret transfer of applicants from Russia', transfers which took place 'in breach of interim measures applied under Rule 39'.[39] Ermakov was also anxious. His lawyer reports that he expressed concerns that he would be transferred to Uzbekistan on his release from prison. In a meeting on 26 October 2012, one week before his release, he repeated these concerns and agreed to telephone his lawyer on leaving prison.

On 2 November 2012 at 6 a.m. – an unusually early time – Ermakov was released from prison in the Russian city of Nizhny Novgorod. His lawyer visited at 8 a.m. but was not told of his client's release. According to court documents, 'the applicant never contacted his representatives after his release, and they have not seen him and have been unable to contact him ever since'.[40] That night, apparently at 11.45 p.m., the applicant departed Moscow's Domodedovo Airport for Tashkent aboard Uzbek Airlines flight HY602 using a ticket issued in Tashkent. The distance between Nizhny Novgorod and Domodedovo is approximately 420 kilometres. Ermakov had no money or documents in his possession other than his passport, making it rather difficult for him to have made this journey of his own accord. His transit to Domodedovo has not been explained by the Russian authorities, who have refused three official requests to mount an investigation into his disappearance. On 18 December 2012, Ermakov's lawyers submitted, with reference to a 'confidential source whose identity has not been disclosed because of fears for his security', that the applicant was being held in detention in Andijan, Uzbekistan, but stressed that no official confirmation of that information was available.[41] Amnesty International issued an Urgent Action in March 2013 expressing concern about Ermakov's abduction and likely torture in Uzbekistan. In June 2013, Ermakov's lawyer submitted a letter dated 4 April 2013 from the Ministry of the Interior of the Republic of Uzbekistan, in reply to a request by an unspecified person, confirming that their client was being held in pre-trial detention in Andijan.[42]

The court, in its judgment of 7 November 2013 which awarded the applicant the maximum amount in damages, was scathing of the culpability of the Russian government in Ermakov's rendition and its complete failure to abide by its treaty obligations. 'It was clear,' the judges argued, 'that the applicant could not have crossed the State border freely and unaccompanied. He had been on the Interpol wanted list, and the search for him in Russia had not been discontinued; furthermore, he was a foreign national against whom criminal proceedings were pending in Russia. Any of these factors, taken alone, would prompt the authorities to arrest the applicant or at least to stop him for a further check in the normal course of events.'[43] The Russian government's account was found to include contradictions and falsehoods. ECHR concluded that:

> the Court finds it established that (a) the applicant did not travel from Russia to Uzbekistan of his own free will but was forcibly transferred to Uzbekistan by an unknown person or persons following his release from SIZO-1 in Nizhniy Novgorod on 2 November 2012, and (b) his transfer through the Russian State border at Domodedovo Airport took place with the authorisation, or at least acquiescence, of the State agents in charge of the airport.[44]

It is rare for the ECHR to directly accuse one of its member states of participation in an illegal rendition, an act of refoulement, a return to torture. The life of Azamat Ermakov, aged 40 at the time of his return to Uzbekistan, has effectively been ended by this act. He has now become a statistic. As the journalist Murat Sadykov (a pseudonym) describes, he is 'one of dozens of Uzbek citizens accused by Tashkent of religious extremism or terrorism, then kidnapped or otherwise forcibly returned to Uzbekistan from Russia and other post-Soviet states'.[45]

The attempted assassination of Obidkhon qori Nazarov

A pattern has emerged of the enforced return of Andijan exiles to face torture, by formal legal extradition or by extralegal rendition, from their exile in other post-Soviet states adhering to the Minsk Convention. But what happens when such exiles have found asylum in Western countries which lie beyond this established infrastructure of extraterritorial security? Andijan exiles have for many years reported informal intimidation and formal measures to restrict their peace and safe haven abroad. For example, Lutfullo Shamsutdinov, an activist who reported on Andijan and was granted asylum in the United States, had to wait five years for a green card that would give him permission to travel abroad after the Uzbek authorities successfully lodged an Interpol Red Notice against him.[46] It is not just freedom of travel that is restricted, however, but peace of mind and body. Rumours abound of Uzbek security services' informants entering refugee communities in Scandinavia and North America, either via online communication or in person. Cynicism and fear – modes of being which are typical of dissidents within authoritarian states – are also commonplace in exile. In her article 'Digital Distrust', the Uzbek-speaking American scholar and journalist Sarah Kendzior discusses the boundaries to *solidarność* (solidarity) in exile communities such as that in St. Louis, Missouri, where her research was undertaken. 'There is no *solidarność* of Uzbek dissidents,' she explains, 'only a scattered body of disparate individuals connected by their enmity toward the Karimov regime – and by the internet where they engage in intense and insular debate with each other.'[47]

It is the case of the attempted assassination of Obidkhon qori Nazarov, a peaceful but conservative Salafi cleric, which most dramatically illustrates the ways in which the Uzbek security services have made inroads into their exile communities. From 1990 to 1996, Nazarov was the imam of Tukhtaboi, a Friday mosque in Tashkent. In 1995 he spoke out about the disappearance of a cleric, Abduvali qori Mirzayev, and was met with calls for his dismissal from his position as imam and, subsequently, criminal charges. In 1998, Nazarov was placed on a national wanted list and went into hiding in Uzbekistan. In 2000, he was able to leave Uzbekistan, relocating to Kazakhstan, where he received political refugee status from the UNHCR. In 2006, he gained political asylum in Sweden and was joined by many of his followers.[48] The community settled in Strömsund, in the north of Sweden, where it was able to practise its conservative faith.

However, as more Uzbek refugees came to Sweden after Andijan, the Uzbek state began to pay more attention to Nazarov and started to portray him in public forums as a violent extremist linked to the banned Islamic Movement of Uzbekistan, an exile organisation which was militarily active throughout the 2000s alongside other violent extremists in northern Pakistan. He was thought to have tens of thousands of followers and, after his move to Sweden, became more visible in the public sphere.[49] In 2006 he gave an interview where he spoke out against violent methods and an Islamist theocracy, but strongly criticised the Karimov regime. 'Allah wants people to live freely and have lots of opportunities', he commented. But Uzbek officials, he argued, 'wanted to rule using communist methods. I told them that times are different and I didn't want to carry out their orders.'[50] In the light of such comments, the Uzbek authorities viewed Nazarov as a security threat and sought his extradition, but without success. In a 2010 Uzbek television documentary laced with conspiracy theories it was alleged that foreign intelligence agencies – not the UNHCR – had enabled Nazarov's transfer to Sweden from where 'he is still trying to set up his jihad group'.[51] His supposed terrorist group was identified by the government as being behind attacks in Uzbekistan in 2004 and 2009.

On 22 February 2012, Nazarov was shot in the head outside his apartment. He survived but went into a coma. The Swedish prosecutor, who suspected a politically motivated contract killing, arrested two Uzbek citizens resident in Sweden, Bakhodyr Pulatov and Nodira Aminova, and charged them with aiding the alleged killer who had rapidly fled the country.[52] The prosecution's case failed due to lack of evidence, but not before the judge confirmed several 'strange' episodes prior to the attack: the suspects tried to trace Nazarov's whereabouts, one of them tried to conceal their real name, they deleted data from their personal computers, and they discarded the killer's clothes. Pulatov and Aminova, meanwhile, claim they only knew the killer as a creditor attempting to collect his money from Nazarov.[53] Some think the case speaks not only to Uzbek state complicity but also to tensions in the Uzbek refugee community between more secular and more conservative Muslims, and distrust between persons still subject to threats against their relatives at home and demands that they inform on their fellow exiles.

In December 2015, a Swedish court sentenced an Uzbek man, Yuri Zhukovsky, to eighteen years in prison for the attempted murder of Nazarov. It noted that the would-be assassin 'acted on behalf of someone in Russia' whilst concluding that there was insufficient evidence to say that the attack was ordered by the government of Uzbekistan.[54] Although evidence to link the Karimov regime to the attack was insufficient for prosecution in a Swedish court, Uzbek exiles and supporters are convinced that the assassination was commissioned by the government of Uzbekistan as a contract killing. Indeed, the judge himself concluded that this was the likely explanation.[55] 'It is obvious that this was an attempted assassination that has been ordered by the Uzbekistan security services', the Nazarov family's lawyer reported to the BBC. 'I'm absolutely convinced that that is the case.'[56] According to the president of the Association for Human Rights in Central Asia, Nadejda Atayeva, herself an exile who is despised by the Uzbek security services and defamed on national television in Uzbekistan, the attack on Nazarov 'should be qualified as an attempted political assassination. These actions of the Uzbek security services could and should be characterised as an act of international terrorism and as their modus operandi for suppressing dissent in the country.'[57]

Together with the assassination of Fuad Rustamkhojayev in 2011 and the disappearance of Lutpiddin Mukhitdinov in 2014, both in Russia, the Nazarov attack is consistent with a pattern of using all necessary measures against imams and supposed 'radicals' exiled overseas.[58] Figure 7.2 maps fifteen cases of attacks, deaths in custody, disappearances and renditions of Uzbek exiles, most of which have taken place since 2010.[59] The sheer number of cases of collusion between the Russian and Kyrgyz authorities speaks to the existence of informal institutions in the realm of security between former Soviet states, even those with troubled diplomatic relations.

Tajikistan: eradicating the secular opposition

While Central Asian regimes are quick to associate banned clerics with extremism and accuse them of terrorism, they are no less severe in their

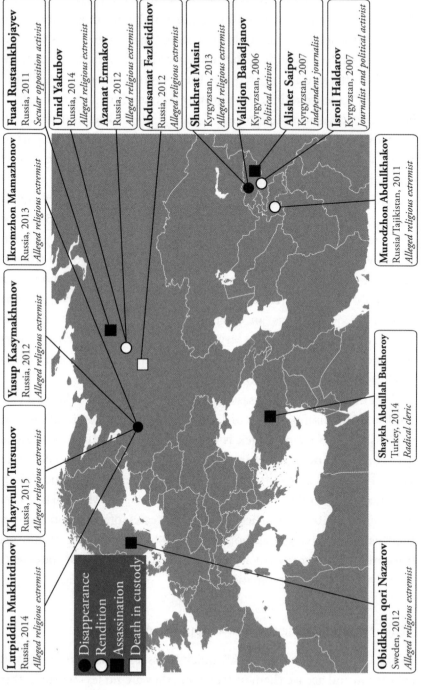

Lutpiddin Mukhitdinov
Russia, 2014
Alleged religious extremist

Khayrullo Tursunov
Russia, 2015
Alleged religious extremist

Yusup Kasymakhunov
Russia, 2012
Alleged religious extremist

Ikromzhon Mamazhonov
Russia, 2013
Alleged religious extremist

Fuad Rustamkhojayev
Russia, 2011
Secular opposition activist

Umid Yakubov
Russia, 2014
Alleged religious extremist

Azamat Ermakov
Russia, 2012
Alleged religious extremist

Abdusamat Fazletidinov
Russia, 2012
Alleged religious extremist

Shukhrat Musin
Kyrgyzstan, 2013
Alleged religious extremist

Validjon Babadjanov
Kyrgyzstan, 2006
Political activist

Alisher Saipov
Kyrgyzstan, 2007
Independent journalist

Isroil Haldarov
Kyrgyzstan, 2007
Journalist and political activist

Murodzhon Abdulkhakov
Russia/Tajikistan, 2011
Alleged religious extremist

Shaykh Abdullah Bukhoroy
Turkey, 2014
Radical cleric

Obidkhon qori Nazarov
Sweden, 2012
Alleged religious extremist

● Disappearance
○ Rendition
■ Assassination
□ Death in custody

Figure 7.2 Map of citizens of Uzbekistan extradited to face torture, rendered, disappeared and/or assassinated

attempts to track down their secular opponents. The equal treatment meted out to former regime insiders and non-religious opposition activists suggests that the targets are selected according to their opposition to the regime, not to the actual harm they may cause to national or international security. This claim is borne out in our second case study of how a nascent, weak and disparate Tajik opposition movement, Group 24, has been decimated by the arrests of its members, attacks on its associates and the assassination of its leader in the street in Istanbul. But to put this into context we need to understand how the 'opposition' in Tajikistan has been progressively weakened at home and aggressively targeted overseas since the country's peace agreement normalised political affairs in the country after 1997.

The opposition goes into exile

No sooner did the government declare national reconciliation with the United Tajik Opposition to have been fully implemented in 2000 than the Tajik opposition found itself under attack. The peace agreement's provision to award 30 per cent of state posts to UTO representatives was never fully implemented. One by one, senior opposition figures were dismissed from their positions. For example, Mahmadruzi Iskandarov, head of the Democratic Party of Tajikistan (DPT), had been in exile in Kazakhstan during the war but returned to a potentially lucrative post as the head of Tajikgaz. He came under pressure after he made statements critical of the president. On 25 November 2004 he was charged with 'terrorism, gangsterism, unlawful possession of firearms and embezzlement' and soon after fled to Russia.[60] Tajikistan's application for extradition was refused by a Russian court, but in evidence presented to and affirmed by the ECHR, Iskandarov gives a vivid account of how he was detained while walking his dog by persons wearing the uniform of the Russian State Inspectorate for Road Safety, and within forty-eight hours extralegally rendered to Tajikistan with the assistance of Russian security officers.[61] Later that year, Iskandarov was tried, convicted and sentenced to twenty-five years. Iskandarov's party was effectively split that same year with Masud Sobirov taking over as the state-recognised head of a newly quietist DPT. A similar fate met the Socialist Party of Tajikistan (SPT), which after its leader was assassinated in the late 1990s was split into two factions in 2004, as well as the Social Democrat Party (SDPT), led by the lawyer Rahmatullo Zoirov, whose members were jailed after it became more oppositional before the 2005 elections.

What looked like a multiparty system in 2000 had been weakened severely by 2005, partly as a result of extraterritorial measures. The Islamic party was the only remaining opposition party in the system with two seats in parliament until 2015. The non-religious democratic opposition was wiped out. It was therefore quite a news story when Zayd Saidov, a secular former minister and businessman, announced the formation of a new political movement in early 2013. Zhani Tojikiston ('New Tajikistan') would not contest the 2013 presidential elections but was preparing, Saidov said, to field candidates in the parliamentary elections of 2015. Saidov – an opponent who was also a former regime insider – was, from the perspective of the inner circle around President Rahmon, the most dangerous kind of politician: he took with him into opposition various secrets about how the business of government really works in the country. He had apparently visited Moscow shortly prior to announcing the new group, a move made by Central Asian opposition movements that seek Russia's seal of approval, as much to give an appearance of credibility as to receive any concrete support. His standing made his party a rallying point for a dwindling group of non-religious activists. It therefore took little time for the state to move against Saidov. On 25 December 2013, he was tried and sentenced to twenty-six years' imprisonment after being convicted of financial fraud, polygamy and sexual relations with a minor.[62]

The extraterritorial struggle with Group 24

Saidov failed because he remained in Tajikistan and overestimated the latitude he might be allowed as a former insider who had good relations with the president. But some of those who allied themselves with New Tajikistan after its formation were already in exile and sought to avoid

Saidov's fate. One of these individuals was Umarali Kuvvatov. Until 2012 Kuvvatov had been in business with Shamsullo Sokhibov, a son-in-law of the president, supplying fuel to the NATO base in Afghanistan. Kuvvatov claimed that his share in these businesses was taken by force by Sokhibov, and made his conversation with a person who he claims is Sokhibov available on YouTube. In summer 2012 Kuvvatov fled from what he claimed was imminent arrest by the Tajik authorities to Russia, living in Moscow for about four months. During this period, he founded Group 24, an alliance of some of Rahmon's most vocal opponents, and announced his intention to take part in presidential elections. Kuvvatov proved an effective exponent of online communication from exile with video messages and communication through *Platforma*, the largest Tajik-language political page on Facebook.[63] It is at this time he began to work with Saidov and his associates.

Facing the formation of an opposition movement with 'onshore' and 'offshore' dimensions, the Tajik government moved quickly both inside and outside the country. Around the time they were mobilising against Saidov they increased pressure on his and Kuvvatov's associates in Moscow. Bakhtiyor Sattori, who had previously worked for the Tajik embassy in Moscow and been the representative of the Tajik Migration Service before his sacking in 2012, was one of the first to be targeted. He had become very critical on the web after being dismissed, and made contact with Kuvvatov's Group 24. On 19 February 2013 he was badly wounded in a stabbing in Moscow which was interpreted by the Tajik opposition as a warning to dissenters.

Kuvvatov, aware of the threat to his own person, was on the move at this time. He travelled to Dubai, another favoured bolthole of Central Asian opposition activists due to its visa-free entry. In December 2012 he was detained at the request of the Tajik government on charges of fraud and was expected to be extradited in early 2013. To the surprise of many, Kuvvatov's lawyers prevented his extradition and he was released.[64] His freedom from detention apparently did not come with an invitation to remain. After a brief sojourn in Bishkek, where he applied to the UNHCR for international protection, he moved to Istanbul. In July 2014 he entered Turkey on a passport in someone else's name, explaining that it was the only way to avoid arrest on his departure from Bishkek. This was the first of a number of administrative violations that placed Kuvvatov in jeopardy. He immediately registered with the UNHCR Office in Istanbul but did not register with the Turkish police, which led to a further violation of administrative law in Turkey.[65]

Despite being under considerable pressure, Kuvvatov decided to up the stakes. Prior to this point, Group 24 had been exclusively extraterritorial, with its political activity limited to berating the Rahmon regime in online media. At the beginning of October 2014, however, Kuvvatov publicly called on Tajikis to gather for a political protest at Dusti ('Friendship') Square in the capital Dushanbe on the tenth of that month. His ally in Moscow, Maksud Ibragimov, a member of the council of Saidov's New Tajikistan, founded Youth for the Revival of Tajikistan, a new movement, and joined the call for protests. What happened next was both a colossal overreaction and a publicity coup for an extraterritorial movement wanting to show its relevance to the country. The Tajik authorities blocked websites and deployed armoured cars outside public buildings. On 9 October, the supreme court in an emergency measure declared Group 24 to be a terrorist movement, banned in the country.[66] Unsurprisingly, given the movement's lack of support inside the country, no one showed up on the 10th. The day before the no-show, *Eurasianet*'s David Trilling described the hysteria surrounding the announcement of protests in a country which simply does not allow demonstrations:

> A band of treacherous radicals will swoop into Tajikistan's capital and seize power tomorrow at 3 p.m. – at least that's what senior government officials seem to fear. To thwart their nefarious plans, prosecutors are visiting schools, telling children to avoid provocations; someone in government has shut down a bunch of Internet sites; and with a straight face the nation's highest court has branded the hazy, little-known Facebook group terrorists.[67]

After elevating Group 24 – hitherto a band of online rabble-rousers led by a man who happened to know something of the inner workings of the family state (see Chapter 3) – to the status of terrorists, the security services acted accordingly by tracking Kuvvatov and his allies with renewed urgency (see Figure 7.3).

The demise of Ibragimov and Kuvvatov

Ibragimov was quickly targeted in Moscow. Tajikistan pronounced Youth for the Revival of Tajikistan illegal on 7 October and requested the extradition of Ibragimov from Russia. Complying with the request, Russia's authorities arrested Ibragimov on 9 October but the Russian court denied the extradition and freed Ibragimov two days later. However, Ibragimov had been fast-tracked through the extraterritorial security process and, in accordance with the pattern of previous cases, remained a target for return or eradication. On 26 November 2014, Ibragimov was stabbed in Moscow but survived the attack. His assailants disappeared. Soon, he found himself effectively stateless. He was a citizen of Russia, having renounced his Tajikistan citizenship after arriving in Moscow in 2004, but in December 2014 the Russian Federation stripped him of his Russian citizenship. He was now without protection. Before his lawyers

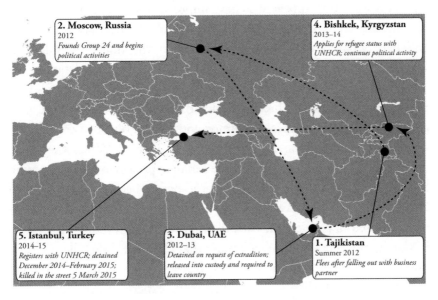

Figure 7.3 The tracking of Umarali Kuvvatov, 2012–15

could appeal to the ECHR on his behalf, Ibragimov was arrested again by the Russian authorities on 20 January 2015 and immediately extradited to Tajikistan.[68] Seven of his associates were arrested in Russia and three more in Tajikistan.[69] In July 2015 he was convicted of extremism charges and sentenced to seventeen years in prison.[70]

Kuvvatov's fate came more quickly and was more final. On 19 December 2014 he was arrested by Turkish police following an anonymous call. His earlier administrative violations came back to haunt him as they became the ostensible reasons for this detention. In the meantime, Western human rights groups battled to protect him from politically motivated extradition. On 21 January 2015, the US group Freedom House reported that they were 'deeply concerned for the safety of Umarali Kuvvatov if he is sent to Tajikistan or to another country where he could be subject to torture'.[71] Such statements may have helped bring about his release on 3 February 2015. But freedom from detention came on condition that he leave Turkey within a month, due to his previous administrative violations. When at the end of February he was granted temporary permission to stay in Turkey legally and received a letter from the UNHCR informing him that his refugee status was confirmed, Kuvvatov's position appeared to have improved considerably.

This proved to be a false dawn. On 5 March 2015, Kuvvatov, his wife and two children were invited to dinner at the house of Sulaimon Qayumov, a 30-year-old Tajik citizen who had been in Istanbul for several months and expressed sympathy for Group 24. Kuvvatov's wife told Radio Ozodi that she, her husband and their sons 'felt sick after consuming food offered by Qayumov and rushed out for fresh air. An ambulance eventually arrived at around 10.30 p.m. When they were outside, Hafizova said, an unidentified man approached Kuvvatov from behind and fired a single shot to his head before fleeing. Kuvvatov died at the scene.'[72] A few days later, Qayumov and two other Tajik citizens were arrested in connection with the murder. At Kuvvatov's funeral on 9 March, mourners unfurled a banner that claimed: 'The killer of Tajik opposition leader, martyr Umarali Kuvvatov, is dictator Emomali Rahmon.'[73] In Dushanbe, pro-government experts suggested that he might have been killed by business rivals. But, as the Tajik security services had tracked Kuvvatov for almost three years, few doubted their hand in the assassination. In February 2016, Qayumov was sentenced in Turkey to life imprisonment for Kuvvatov's murder.[74]

Kuvvatov's assassination occurred within days of Tajikistan's fraudulent parliamentary election, the assassination of Russian opposition activist Boris Nemtsov in Moscow, and the suspicious death in Austria of Rakhat Aliyev, the former son-in-law and now opponent of President Nazarbayev. It all seemed to add up to the further darkening of politics in and beyond the post-Soviet world. Figure 7.4 illustrates fourteen cases of Tajik exiles subjected to rendition, disappearance and attacks. Most of these have occurred since 2014, indicating the hardening of the regime's stance against its exiles as it seeks to close down political space both at home *and* abroad.[75]

Opposition politics abroad and extraterritorial security

At the time of writing, political opposition to the Uzbek and Tajik regimes exists in little more than name. Both states, fearing political

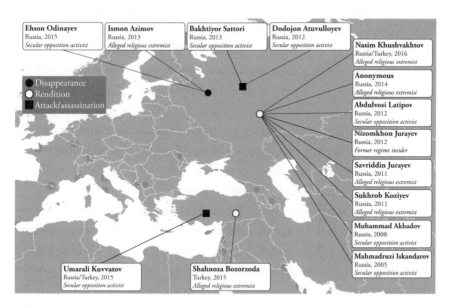

Figure 7.4 Map of citizens of Tajikistan extradited to face torture, rendered, disappeared and/or assassinated

instability and the loss of power, criminalised political parties in the early 1990s. In the case of Tajikistan this took place in the midst of a brutal civil war. The peace agreement of 1997 opened up new but limited space for a loyal opposition. But in the last decade, even nominal opponents within the territory of the state have been driven out – a process confirmed by the removal of all opposition from parliament after the March 2015 parliamentary elections, the harassment and flight of Muhiddin Kabiri, the leader of the Islamic Revival Party of Tajikistan, and the rounding up of the party's remaining leadership on spurious terrorism charges in September 2015. In Uzbekistan, the opposition has been wiped from the country long ago. These states once hosted credible opposition parties; they now terrorise their barely credible remnants overseas.

Making exiles out of political opponents was not enough. As the opposition moved offshore so did the strategies and practices of political control and security.[76] In facilitating these practices and spaces of extraterritorial security within its own territory, Russia has consistently violated its commitments as a member of the Council of Europe.

However, these practices extend beyond the post-Soviet region and its institutions right into the Western world. The abuse of Interpol Red Notices has restricted the movement of exiles who have been granted asylum in democracies including the United States. In France and Spain, Ablyazov's associates have been arrested and detained. In Italy, Ablyazov's family were secretly rendered to Kazakhstan in an extraordinary case of connivance by a major Western state. In Austria, Kazakh exiles have been beaten and died in suspicious circumstances. The image-conscious emerging economies of UAE and Turkey have also become centres of these extraterritorial security measures – as Kuvvatov's killing in Istanbul vividly illustrates.

Increasing rates of migration, the stalling and even reversal of democratisation in Central Asia, and growing hostility towards asylum seekers across the world, suggests that genuinely safe havens will become harder to find. More accurately, such havens depend on the ability to pay for the lawyers and security protection necessary to access them. As Chapter 1 showed, the UK's Tier 1 investment visas offer a convenient route for former regime insiders like Maxim Bakiyev, willing to invest in government bonds and launder their ill-gotten gains. Inflows of wealthy former regime insiders into London and other prime destinations have brought these uses of extraterritorial security measures to light, most prominently in the cases of Russian exiles (the assassination of Alexander Litvinenko and the suspicious death of Boris Berezovsky).

Extraterritorial security is not unfamiliar to Western states. The United States' use of extraordinary rendition and secret detention centres, assisted by a number of Western states including the UK, surrendered any moral high ground they might previously have claimed. In the words of Amnesty International:

> The US led renditions programme was, at least briefly, secret. Its exposure did much to reverse it. Something less centralized, and less coordinated, but no less widespread is taking place across the former Soviet Union – and there is nothing secret about it . . . It is going on today, right now, right under the nose of the international community and no one is saying anything about it.[77]

This powerful statement, made in 2013, needs only a little revision today. In the three years since, more reports have been released and some moves have been made by Interpol to tighten their system. However, across the former Soviet states, the system of the unquestioned extradition of suspects continues unabated and suggests a high degree of coordination between national security agencies in the transnational space of extraterritorial security. Western states cannot reverse their own unfortunate recent history of torture and rendition but, as we shall discuss in the following Conclusion, they can make sure they are no longer complicit in such acts by refusing to support the security services of states engaged in these practices.

CONCLUSION

CONFRONTING THE CHALLENGE OF GLOBAL AUTHORITARIANISM

Central Asian security services and their agents roaming with impunity in Europe, US federal judges freezing the assets of Central Asian presidential relatives, and a mounting docket of court cases – from London to California to Geneva – determining the future of political dissidents and the ownership of key state assets: we are not accustomed to thinking of these as matters of Central Asian political contestation, yet with each passing month it becomes clear that, in fact, these extraterritorial places are the primary sites for the battle between regime power and regional opposition. At the same time, autocratic elites and their allies routinely use the professional services and institutions of the West to elevate their status, play up their cosmopolitanism, relocate personal funds and camouflage their identities, all the while retaining the legal protections for transacting in the West that are usually denied to their political opponents back home. The traditional academic distinctions between democratic and authoritarian spaces, clean and corrupt polities, political dissidents and international fugitives – in short, the defined political spheres of 'here' and 'there' – are rapidly dissolving into a global patchwork of autocratic zones and enabling practices and institutions.

In recent years we have witnessed the intensification of both authoritarianism in and outside the region, but also an increased scrutiny of many of these same dynamics in the West. Just as the colour revolutions led to a renewed crackdown on civil society organisations and media outlets throughout the region, the toppling of Middle Eastern governments during the Arab Spring has further intensified regime paranoia about the power of street protests, social media and even the conducting of basic research and advocacy within their countries.

The 2014 crisis in Ukraine, during which President Viktor Yanukovych fled in response to the Euromaidan street protests against his corrupt administration, and which triggered Russia's annexation of Crimea and support for separatists in the Donbas, has further fuelled regime anxiety and closed political space. Certainly, Central Asian autocrats fear the possibility that Russia will find a pretext to intervene in their domestic affairs, perhaps using forces from the overseas military or defence facilities in Kazakhstan, Kyrgyzstan and Tajikistan. Statements such as that uttered by President Putin in July 2014 questioning the historical statehood of Kazakhstan sent alarm bells ringing throughout the region. Tellingly, during the April 2014 UN General Assembly vote affirming Ukraine's sovereignty over Crimea, Uzbekistan and Kazakhstan abstained, while representatives of Kyrgyzstan, Tajikistan and Turkmenistan failed to show up for the historical vote altogether.[1]

But whatever fears Central Asian rulers harbour about Russia, their anxiety about future destabilising waves of Maidan-like street protests is a greater cause of regime insecurity. A growing regional economic crisis, compounded by falling oil and commodity prices, the devaluation of the ruble and other local currencies, declining remittances and slowing regional trade – in part the result of Ukraine-related sanctions and counter-sanctions – has added to a mounting sense of deep uncertainty. Not surprisingly, it is precisely in these times of uncertainty that the autocratic discourse of 'preserving stability' is most effective: small wonder, then, that, according to public opinion surveys, the Central Asian publics are among the most approving in the world of the strongman leadership of Vladimir Putin.[2] A wave of insecurity has swept the region that has not been seen since late Soviet times.

At the same time, only recently have we seen renewed scrutiny in the West of the transnational and global activities of the Central Asian elite, whether in a growing collection of stories about Central Asians buying luxury real estate, the unfolding of international corruption investigations and court proceedings, or the widespread fallout of the Panama Papers, which revealed the industrial scale on which shell companies are manufactured and routinely used by the global elite to move money and hide assets. Moreover, the perennial concern about the succession issue across the region now has a new twist: what will become of frozen and stranded assets, associated with the corrupt activities of Central Asian regimes, when these countries undergo a political transition? The issue has assumed renewed importance in the post-Karimov era as Uzbek authorities campaign to reclaim overseas assets frozen by international courts, but this is the latest example of how these global developments and court proceedings feed back into the local.

Policy recommendations: how to confront dictators without borders

What then is to be done from a policy perspective? Over twenty-five years since gaining independence, the political systems of the Central Asian states continue to be closed or closing, even as Central Asian elites show an ever-greater appreciation for navigating global spaces, strengthening their transnational networks and defining themselves as global citizens.

The most pressing recommendation that emerges from our study is that the landscape for policy intervention needs to be significantly broadened. In both academia and the policy world, we have been trained to think of democracy and governance as purely internal characteristics of states; indeed, over the last two decades the practice of rating and ranking states on the quality of their performance has further entrenched this methodologically nationalist move. And, whilst several authors have offered constructive critiques of how the Western democracy-promotion industry needs to evolve and adapt,[3] we are still hesitant to acknowledge the integral role that Western institutions, intermediaries, regulations and practices play in aiding the transnational reach and practices of supposedly distant authoritarians. Promoting civil society, open dialogue, transparency and the rule of law are all vital to democratic governance;

our book suggests that important deficits in these areas actually have emerged in the West and within transnational spaces that are vital to the so-called 'democracy and governance' agenda.

Training civil society to confront new extraterritorial legal practices

A favourite practice among democratic practitioners is to train local civil society organisations and representatives in litigation and the promotion of their rights within their countries. Civil society training has traditionally involved gathering committed activists and organisations, instructing them in advocacy techniques and protections, and networking them with peer groups from the same region or around the world. Our study suggests that activists and groups now are in urgent need of similar levels of training and competence about international and transnational legal practices. In particular, regional activists need both to be aware of and campaign for greater clarity in how regional anti-terror laws and frameworks, such as the SCO anti-terror treaty, operate in practice. Second, on the international front, activists need to be better equipped to understand and document how the Red Notice system at Interpol is subject to abuse, and be made aware of the technical criteria involved when home countries initiate international anti-money-laundering investigations and accusations. In short, rule-of-law training, for decades a core practice of democracy-promotion efforts, needs to be made both more regional and more global in its scope.

Pressure universities and think tanks to be open about reporting international funding sources

Another critical area concerns Western centres of knowledge production. As authoritarians have gone global, their activities, agendas and regime character have often been ignored or whitewashed by institutions that have received funds from these regimes or their agents. Exposés such as 'Caviar Diplomacy', which documented how European parliamentarians were wooed with free luxury trips to Azerbaijan, have been important in raising awareness about the growing influence of authoritarians and their outreach in formal corridors of power.[4]

Less attention has been given to how international donations from these same autocratic countries affect or compromise Western coverage and programming in think tanks and universities about non-democratic trends and corruption in the region. In the United States, the disclosure rules governing the formal practices of lobbyists differ from those covering more informal efforts at 'image-crafting' and influencing the academy and policy institutes. Under the Foreign Agents Registration Act (FARA), any lobbyist or organisation hired by a foreign government must register as such with the Department of Justice and describe its activities in considerable detail. However, these same standards of disclosure do not apply when foreign governments give funds to knowledge-making institutions, especially think tanks and universities. As one prominent report on international funding for think tanks exposed, foreign governments, including those of Azerbaijan and Kazakhstan, have paid tens of millions of dollars to prominent public policy institutes in recent years, but the exact amount of this funding and its purpose are not usually reported.[5]

Universities suffer from a similar lack of transparency. Most established universities have committees tasked with vetting and scrutinising foreign donations, but in practice the allure of international income often seems to trump public perception that for institutions to accept funds from authoritarian countries might taint their academic autonomy. For example, an inquiry into a donation to the London School of Economics from Saif al-Islam Gaddafi, the son of then Libyan dictator Muammar Gaddafi, found that the funds contributed to LSE's 'global governance' programme may have been originally paid as bribes and that the 'Libyan gift proceeded to Council [LSE's governing body] when due diligence remained, at best, embryonic'.[6]

Think tanks and universities should acknowledge the origin of international and project-specific donations in their annual reporting. If a particular project, initiative or report has been supported by an international contribution, this should be disclosed in the publication itself or in the public announcement of the initiative.

Support the establishment of beneficial ownership registries worldwide

More broadly, our chapters give additional impetus to the global campaign to disclose the beneficial owners of anonymous companies. Our study has shown how Central Asian elites routinely use anonymous shell companies to structure private pay-offs from international transactions or to hide their acquisition of foreign assets such as luxury real estate. The leak of the Panama Papers has brought even greater urgency to the problem of providers establishing shell companies on an industrial scale. But as Jason Sharman has pointed out, the 200,000 companies established by provider Mossack Fonseca are dwarfed by the 15 million registered in the United States alone, and this is especially worrying given that US-based incorporation firms were just as likely to do business with high-risk clients as low-risk clients and violate international 'know thy client' procedure more than their non-OECD or 'tax haven' counterparts.[7]

The central role played by OECD jurisdictions in shell company formation underscores the need for the West to ascertain and make public information about the beneficial owners of all companies in a public registry. This needs to happen both at a national and global level and needs to be made completely public so that citizens, journalists and civil society have access to such information. Nationally, regulators should ascertain the beneficial owners of all companies registered by in-country providers – while the UK has made some progress here, a number of exceptions (such as trusts) have limited the effectiveness of these measures. New rules announced in the wake of the Panama Papers by the US Treasury in May 2016 proposing that all financial institutions ascertain the identity of the individual who controls and manages the business may be positive, but their efficacy will depend on the definition of beneficial ownership and their broad enforcement.[8] A related policy proposal gaining support among transparency activists is the adoption of a similar global, searchable registry of companies. In turn, completely public registries of beneficial owners have the potential to dramatically improve companies' due diligence by eventually making even the appearance of an anonymous corporation in and of itself a red flag, rather than the norm, in the international financial architecture.

Increase transparency in Western luxury real estate markets

Another related recommendation concerns the role of real estate in the West. As we have seen, luxury real estate is a source of great prestige for autocrats and their families and also potentially a way for kleptocrats to launder funds into legitimate purchases. One recommendation is that countries, similar to company registries, should publish national registries of the beneficial owners of all real estate and property transactions. But another is to target the role of real estate brokers across Western markets who actively guard the privacy of their clients and fail to follow established rules of disclosure and transparency. The right to privacy needs to be weighed against the public interest in countering money laundering and corruption. Consequently, all cash transactions above a certain threshold should be subject to mandatory reporting and the ascertaining of the purchaser's identity.

Develop dedicated international institutions for asset recovery and disbursal in authoritarian countries

The emergent international regime on asset recovery and return assumes that assets that prove to be the results of criminal activities should be returned to their countries of origin. As our chapter on Uzbekistan revealed, returning these assets to their originating countries, when they are generally characterised by authoritarian and closed patrimonial rule, risks simply returning funds to the networks that spawned them. On the other hand, civil society and legal advocates remain weak and embattled, and often lack the necessary expertise to advocate for a responsive institutional structure to disburse funds.

One solution might be for the international community, under the auspices of an international organisation or an international financial institution like the World Bank, to hold the fund in escrow and develop a repatriation plan intended to rectify or compensate populations that were harmed by criminal and corrupt activities. For example, if the proceeds were linked to the payments of bribes in the telecoms industry, they could be used to subsidise consumer tariffs from that company for a selected period of time.

Really enforce anti-corruption laws and require the publication of due diligence studies

We also draw attention to the role of Western financial services actors in greasing the wheels of the business dealings of Central Asian autocrats. We have touched upon the role of such 'intermediaries' – due diligence consultants, financial services lawyers and other company services providers – throughout this book. More often their activities are hidden from view, but they are absolutely essential to the functioning of the system. By law, very little foreign direct investment by the private sector, either from OECD states or so-called emerging economies, can take place without adherence to international anti-corruption standards. In particular, the extraterritorial reach of the US Foreign Corrupt Practices Act means that, to take a hypothetical case, a Chinese company investing in a Tajik gold mine which raised finance from a bank listed on the New York Stock Exchange must conduct a due diligence exercise to demonstrate that it is compliant with the FCPA. In such a case, any credible analysis ought to conclude that a significant proportion of that Chinese investment is highly likely to find its way into the pockets of Dushanbe's cronies, perhaps via offshore accounts that may be built into the structure of the deal. The apparent heightening of anti-corruption standards in recent years, at least in the rhetoric of Obama and Cameron, among others, is all the more reason for such a high standard of due diligence work. Such studies are often carried out by immensely talented and well-compensated people, but there will never be enough evidence available for these analysts to *prove* corrupt links in the vast majority of cases. Rather, they can only say instead that corruption is highly *probable*.

Our research and experiences have led us to believe that the reason why many such deals go ahead is that due diligence reports are *deliberately* written to maintain ambiguity on the question of the likelihood of corruption. It is very difficult to see how any investment into a major commodities business in any of the five Central Asian states could be deemed FCPA-compliant if the due diligence work draws unambiguous conclusions about the high probability of corruption. Given the neo-patrimonial political economies of these countries, how can they be deemed low risk?

But there's the rub: maintaining ambiguity is a multi-billion-dollar business. It allows the client the freedom of choice as to whether to go ahead with the deal or not. All this points to the fact that international financial services intermediaries are directly complicit in the emergence of Central Asia's crony capitalism and its consolidated dictatorships. If there was a huge reduction in such investment, it is a matter of interpretation as to whether this would lead to the destabilisation of Central Asian states or the gradual raising of transparency and accountability standards. A little of both may occur. But if Western leaders are actually serious about reducing corruption in developing countries they must demand transparency and accountability in their own financial services industries, perhaps including the publication of due diligence studies, as well as in business and politics within Central Asia and other regions where corruption is high. It may be time to make firms legally liable for the performance of their intermediaries.[9] Otherwise, all the anti-corruption announcements and conferences are just talk.

Ensure Interpol is not abused; make security assistance conditional

We have documented several cases where the Interpol Red Notice system has been abused by requesting states, or implemented without appropriate review by arresting states. As several studies have now shown, there is inadequate implementation of Interpol's human rights obligations and a lack of an effective avenue of redress for individuals wishing to challenge misuse of Interpol's systems.[10] The organisation claims to have embarked on a comprehensive process of reform which must be seen through to completion. It has reasserted control over the data published on its databases and, since March 2015, committed not to publish Red Notices on individuals with refugee status. It has also begun working with the UN in an attempt to reduce the risk of refoulement and reliance on torture evidence. It has also tasked an internal working group with reviewing its data-processing methods and the procedures of its complaints commission (the CCF) – the only form of redress to victims of abuse.[11] At present, the CCF meets just three times a year and it can take several years to get an improper Red Notice removed.

Such cases continue to occur. Shortly before we went to press, Interpol agreed to a Tajik request to put out a Red Notice for the arrest of opposition leader Muhiddin Kabiri.[12] A genial man who for years maintained a persistently moderate stance in opposition, Kabiri is now wanted globally on preposterous charges of terrorism. Tajikistan's brutal crackdown on the opposition has been well documented by human rights groups and condemned by the US and EU among others. This is as clear a case of a politically motivated request for a Red Notice as one is likely to see.

The reform proposals for Interpol were out for consultation with member states as we finished this book, with a decision to be made at the General Assembly of Interpol in November 2016. Groups such as Foreign Policy Centre, Fair Trials International and the International Committee of Jurists are lobbying the organisation and member states to ensure Interpol's activities uphold human rights standards.

But whilst Western states will affirm the nonpolitical role of Interpol, they continue to train and supply equipment and funding to the security services of states such as Tajikistan and Uzbekistan which extrajudicially kill, disappear and render their exiles overseas. While Tajikistan arrested the leaders of its moderate Islamic political party on terrorism charges in September 2015, US Central Command launched the counter-terrorism exercise Regional Cooperation 2015 in Tajikistan with 400 military personnel involved. Such support must surely be made conditional on not-quite-so-bad standards of governance. If not, the United States may find that its 'counter-terrorism' activities are supporting regimes that are one of the major causes of instability in their countries.

Self-reflection about the West's role and shortcomings

Last but not least, taking seriously the West's role in supporting the political and financial dealings of authoritarians should also become a routine part of Western public diplomacy when discussing the promotion of democracy and good governance. Across the world, but in Eurasia in particular, Western credibility on so-called 'values issues' is at an all-time low and has been badly damaged by accusations of double standards, scandals that highlight hypocrisy – such as NSA wiretapping and Guantanamo Bay – and the growing role of non-Western media outlets in highlighting Western shortcomings. As focus groups suggest, values such as democracy and human rights are not in and of themselves unpopular – but the West as a messenger has lost a great deal of moral authority.[13]

Acknowledging our own struggles with issues like striking the right balance between guarding civil liberties and security, as well as pointing to our own institutional shortcomings in areas such as identifying beneficial ownership, would make us a part of the conversation and move towards more collective and transnational solutions.

The no-longer-hidden connections of a global world

Autocrats operate in two spaces: on the one hand, they are vigorous self-proclaimed defenders of their countries' sovereignty, tradition and security. They crack down on political opposition, restrict civil society organisations and dominate the media. But even as they control their political and social spaces, they actively seek to target political opponents and dissidents overseas through a variety of global practices and foreign policy tools. Autocrats and their families regularly travel, holiday and purchase luxury residences across the world; they employ international consultants and public relations firms to craft their images; and they eagerly consort with celebrities, politicians and high-profile socialites to underscore their global status. It is this constant navigation between defending their authoritarianism in terms of promoting 'national interest' and safeguarding their activities as global individuals that is the hallmark of autocrats in the twenty-first century. In this regard, the dealings of Central Asian elites are little different from the similar dynamics that characterise authoritarians of the Middle East and Gulf states, sub-Saharan Africa and Southeast Asia.

The pressing issue at hand, both analytically and in terms of policy actions, is not one of achieving greater 'connectivity', but rather honestly assessing and exposing the myriad actual connections and networks forged by authoritarians on a global scale. Only now, shamed by massive leaks and public exposés, are we beginning to appreciate the scale by which authoritarian actions and networks are systematically embedded in Western institutions, legal spaces and professional practices. Our book is but a small step towards catching up with a phenomenon well underway. All of us must do better.

APPENDIX 1: MAJOR REPORTED FOREIGN REAL ESTATE HOLDINGS OF CENTRAL ASIAN ELITES

Name	Location	Price, date	Shell company?
Mukhtar Ablyazov	Oaklands Park Estate, Surrey	£18.15m, 2006; sold for £25m in April 2015	Yes: Seychelles-based Lafe Technology Ltd[1]
Mukhtar Ablyazov	Carlton House, Bishop's Avenue, London	£15.5m, 26 April 2006	Yes: BVI-based Mount Properties Ltd[2]
Mukhtar Ablyazov	Apartment at 79 Elizabeth Court, London[3]	£650,000, January 2002	Yes: BVI-based Rocklane Properties Ltd[4]
Mukhtar Ablyazov	Apartment at 17 Albert's Court, London	£965,000, 27 June 2008	Yes: BVI-based Bensborough Trading Inc.[5]
Rakhat Aliyev (or close associate)*	Various properties between 215 and 237 Baker Street, London	Valued at approximately £137m, bought between April 2009 and March 2010	Yes: BVI-registered; bought through two UK companies[6]
Rakhat Aliyev (or close associate)*	Two properties near Hyde Park, London	One valued at £1m, the other unknown; bought between 2008 and 2010	Yes: BVI-registered; bought through UK companies[7]
Rakhat Aliyev (or close associate)*	Mansion in Highgate, London	£9.3m, April 2008	Yes: BVI-registered but also using a UK shell. Transferred in 2013 to Panamanian Villa Magna Foundation[8]
Maxim Bakiyev[9]	Mansion in Reigate and Banstead, Surrey	£3.5m, August 2010	Yes: Belize-registered Limium Partners Ltd[10]

Gulnara Karimova	Geneva	18m Swiss francs, 2009	Unknown[12]
Gulnara Karimova	80th-floor penthouse in The Arch, Hong Kong	$14m, February 2009	Yes: location unclear[13]
Gulnara Karimova	Villa at 32 Allée de la Cheneraie near St Tropez, France	Undisclosed amount, 2009; seized by French authorities, September 2014	Unknown[14]
Gulnara Karimova	Paris apartment	Undisclosed amount, 2009; seized by French authorities, September 2014	Unknown[15]
Lola Karimova	904 N. Crescent Drive, Beverly Hills, California	$32.75m, 13 June 2013 (reportedly)	Reportedly through company based in Culver City, CA[11]
Lola Karimova	Vandoeuvres, Geneva	43.4m Swiss francs, 2010 (reportedly)	Unknown[16]
Viktor Khrapunov	Mansion on Lake Geneva	32m Swiss francs, year unclear	Unknown[17]
Timur Kulibayev	Sunninghill Park, Berkshire	£15m, September 2007	Yes: BVI-registered Unity Assets Corporation[18]
Timur Kulibayev	Four adjoining houses in Mayfair, London (41 and 42 Upper Grosvenor Street, 41 and 42 Reeves Mews)	£44.4m combined, 2007	Yes: three shell companies: Merix International Ventures is BVI-registered[19]
Dinara Kulibayeva-Nazarbayeva	Mansion in Anières, Geneva	74.7m Swiss francs, 23 December 2009	Unknown[20]
Rustam Madumarov (Gulnara Karimova associate)	French properties: chateau de Groussay, Île-de-France; villa in Gassin; and apartment in the 6th arrondissement, Paris	€50m, 2009–11	Yes: three shell companies: Invest Studio, Invest Service Group and Ruby International[21]

* These shell companies have denied that Aliyev was their owner but Global Witness traces close links between him and them.

[1] High Court of Justice, *BTA v Ablyazov: Judgment*, EWHC 237 (16 February 2012), point 148, available at: http://www.bailii.org/ew/cases/EWHC/Comm/2012/237.html

[2] Ibid., point 128.

[3] The judge found that although various pieces of evidence 'strongly support' the case that Ablyazov owned it, they were not 'sufficiently cogent to expel all reasonable doubt that it is correct, though it may well be'.

[4] High Court of Justice, *BTA v Ablyazov: Judgment*, point 159.

[5] Ibid., point 165.

[6] Global Witness, *Mystery on Baker Street* (July 2015), p. 6–7, available at: https://www.globalwitness.org/en-gb/campaigns/corruption-and-money-laundering/mystery-baker-street/

[7] Ibid.

[8] Ibid.

[9] Bakiyev's direct ownership of the shell company has not been conclusively proven, but it was established days after his arrival in the UK, while he lives in the property itself and listed it as his address in a 2012 US court case.

[10] Global Witness, *Blood Red Carpet* (March 2015), p. 2, available at: https://www.globalwitness.org/en/reports/surrey-mansion-used-hide-suspect-funds/

[11] 'The 10 Most Expensive Luxury Real Estate Sales in Los Angeles for 2013', *Pinnacle List* (13 February 2014), available at: http://www.thepinnaclelist.com/2014/02/13/13463/the-10-most-expensive-luxury-real-estate-sales-in-los-angeles-for-2013/; 'Your Mama Hears . . .', *Variety* (2 July 2013), available at: http://variety.com/2013/dirt/real-estalker/your-mama-hears-21-1201236007/; 'UPDATE: Le Palais', *Variety* (24 July 2013), available at: http://variety.com/2013/dirt/real-estalker/update-le-palais-429/

[12] 'Uzbek president's daughter faces Swiss money-laundering investigation', *Guardian* (12 March 2014), available at: http://www.theguardian.com/world/2014/mar/12/uzbek-president-daughter-money-laundering-investigation-switzerland

[13] OCCRP, 'Following Gulnara's Money' (21 March 2015), available at: https://www.occrp.org/en/corruptistan/uzbekistan/gulnarakarimova/following-gulnaras-money

[14] Ibid.

[15] Ibid.

[16] 'Uzbekistan's Lola Karimova-Tillyaeva Reveals Rift in First Family', *BBC* (27 September 2013), available at: http://www.bbc.co.uk/news/world-asia-24179949; 'In Switzerland, No Bubble Yet as Real Estate Prices Soar', *Wall Street Journal* (20 July 2012), available at: http://www.wsj.com/articles/SB10000872396390443309045775388803160170434

[17] 'La Suisse, eldorado des dynasties de l'Asie centrale', *Le Monde* (15 January 2010), available at: http://www.lemonde.fr/europe/article/2010/01/15/la-suisse-eldorado-des-dynasties-de-l-asie-centrale_1292121_3214.html; 'Amitiés kazakhes', *Le Monde* (11 February 2013), available at: http://www.lemonde.fr/international/article/2013/02/11/amities-kazakhes_1830157_3210.html

[18] D. Foggo and Jack Grimston, '"Andrew should not look as if he is for sale or rent": A Kazakh Tycoon used a web of firms to hide his dealing with the prince', *The Sunday Times* (14 February 2010), p. 12.

[19] Ibid.

[20] 'La Suisse, eldorado des dynasties de l'Asie centrale'; 'Le clan des Kazakhs riposte et critique la justice suisse', *Tribune de Geneve* (9 March 2012), available at: http://www.tdg.ch/geneve/actu-genevoise/Le-clan-des-Kazakhs-riposte-et-critique-la-justice-suisse/story/10833778

[21] OCCRP, 'Following Gulnara's Money'; 'France: saisie de biens appartenant à la fille du président ouzbèke', *AFP* (10 February 2015), available at: http://www.lexpress.fr/actualites/1/societe/france-saisie-de-biens-appartenant-a-la-fille-du-president-ouzbeke_1650122.html

APPENDIX 2: UZBEKISTAN'S 'STAGE 3' EXILES

Name	Year	Country of exile	Category of exile	Description of fate
Khayrullo Tursunov	2015	Russia	Alleged religious extremist	Disappearance: Tursunov was detained in Russia in November 2009 under charges of extremism, though this has been used to silence critics of the Andijan massacre (2005). Tursunov spent the following years in and out of prison, though in 2015 he disappeared. His current whereabouts are unknown.[1]
Shaykh Abdullah Bukhoroy	2014	Turkey	Radical cleric	Attack: Bukhoroy, a prominent imam who left Uzbekistan in around 2004 and moved to Istanbul in Turkey, was considered a radical Islamist by the Uzbek authorities. He was shot near his house in Istanbul and later died from his injuries.[2]
Lutpiddin Mukhitdinov	2014	Russia	Alleged religious extremist (Islamic Movement of Uzbekistan)	Disappearance: in 2013, Mukhitdinov was arrested in Russia – where he had lived since 1997 – charged with involvement with the IMU. The ECHR warned against extradition. In July 2014 Mukhitdinov was taken from his home by the Federal Migration Service, yet when his family reached the local office, they were informed that he had been released. Mukhitdinov's current whereabouts are unknown.[3]
Umid Yakubov	2014	Russia	Alleged religious extremist (Hizb ut-Tahrir)	Rendition: between 1999 and 2008, after coming under police surveillance, Yakubov was repeatedly detained by Uzbek authorities for various periods of time. On 29 April 2014, Yakubov was abducted in Moscow, despite being recognised as a refugee by the UN.[4]
Ikromzhon Mamazhonov	2013	Russia	Alleged religious extremist (Islamic Movement of Uzbekistan)	Disappearance: Mamazhonov fled to Russia in 2008 on a forged Kyrgyz passport, fearing religious persecution. An international arrest warrant was issued against him in 2009; later he was held in a pre-trial detention facility, SIZO-3 in Orenburg. Mamazhonov was released in June 2013, but has since disappeared with no ongoing investigation into his whereabouts.[5]
Shukhrat Musin	2013	Kyrgyzstan	Alleged religious extremist	Disappearance: Musin fled to Kyrgyzstan with his family in 2008, fearing religious persecution. He was detained by Kyrgyz authorities in October 2010 following an Uzbek extradition request, but was released in February 2011 after Kyrgyz courts refused to extradite as he had been awarded UNHCR status. Musin was reported missing in February 2013.[6]
Yusup Kasymakhunov	2012	Russia	Alleged religious extremist (Hizb ut-Tahrir)	Disappearance: after Kasymakhunov left Uzbekistan in 1995, the Uzbek authorities opened criminal proceedings against him in 1999 on suspicion of involvement with Hizb ut-Tahrir. Kasymakhunov was arrested in Russia in 2004, and served seven years in prison. After a further detention period, Kasymakhunov was released in December 2012, but disappeared shortly after.[7]

Name	Year	Country	Category	Details
Abdusamat Fazletidinov	2012	Russia	Alleged religious extremist (Hizb ut-Tahrir)	Death in custody: Fazletidinov moved to Russia between 2010 and 2012 in search of work, though the Uzbek authorities later claimed he left to escape prosecution. He was detained in November 2012 at Vnukovo airport, Moscow, while trying to fly to Uzbekistan. After Uzbek security services visited Fazletidinov in a Russian detention centre and openly threatened torture, Fazletidinov committed suicide in his cell on 9 December 2012.[8]
Azamat Ermakov	2012	Russia	Alleged religious extremist ('Akramiya')	Rendition: Ermakov lived in the Andijan region of Uzbekistan but fled in 2009 after learning of the arrest of his neighbour, with whom he had practised *salat*. In November 2009, Ermakov was arrested by Russian police on an Uzbek extradition request, though this was rejected by the Supreme Court of the Russian Federation. Ermakov was later arrested for the possession of a hand grenade and was held in SIZO detention facility until his disappearance on 2 November 2012. He was later confirmed to be in prison in Uzbekistan.[9]
Obid qori Nazarov	2012	Sweden	Alleged religious extremist (Salafi)	Attack: as the imam of a Tashkent Friday mosque, Nazarov made several critical statements about the Uzbek authorities, who called for his dismissal. In 2000, Nazarov relocated to Kyrgyzstan and later received political asylum in Sweden. In Stockholm, February 2012, Nazarov was shot in the head and remains in a coma.[10]
Fuad Rustamkhojayev	2011	Russia	Secular opposition activist (People's Movement of Uzbekistan)	Attack: Rustamkhojayev, the founder of the People's Movement of Uzbekistan, had been threatened by the authorities if he continued his political activities. He was shot dead outside his home in Ivanovo, Russia, on 24 September 2011.[11]
Murodzhon Abdulkhakov	2011	Russia/ Tajikistan	Alleged religious extremist (Wahhabism)	Rendition: after a series of arrests and torture in Andijan, Abdulkhakov fled in August 2009. Abdulkhakov was arrested on arrival in Moscow on 9 December 2009, though was released in June 2011 after his detention period had expired. On 23 August 2011, he was abducted and taken to Tajikistan, where he is thought to be in exile.[12]
Usmanzhan Khalmirzayev	2011	Kyrgyzstan	Other	Death in custody: on 7 August 2011, Khalmirzayev was detained in the village of Bazar-Korgon, Kyrgyzstan, in unclear circumstances. The police threatened that if he did not pay them $6,000 they would charge him with violent crimes relating to the June 2010 violence. Khalmirzayev died as a result of injuries sustained during the incident and subsequent detention.[13]

Alisher Saipov	2007	Kyrgyzstan	Independent journalist	Attack: Saipov was editor of the region's only Uzbek-language publication, which frequently challenged the government. While living in Kyrgyzstan, Saipov had told friends that he feared he was being followed by the Uzbek authorities. He was shot dead in October 2007.[14]
Isroil Haldarov	2007	Kyrgyzstan	Journalist and political activist	Rendition: Haldarov, an activist from Andijan, fled to Kyrgyzstan after the Andijan massacre of 2005 before disappearing in July 2006. It is thought he was abducted by the Uzbek security services. Haldarov was arrested in September 2006 for crossing the Kyrgyzstan–Uzbekistan border and was sentenced to six years' imprisonment.[15]
Validjon Babadjanov	2006	Kyrgyzstan	Political activist	Disappearance: Babadjanov escaped to Kyrgyzstan after the Andijan massacre of 2005. In August 2006, he was abducted by the Uzbek security services and transferred to Uzbekistan. His current whereabouts are unknown.[16]

[1] Murat Sadykov, 'Uzbekistan: No Former Soviet State a Safe Place for Uzbek Refugees', *Eurasianet* (24 April 2013), available at: http://www.eurasianet.org/node/66873

[2] 'Radical Uzbek Imam Shot Dead In Istanbul', *RFE/RL* (10 December 2014), available at: http://www.rferl.org/content/uzbekistan-imam-shot-dead-istanbul/26736111.html

[3] European Court of Human Rights, *Press Release: Judgments and Decisions on Mukhitdinov v Russia* (21 May 2015), available at: hudoc.echr.coe.int/webservices/content/pdf/003-5086646-6265270

[4] Amnesty International, *Urgent Action: Refugee Abducted by Police in Broad Daylight* (2 May 2014), available at: https://www.amnestyusa.org/sites/default/files/uaa10714.pdf

[5] European Court of Human Rights, *Case of Mamazhonov v Russia: Judgment* (23 October 2014), available at: http://hudoc.echr.coe.int/eng?i=001-147333

[6] Human Rights Watch, *Kyrgyzstan: Locate Missing Uzbek Refugee* (25 February 2013), available at: https://www.hrw.org/news/2013/02/25/kyrgyzstan-locate-missing-uzbek-refugee

[7] European Court of Human Rights, *Case of Kasymakhunov v Russia: Judgment* (14 November 2013), available at: http://hudoc.echr.coe.int/eng?i=001-119416

[8] Vitaly Ponomarev, 'Гражданин Узбекистана совершил самоубийство в московском СИЗО после угроз сотрудников узбекских спецслужб [A Citizen of Uzbekistan Committed Suicide in a Moscow SIZO after Threats from Uzbek Special Services Officials]' (10 December 2012), available at: http://www.memo.ru/d/139176.html

[9] European Court of Human Rights, *Case of Ermakov v Russia: Judgment* (7 November 2013), available at: http://hudoc.echr.coe.int/eng?i=001-127816

[10] Nadejda Atayeva, 'The Karimov Regime is Accused of Terrorist Activities: An Attempt on the Life of Political Émigré Obidkhon Nazarov' (29 February 2012), available at: http://nadejda-atayeva-en.blogspot.co.uk/2012/02/karimov-regime-is-accused-of-terrorist.html

[11] 'Exiled Uzbek Political Activist Shot Dead In Russia', *RFE/RL* (26 September 2011), available at: http://www.rferl.org/content/exiled_uzbek_political_activist_shot_dead_in_russia/24340471.html

[12] European Court of Human Rights, *Case of Abdulkhakov v Russia: Judgment* (2 October 2012), available at: http://hudoc.echr.coe.int/eng?i=001-113287

[13] Amnesty International, *Return to Torture: Extradition, Forcible Returns and Removals to Central Asia* (London: Amnesty International, 2013), pp. 5–68, extract at 49–50.

[14] Natalia Antelava, 'Outspoken Uzbek Reporter Killed', BBC News (27 October 2007), available at: http://news.bbc.co.uk/1/hi/world/asia-pacific/7061171.stm

[15] Human Rights Watch, 'Uzbekistan: Events of 2007', available at: https://www.hrw.org/world-report/2008/country-chapters-0

[16] Atayeva, 'The Karimov Regime is Accused of Terrorist Activities'.

APPENDIX 3: TAJIKISTAN'S 'STAGE 3' EXILES

Name	Year	Country of exile	Category of exile	Description of fate
Nasim Khushvakhtov	2016	Russia/ Turkey	Alleged religious extremist (Islamic State)	Rendition: in March 2015, Khushvakhtov left Tajikistan to work in Russia, where he communicated with members of Islamic State using the Telegram app. Khushvakhtov flew to Istanbul in February 2016, where he was detained on arrival by the Russian security services. He was subsequently abducted and transferred to Tajikistan, where he is believed to be serving six years in prison for attempting to join IS.[1]
Ehson Odinayev	2015	Russia	Secular opposition activist (Group 24)	Disappearance: Odinayev – an opposition blogger associated with Group 24 – was sought by the Tajikistan authorities for extradition on charges of 'cyber-crime'. Odinayev disappeared from Moscow in May 2015: his whereabouts remain unknown. After his disappearance, his apartment was discovered to have been bugged.
Umarali Kuvvatov	2015	Russia/ Turkey	Secular opposition activist (Group 24)	Attack: Kuvvatov had worked alongside Shamsullo Sokhibov – son-in-law of President Rahmon – but fled to Moscow in 2012 fearing arrest on politically motivated charges. In Russia, Kuvvatov founded Group 24; the organisation was declared illegal by the Tajik authorities in October 2014. Although Kuvvatov was detained in Dubai in December 2012, he was pardoned and travelled to Turkey – on someone else's passport – in July 2014. He was shot dead in Istanbul on 6 March 2015, after he and his family had been poisoned – his family survived.[2]
Shahnoza Bozorzoda	2015	Turkey	Alleged religious extremist (Islamic State)	Rendition: Bozorzoda, a medical student, travelled to Turkey in February 2015 and called a friend in Tajikistan to inform them of her plans to join IS. Bozorzoda was detained in Istanbul shortly afterwards; her deportation appears to have been conducted unilaterally by the Tajik government.[3]
R. Yu	2014	Russia	Alleged religious extremist (Jamaat Ansarullah)	Rendition: originally from the city of Istaravshan in Sughd Province, Tajikistan, Yu was detained in St Petersburg in June 2014. Yu was alleged to have promoted the ideas of Jamaat Ansarullah, an organisation funded by Al-Qaeda. He was subsequently sentenced to nine years in prison.[4]
Ismon Azimov	2013	Russia	Alleged religious extremist (Islamic Movement of Uzbekistan)	Disappearance: Azimov was charged with involvement in plotting an attack on police headquarters in the northern city of Khujand, which killed four people in March 2010. After his arrest in Russia on 3 November 2010, interim measures were issued by the European Court of Human Rights to prevent Azimov's extradition. However he was abducted from a detention centre in Tver in December 2013: his current whereabouts remain unknown.[5]

Name	Year	Country	Role	Details
Bakhtiyor Sattori	2013	Russia	Secular opposition activist (Group 24)	Attack: Sattori lived in Moscow and worked as a journalist in cooperation with Tajik opposition activists, most notably Group 24 leader Umarali Kuvvatov. Sattori was attacked by an unknown assailant near his apartment on 19 February 2013: stabbed in the stomach, he survived.[6]
Abdulvosi Latipov	2012	Russia	Secular opposition activist (United Tajik Opposition)	Rendition: Latipov had been an active member of the UTO during the Tajik civil war of 1992–97. In November 2010 he was detained in Russia, but Tajikistan's extradition requests were blocked by the European Court of Human Rights, due to the potential harm facing Latipov on return. Latipov was released on 15 October 2012 but was forcibly removed from his flat just days later and transported back to Tajikistan.[7]
Nizomkhon Jurayev	2012	Russia	Former CEO of the Kimie chemical plant	Rendition: Jurayev left Tajikistan in 2007 after falling out of favour with President Rahmon's family; he was arrested in Moscow in August 2010. Jurayev's detention ended in February 2012, after which he was held on no new charges. Jurayev's lawyer was 'unofficially' informed that her client had been released on 29 March 2012 and that he had returned to Tajikistan to face charges; however, his passport was in his lawyer's possession. He is currently serving twenty-six years in prison.[8]
Dodojon Atuvulloyev	2012	Germany/ Russia	Former publisher of *Charogi Ruz* ('Daylight')	Attack: Atuvulloyev fled Tajikistan in 2001 after being accused of insulting the president; in 2011 an extradition request was rejected by Russian authorities. Atuvulloyev was stabbed by two unidentified assailants on a visit to Moscow in 2012, but survived the attack. Atuvulloyev currently resides in Germany as a political refugee.[9]
Savriddin Jurayev	2011	Russia	Alleged religious extremist (Islamic Movement of Uzbekistan)	Rendition: Jurayev fled Tajikistan in 2006 after being accused of associating with banned Islamist organisations. He was arrested in Moscow in 2009. Jurayev received temporary asylum status from the European Court of Human Rights to prevent his extradition and was released in May 2011. However, on 31 October 2011 Jurayev was transferred to Tajikistan, without his passport, where he was sentenced to twenty-six years in prison.[10]
Sukhrob Koziyev	2011	Russia	Alleged religious extremist (Islamic Movement of Uzbekistan)	Rendition: Koziyev was accused of being an accomplice of Savriddin Jurayev. He was arrested in Russia in November 2009 and his extradition was approved in June 2010. Interim measures against the extradition were issued by the European Court of Human Rights in October 2010. Koziyev was released on 23 August 2011 but was kidnapped by plainclothes security officers and returned to Tajikistan, where is he serving a twenty-eight-year prison sentence.[11]

Muhammad Akhadov	2008	Russia	Secular opposition activist (United Tajik Opposition)	Rendition: Akhadov, a Tajik national, fled to Russia due to fear of persecution over his involvement with the UTO. He was arrested in 2007 before being handed over to the Tajik Ministry of Internal Affairs at Moscow's Vnukovo airport in September 2008. Akhadov was given a nine-year prison sentence for 'unlawful intrusion'.[12]
Mahmadruzi Iskandarov	2005	Russia	Secular opposition activist (Democratic Party of Tajikistan)	Rendition: Iskandarov, the former leader of the UTO and a presidential hopeful, moved to Russia in August 2004 after a dispute with President Rahmon. The government implicated Iskandarov in an attack on two government offices in Tojikobod in August 2004, resulting in his arrest in Russia in December 2004, though he was soon released. In 2005, Iskandarov was arrested on a warrant requested by the Tajik authorities, rendered to Tajikistan and sentenced to twenty-three years in prison.[13]

[1] 'Шесть лет тюрьмы "за намерение" участвовать в войне в Сирии [Six Years in Prison 'For the Intention' of Participating in the War in Syria]', RFE/RL (23 April 2016), available at: http://rus.ozodi.org/content/article/27692517.html

[2] Global Voices, Tajik Dissident's Murder Rattles Opposition (16 March 2015), available at: https://iwpr.net/global-voices/tajik-dissidents-murder-rattles-opposition

[3] 'Tajikistan Says Detained Woman Who Planned to Join IS in Syria' (11 March 2015), RFE/RL, available at: http://www.rferl.org/content/tajikistan-says-detained-woman-who-planned-to-join-is-in-syria/26893638.html

[4] Mavlouda Rafiyeva, 'One More Activist of Jamaat Ansarullah Jailed in Sughd Province', Asia Plus (4 March 2015), available at: http://news.tj/en/news/one-more-activist-jamaat-ansarullah-jailed-sughd-province

[5] Amnesty International, Russia: Urgent Action: Fear for Safety of Tajikistani Asylum Seeker: Ismon Azimov (6 December 2013), available at: http://www.refworld.org/docid/52a723864.html

[6] 'Bakhtiyor Sattori Gives His First Interview after Stab Attack', Asia Plus (21 February 2013), available at: http://www.news.tj/en/news/bakhtiyor-sattori-gives-his-first-interview-after-stab-attack

[7] Amnesty International, Public Statement: Tajikistan Urged to Disclose Whereabouts of Suspect Held Incommunicado (5 November 2012).

[8] Amnesty International, Urgent Action: Tajik Refused Asylum Seeker Disappeared (3 April 2012); 'Nizomkhon Juraev Faces Trial', Asia Plus (22 May 2015), available at: http://news.tj/en/news/nizomkhon-juraev-faces-trial

[9] Reporters Without Borders, Tajik Opposition Journalist Stabbed in Moscow (13 January 2012), available at: http://en.rsf.org/russia-tajik-opposition-journalist-13-01-2012,41676.html; 'Russia Denies Entry To Tajik Opposition Journalist', RFE/RL (15 July 2013), available at: http://www.rferl.org/content/tajikistan-journalist-russia-entry/25047058.html

[10] Amnesty International, Return to Torture: Extradition, Forcible Returns and Removals to Central Asia (London: Amnesty International, 2013), p. 28.

[11] Ibid., pp. 28–9.

[12] Amnesty International, Shattered Lives: Torture and Ill-Treatment in Tajikistan (London: Amnesty International, 2012), p. 56.

[13] Human Rights Watch, Tajikistan Events of 2005 (2005), available at: http://www.hrw.org/world-report/2006/country-chapters/tajikistan

ENDNOTES

Preface

1. 'Revealed: The London Skyscraper that is a Stark Symbol of the Housing Crisis', *Guardian* (25 May 2015).
2. Global Witness, *Mystery on Baker Street* (July 2015), available at: https://www.global-witness.org/en/campaigns/corruption-and-money-laundering/mystery-baker-street/
3. In fact, Central Asia has only experienced one major armed conflict since independence and saw 0.1 per cent of the world's terrorist attacks in the period 2001–13. See https://www.start.umd.edu/gtd/
4. See https://www.therenditionproject.org.uk/
5. Ewan MacAskill, 'Drone killing of British citizens in Syria marks major departure for UK', *Guardian* (7 September 2015), available at: https://www.theguardian.com/world/2015/sep/07/drone-british-citizens-syria-uk-david-cameron; Adam Taylor, 'The U.S. keeps killing Americans in drone strikes, mostly by accident', *Washington Post* (23 May 2015), available at: https://www.washingtonpost.com/news/worldviews/wp/2015/04/23/the-u-s-keeps-killing-americans-in-drone-strikes-mostly-by-accident/

Acknowledgements

1. Alexander Cooley and J.C. Sharman, 'Blurring the Line between Licit and Illicit: Transnational Corruption Networks in Central Asia and Beyond', *Central Asian Survey* 34:1 (2015), pp. 11–28.
2. Asel Doolotkeldieva and John Heathershaw, 'State as Resource, Mediator and Performer: Understanding the Local and Global Politics of Gold Mining in Kyrgyzstan', *Central Asian Survey* 34:1 (2015), pp. 93–109.
3. John Heathershaw and Nick Megoran, 'Contesting Danger: A New Agenda for Central Asian Studies', *International Affairs* 87:3 (2011), pp. 589–612.
4. Global Witness, *Mystery on Baker Street*.

Introduction: Central Asia Beyond Borders

1. Global Witness, *It's a Gas* (2007). With thanks to Tom Mayne, formerly of Global Witness, for sharing his own research on this case, which has informed the example.

See also US Embassy Ashgabat, 'Unsettled Times but no Revolution in Sight', 08ASHGABAT652_a (21 May 2008), available at: https://wikileaks.org/plusd/cables/08ASHGABAT652_a.html

2. US Embassy Ashgabat, 'SCA DCA Feigenbaum Meets Ashgabat Businessmen on Post-Niyazov Scenarios', 07ASHGABAT56_a (27 January 2007), available at: https://wikileaks.org/plusd/cables/07ASHGABAT56_a.html

3. Freedom House, *World's Worst Regimes Unveiled* (2003–05), available at: https://freedomhouse.org/article/worlds-worst-regimes-unveiled-0#.VW43-M9Viko, https://freedomhouse.org/article/worlds-worst-regimes-unveiled#.VW44O89Viko, and https://freedomhouse.org/article/worlds-worst-regimes-revealed#.VW438c9Viko

4. Freedom House, *Turkmenistan* (2014), available at: https://freedomhouse.org/report/freedom-world/2014/turkmenistan#.VXCtF89Viko.

5. TAPI is the Turkmenistan–Afghanistan–Pakistan–India pipeline that is a key part of the US-proposed New Silk Road, but which is beset by security concerns about the infrastructure through Afghanistan and Pakistan.

6. US Embassy Ashgabat, 'German Business in Turkmenistan', 09ASHGABAT859_a (9 July 2009), available at: https://wikileaks.org/plusd/cables/09ASHGABAT859_a.html.

7. Iranian, Turkish and Pakistani banks also operate but lack this status. US Embassy Ashgabat, 'The Few Foreign Banks in Turkmenistan', 09ASHGABAT1428_a (6 November 2009), available at: https://wikileaks.org/plusd/cables/09ASHGABAT1428_a.html.

8. US Embassy Ashgabat, 'German Business in Turkmenistan'.

9. The other being Liechtenstein.

10. Heathershaw and Megoran, 'Contesting Danger'.

11. Kyrgyzstan and Tajikistan eventually became a greater priority for donors when their poverty began to be understood in the late 1990s, and they became target countries under the UN's Millennium Development Goals.

12. Alexander Cooley, *Great Games, Local Rules: The New Great Power Contest in Central Asia* (New York: Oxford University Press, 2012), Chapter 3.

13. See e.g. Colin Thubron's excellent travelogue of the region, *The Lost Heart of Asia* (London: Vintage, 1994).

14. See Nick Megoran and Sevara Sharipova, *Central Asia in International Relations: The Legacies of Halford Mackinder* (London: Hurst & Co., 2013).

15. For an argument for the importance of these factors in explaining the divergence between Central and Eastern Europe and the former Soviet states, see Steven Levitsky and Lucan A. Way, *Competitive Authoritarianism: Hybrid Regimes after the Cold War* (New York: Cambridge University Press, 2010).

16. David C. Kang, *Crony Capitalism: Corruption and Development in South Korea and the Philippines* (New York: Cambridge University Press, 2002), p. 3

17. Anders Åslund, *Building Capitalism: The Transformation of the Former Soviet Bloc* (New York: Cambridge University Press, 2002).

18. Thomas Carothers, 'The End of the Transition Paradigm?', *Journal of Democracy* 13:1 (2002), pp. 5–21.

19. Roberto Roccu, 'Gramsci in Cairo: Neoliberal Authoritarianism, Passive Revolution and Failed Hegemony in Egypt under Mubarak, 1991–2010' (PhD dissertation, London School of Economics and Political Science, 2012); Catherine Owen 'Obshchestvennyi Kontrol ("Public Scrutiny") from Discourse to Action in Contemporary Russia: The Emergence of Authoritarian Neoliberal Governance' (PhD dissertation, University of Exeter, 2014).

20. Åslund, *Building Capitalism*.

21. Cooley and Sharman, 'Blurring the Line'.

22. For a similar argument, see Sarah Chayes's account of how the Karzai regime in Afghanistan used financial sector openness to facilitate the laundering of foreign assistance. Sarah Chayes, *Thieves of State: How Global Corruption Threatens Global Security* (New York: W.W. Norton, 2013).

23. Alexander Cooley, 'Countering Democratic Norms', *Journal of Democracy* 26.3 (2015), pp. 49–63.

24. Ahmed Rashid, *Descent into Chaos: The U.S. and the Disaster in Pakistan, Afghanistan, and Central Asia* (New York: Penguin, 2009).

25. Adeeb Khalid, *Islam after Communism: Religion and Politics in Central Asia* (Berkeley: University of California Press, 2007).

26. The last major armed conflict in Central Asia was Tajikistan's civil war, the main fighting in which ended in 1996. See the Uppsala Conflict Database Project, available at: http://ucdp.uu.se/

27. University of Maryland, 'Global Terrorism Database' (2012), available at: http://www.start.umd.edu/gtd

28. Thomas Barnett, *The Pentagon's New Map: War and Peace in the Twenty-First Century* (New York: Berkeley Books, 2004).

29. Chris Seiple, 'Uzbekistan: Civil Society in the Heartland', *Orbis* 49:2 (2005), pp. 245–59.

30. Donald Rumsfeld, *Annual Report to the President and to Congress* (Washington, DC: Department of Defense, 2002), p. 11, available at: http://www.nti.org/e_research/official_docs/dod/2002/81502DOD.pdf

31. See Heathershaw and Megoran, 'Contesting Danger'.

32. Edward Schatz, *Modern Clan Politics: The Power of 'Blood' in Kazakhstan and Beyond* (Seattle: University of Washington Press, 2004); Kathleen Collins, *Clan Politics and Regime Transition in Central Asia* (New York: Cambridge University Press, 2006).

33. Olivier Roy, *The New Central Asia: The Creation of Nations* (London: I.B. Tauris, 1998).

34. Scott Radnitz, *Weapons of the Wealthy* (Ithaca: Cornell University Press, 2010); Jesse Driscoll, *Warlords and Coalition Politics in Post-Soviet States* (New York: Cambridge University Press, 2015); Madeleine Reeves, *Border Work: Spatial Lives of the State in Rural Central Asia* (Ithaca: Cornell University Press, 2014).

35. Doolotkeldieva and Heathershaw, 'State as Resource, Mediator and Performer'.

36. Nicholas Shaxson, *Treasure Islands: Tax Havens and the Men Who Stole the World* (London: Random House, 2011), p. 70.

37. Ibid., p. 8; Ronen Palan, Richard Murphy and Christian Chavagneux, *Tax Havens: How Globalization Really Works* (Ithaca: Cornell University Press, 2009), p.51.

38. Steve LeVine, *The Oil and the Glory: The Pursuit of Empire and Fortune on the Caspian Sea* (New York: Random House, 2007); Global Witness, *Risky Business: Kazakhstan, Kazakhmys Plc and the London Stock Exchange* (July 2010).

39. Global Witness, *Grave Secrecy: How a Dead Man Can Own a UK Company and Other Hidden Stories about Hidden Company Ownership from Kyrgyzstan and Beyond* (June 2012); Cooley, *Great Games, Local Rules*, pp. 120–30.

40. Sumie Nakaya, 'Aid and Transition from a War Economy to an Oligarchy in Post-War Tajikistan', *Central Asian Survey* 28:3 (2009), pp. 259–73; John Heathershaw, 'Tajikistan amidst Globalization: State Failure or State Transformation?', *Central Asian Survey* 30:1 (2011), pp. 147–68; John Helmer, 'The Tajik Arm Wrestle – Rusal Squeezes, Oleg Deripaska Threatens, but President Rahmon Gets the Upper Hand', *Dances with Bears* (21 November 2007), available at: http://johnhelmer.net/?p=9864; John Helmer, 'Tajik Aluminium Court Case Ends in London Defeat for President Rahmon', *Dances with Bears* (23 November 2008), available at: http://johnhelmer.net/?p=632

41. Global Witness, *All that Gas? Five Reasons Why the European Union is Wrong to Bow to the Dictatorship of Turkmenistan* (November 2009).

42. OCCRP, 'Corruptistan' (21 March 2015), available at: https://www.occrp.org/en/corruptistan/uzbekistan/
43. Seymour Hersh, 'The Price of Oil: What Was Mobil up to in Kazakhstan and Russia?', *New Yorker* (9 July 2001), p. 51.
44. Ibid.; LeVine, *The Oil and the Glory.*
45. http://www.bloomberg.com/news/articles/2010-12-16/cold-war-patriot-defense-helps-kazakh-go-between-beat-u-s-bribe-charges
46. In Kazakhstan foreign law firms include Baker & McKenzie (Chicago), Bracewell & Giuliani (Houston), Cadbourne & Parke (New York), Curtis, Mallet-Prevost, Colt & Mosle (New York), Denton Wilde Sapte (London), Dewey & LeBoeuf (New York), MacLeod Dixon (Calgary), McGuire Woods (Richmond, VA), Salans (Paris) and White & Case (New York), as well as the big four accounting firms.
47. United States Senate, *Tax Haven Abuses: The Enablers, the Tools and Secrecy* (Washington, DC: Permanent Subcommittee on Investigations, 2006); United States Senate, *Keeping Foreign Corruption out of the U.S.: Four Case Histories* (Washington, DC: Permanent Subcommittee on Investigations, 2010); World Bank and United Nations Office for Drugs and Crime, *Stolen Asset Recovery (StAR) Initiative: Challenges, Opportunities and Action Plan* (Washington, DC, 2007).
48. Palan, Murphy and Chavagneux, *Tax Havens*, p. ix.
49. Peter Andreas, 'The Politics of Measuring Illicit Flows and Policy Effectiveness', in P. Andreas and K. Greenhill (eds.), *Sex, Drugs, and Body Counts: The Politics of Numbers in Global Crime and Punishment* (Ithaca: Cornell University Press, 2010).
50. Cooley and Sharman, 'Blurring the Line'.
51. John F. Tierney, *Mystery at Manas: Strategic Blind Spots in the Department of Defense's Fuel Contracts in Kyrgyzstan – Report of the Majority Staff* (Washington, DC: United States Congress, House of Representatives, Committee on Oversight and Government Reform: Subcommittee on National Security and Foreign Affairs, December 2010).
52. Nakaya, 'Aid as Transition'; Heathershaw, 'Tajikistan amidst Globalization'.
53. J.C. Sharman, *Havens in a Storm: The Struggle for Global Tax Regulation* (Ithaca: Cornell University Press, 2006), p. 6.
54. Ibid.
55. Ronen Palan, *The Offshore World: Sovereign Markets, Virtual Places, and Nomad Millionaires* (Ithaca: Cornell University Press, 2006); J.C. Sharman, 'Offshore and the New International Political Economy', *Review of International Political Economy* 17:1 (2010), pp. 1–19.
56. M.G. Findley, D.L. Nielson and J.C. Sharman, *Global Shell Games: Experiments in Transnational Relations* (Cambridge University Press, 2014).
57. *From Russia With Cash* (8 July 2015), available at: http://www.channel4.com/programmes/from-russia-with-cash

Chapter 1: Inside-Outside, Onshore-Offshore: How Central Asia Went Global

1. Claus Offe and Pierre Adler, 'Capitalism by Democratic Design? Democratic Theory Facing the Triple Transition in East Central Europe', *Social Research* 58:4 (1991), pp. 865–92.
2. Freedom House, *Nations in Transit 2016: Europe and Eurasia Brace for Impact*, available at: https://freedomhouse.org/report/nations-transit/nations-transit-2016
3. In 2015, all five Central Asian states ranked in the bottom 15 per cent of the 168 states in Transparency International's 'Corruption Perceptions Index'; see https://www.transparency.org/country/
4. See especially Adam Przeworski's warning, drawing upon the Latin American experience, that undertaking disruptive market reforms would lead to bouts of political

backlash and instability: *Democracy and the Market: Political and Economic Reforms in Eastern Europe and Latin America* (Cambridge University Press, 1991).

5. Martha Brill Olcott, *Central Asia's Second Chance* (Washington, DC: Carnegie Endowment, 2005).
6. Eric McGlinchey, *Chaos, Violence, Dynasty: Politics and Islam in Central Asia* (Pittsburgh: University of Pittsburgh Press, 2011).
7. Schatz, *Modern Clan Politics*.
8. Milada Anna Vachudova, *Europe Undivided: Democracy, Leverage, and Integration after Communism* (Oxford University Press, 2005); Anna Grzymala-Busse and Abby Innes, 'Great Expectations: The EU and Domestic Political Competition in East Central Europe', *East European Politics and Societies* 17.1 (2003), pp. 64–73.
9. Alan A. Bevan and Saul Estrin, 'The Determinants of Foreign Direct Investment into European Transition Economies', *Journal of Comparative Economics* 32.4 (2004), pp. 775–87.
10. On values and the influence of OSCE and Council of Europe, see Rick Fawn, *International Organizations and Internal Conditionality: Making Norms Matter* (Basingstoke: Palgrave Macmillan, 2013). On insincere human rights treaty ratifications, see Beth Simmons, *Mobilizing for Human Rights: International Law in Domestic Politics* (Cambridge University Press, 2009).
11. Marlène Laruelle and Sebastien Peyrouse, *Globalizing Central Asia: Geopolitics and the Challenges of Economic Development* (Armonk, NY: M.E. Sharpe, 2013).
12. Cooley, *Great Games, Local Rules*.
13. David Lewis, 'Who's Socialising Whom? Regional Organisations and Contested Norms in Central Asia', *Europe-Asia Studies* 64:7 (2012), pp. 1219–37.
14. As Marlène Laruelle and Sebastien Peyrouse have argued, Central Asia's exposure to economic globalisation has been largely mediated by its economic relations and networks with China. Marlène Laruelle and Sébastien Peyrouse, *The Chinese Question in Central Asia: Domestic Order, Social Change, and the Chinese Factor* (New York: Columbia University Press, 2012).
15. Rawi Abdelal, *Capital Rules: The Construction of Global Finance* (Cambridge, MA: Harvard University Press, 2007).
16. However, scholars disagreed on whether it was EU material incentives or European norms that pushed this transformation. On the importance of incentives, see Frank Schimmelfennig and Ulrich Sedelmeier, 'Governance by Conditionality: EU Rule Transfer to the Candidate Countries of Central and Eastern Europe', *Journal of European Public Policy* 11:4 (2004), pp. 661–79; Judith Kelley, 'International Actors on the Domestic Scene: Membership Conditionality and Socialization by International Institutions', *International Organization* 58:3 (2004), pp. 425–57. On norms, see Alexandra Gheciu, 'Security Institutions as Agents of Socialization? NATO and the "New Europe"', *International Organization* 59:4 (2005), pp. 973–1012; and Frank Schimmelfennig, 'International Socialization in the New Europe: Rational Action in an Institutional Environment', *European Journal of International Relations* 6:1 (2000), pp. 109–39.
17. Cooley, *Great Games, Local Rules*. pp. 31–2.
18. On military assistance as quid pro quo for cooperation on Afghanistan, see Joshua Kucera, 'US Military Aid to Central Asia: Who Benefits?' (New York: Open Society Foundations, 2012).
19. Cooley, *Great Games, Local Rules*, Appendix 1.
20. Rick Fawn, 'Battle Over the Box: International Election Observation Missions, Political Competition and Retrenchment in the Post-Soviet Space', *International Affairs* 82:6 (2006), pp. 1133–53.

21. Katharina Pistor and Igor Logvinenko, 'Legal Globalization and Transitions' (memo prepared for the Legal Globalization and Transitions Workshop, Columbia University, New York, 20 October 2015).
22. See especially Kristian Wilson, 'The Role of Offshore Jurisdictions in Russia', *Russian Law Journal* 3:2 (2015), pp. 119–36. Nougayrède considers the 'weak property' rights explanation in the Russian and Central Asian context, but also offers important critiques emphasising the agency shown by post-Soviet elites; also Delphine Nougayrède, 'Outsourcing Law in Post-Soviet Russia', *Journal of Eurasian Law* 3:6 (2013), pp. 383–449.
23. 'Russian Foreign Direct Investment and Tax Havens', Global Financial Integrity, 24 May 2014. On Russia and Cyprus, see http://www.gfintegrity.org/report/country-case-study-russia
24. Svetlana Ledyaeva, Päivi Karhunen, Riitta Kosonen and John Whalley, 'Offshore Foreign Direct Investment, Capital Round-Tripping, and Corruption: Empirical Analysis of Russian Regions', *Economic Geography* 91:3 (2015), pp. 305–41.
25. International Monetary Fund, as cited in Alexander Cooley and J. C. Sharman, 'Blurring the Line', p. 20. The Kazakh tax commissioner in 2012 publicly announced that 700 Kazakh companies had been registered in the BVI, noting that 'The money is being siphoned off, that's for sure.' Cited in 'Over 700 Kazakhstan companies are registered at British Virgin Islands', Tengrinews.kz (29 October 2012), originally accessed 2 November 2012, at: http://en.tengrinews.kz/companies/Over-700-Kazakhstan-companies-are-registered-at-British-Virgin-Islands-14088/
26. Global Witness, *It's a Gas*, p. 5.
27. International Consortium of Investigative Journalists (ICIJ), 'The Panama Papers: Politicians, Criminals and the Rogue Industry that Hides their Cash', available at: https://panamapapers.icij.org
28. ICIJ, 'The Panama Papers: The Power Players', available at: https://panamapapers.icij.org/the_power_players/
29. OCCRP, 'Kazakhstan: President's Grandson Hid Assets Offshore', available at: https://www.occrp.org/en/panamapapers/kazakh-presidents-grandson-offshores/
30. Ibid.
31. 'Kazakhstan Refuses to Investigate Panama Paper Links to President's Family', *Newsweek* (24 April 2016).
32. Mansur Miroval, 'Uzbekistan: President's Daughter and the Panama Papers', *Al Jazeera* (12 May 2016), available at: http://www.aljazeera.com/news/2016/05/uzbekistan-president-daughter-panama-papers-160512081956459.html
33. Paolo Sorbello and Bradley Jardine, 'Central Asia, the Panama Papers, and the Myth of the Periphery', *OpenDemocracy* (20 May 2016), available at: https://www.opendemocracy.net/od-russia/paolo-sorbello-bradley-jardine/central-asia-panama-papers-and-myth-of-periphery
34. The following discussion draws on the findings in Michael G. Findley, Daniel L. Nielson and Jason Campbell Sharman, *Global Shell Games: Experiments in Transnational Relations, Crime, and Terrorism* (New York: Cambridge University Press, 2014).
35. 'Haven Hypocrisy', *The Economist* (26 March 2009).
36. Findley, Nielson and Sharman, *Global Shell Games*. The Central Asia-related findings are reproduced and summarised in Cooley and Sharman, 'Blurring the Line'.
37. Jun Tang and Lishan Ai, 'Combating Money Laundering in Transition Countries: The Inherent Limitations and Practical Issues', *Journal of Money Laundering Control* 13:3 (2010), p. 219.
38. ICNL, 'A Mapping of Existing Initiatives to Address Legal Constraints on Foreign Funding of Civil Society' (1 July 2014), available at: http://www.icnl.org/research/resources/foreignfund/A%20Mapping%20of%20Existing%20Initiatives%20to%20

Address%20Legal%20Constraints%20on%20Foreign%20Funding%20of%20Civil%20
Society,%20July%202014.pdf

39. Nougayrède, 'Outsourcing Law in Post-Soviet Russia', p. 59, observes:

> The poor state of the legal system in the former Soviet countries, combined
> with the preference of local elites to keep their assets abroad and engage in
> dispute resolution in Europe, provided very significant work opportunities for
> foreign lawyers, litigators, and courts. These disputes represented significant
> proceedings, even at the preliminary or interlocutory stages, which could last for
> years. By expanding party autonomy and reducing judicial discretion in connec-
> tion with *forum non conveniens*, at least in Europe, international jurisdictional
> machinery contributed to the outflow of post-Soviet disputes, but this
> outsourcing to foreign judges and tribunals of commercial dispute resolution
> was primarily led by the litigants themselves.

40. 'Russians in London: Super-Rich in Court', *Financial Times* (7 October 2011).
41. See 'No End in Sight to London Courtrooms' Oligarch Litigation Boom', *Financial Times* (1 October 2013).
42. Nougayrède, 'Outsourcing Law in Post-Soviet Russia', pp. 46–8.
43. Ibid., pp. 48–9.
44. On the patchwork nature of international arbitration, see Gus Van Harten, *International Treaty Arbitration and Public Law* (Oxford University Press, 2008).
45. B. Sabahi and D.M. Ziyaeva, 'Investor State Arbitration in Central Asia', *Transnational Dispute Management* 10:4 (2013), Appendix 1.
46. 'Kyrgyzstan: Arbitration Suits Weighing Kyrgyzstan Down', *Eurasianet* (11 September 2014).
47. *Valeri Belokon v Kyrgyz Republic*, UNCITRAL Tribunal (24 October 2014), available at: http://www.italaw.com/sites/default/files/case-documents/ITA%20LAW%207008_0.pdf
48. 'Canadian Court Freezes Kyrgyz Gold Mine Shares', *Eurasianet* (15 October 2014), available at: http://www.eurasianet.org/node/70446
49. Kahlitov Vikotorovich, 'Settlement of Investment Disputes with Kyrgyz Republic: Expropriation of Investments on the Example of Kyrgyz Commercial Banks' (senior thesis, American University of Central Asia, Bishkek, 2013), p. 28.
50. Sabahi and Ziyaeva, 'Investor State Arbitration in Central Asia'.
51. See, for instance, the Turkmenistan–Turkey dispute over which language version of their 1992 BIT was the agreement's controlling text. 'Heavy Blow to Turkish Investor's Claims against Turkmenistan', *CIS Arbitration Forum* (12 May 2012), available at: http://www.cisarbitration.com/2012/05/30/heavy-blow-to-the-turkish-investors-claims-against-turkmenistan/
52. Michael A. Losco, 'Charting a New Course: Metal-Tech v. Uzbekistan and the Treatment of Corruption in Arbitration', *Duke Law Journal Online* 64 (2014), pp. 37–52.
53. Ibid.
54. In one influential social science experiment that examined parking ticket violations among UN staff members enjoying diplomatic immunity in New York City, Fisman and Migel found high correlations between parking violations and home country corruption measures, suggesting that 'cultural or social norms related to corruption are quite persistent: even when stationed thousands of miles away, diplomats behave in a manner highly reminiscent of government officials in the home country'. Raymond Fisman and Edward Miguel, 'Corruption, Norms, and Legal Enforcement: Evidence from Diplomatic Parking Tickets', *Journal of Political Economy* 115:6 (2007), p. 1045.

55. 'Like Father, Like Daughter', *RFE/RL* (30 September 2009), available at: http://www. rferl.org/content/Like_Father_Like_Daughter/1839891.html
56. See 'Turkmen Gas is a Family Business', *Chronicles of Turkmenistan* (3 February 2010), available at: http://archive.chrono-tm.org/en/?id=1276; and 'Wikileaks: The Turkmenistan Fallout Begins?', *Eurasianet* (22 December 2010), available at: http://www.eurasianet.org/node/62625
57. US Embassy Ashgabat, 'Turkmenistan: Former Deputy Chairman for Oil and Gas Tachberdi Tagoyev Arrested', 09ASHGABAT1288 (13 October 2009), available at: https://www.wikileaks.ch/cable/2009/10/09ASHGABAT1288.html
58. Alexander Cooley and J.C. Sharman, 'Transnational Corruption and the Globalised Individual' (paper presented to the 2016 International Studies Association, Annual Convention Atlanta); 'This Swiss Lawyer Is Helping Governments Get Rich off Selling Passports', *Bloomberg* (11 March 2015), available at: http://www.bloombergcom/news/articles/2015-03-11/passport-king-christian-kalin-helps-nations-sell-citizenship
59. Cooley and Sharman, 'Transnational Corruption and the Globalised Individual'.
60. Two prominent examples include: Maksat Arip, part-owner of the Kazakh paper firm Kagazy plc, whose assets were frozen by the UK High Court on accusations of fraud and tax evasion. He was found in possession of both Cypriot and St Kitts and Nevis passports. See 'London-Listed Firm Raided by Police in Almaty', *Reuters* (11 December 2013). Also see the case involving Rustem Tursunbayev, a Kazakh businessman living in Canada, which he entered with his St Kitts and Nevis passport. Kazakhstan has requested his extradition on the grounds of embezzlement and asset-stripping from a state-owned nuclear company. 'Kazakhstan Asks Canada to Extradite Millionaire Accused of Stealing from State-Owned Nuclear Agency', *National Post* (4 May 2012).
61. Cooley and Sharman, 'Transnational Corruption and the Globalised Individual'.
62. See Ayelete Shachar and Rainer Baubock, 'Should Citizenship be for Sale?', Robert Schuman Centre for Advanced Studies Research Paper 2014/01 (2014).
63. 'Children of Uzbekistan's Elite Find a Playground in Latvia', *RFE/RL* (14 May 2016), available at: http://www.rferl.org/content/children-of-uzbekistan-elite-playground-latvia-golden-visa-program/27734370.html
64. On the role of such firms, see Cooley and Sharman, 'Transnational Corruption and the Globalised Individual'. One citizenship programme provider notes: 'Kazakhstan, part of CIS and former Soviet Union, is another country from where the high-net-worth individuals have shown significant interest in making overseas investment. This is done by some to secure their investment and by some to get a residence status or even citizenship of another country which could then secure future for the investors and their family. Europe has been one of the attractive destinations for these high-net-worth individuals. European financial institutions and real-estate have observed significant investment from the investors of Russia and Kazakhstan.' 'Alternate Residence and Citizenship Options for Russian and CIS investors', HF Corporation, available at: http://www.hfcorporation.co/2010/10/11/alternate-residence-in-an-eu-country-for-russian-and-cis-investors/
65. Migration Advisory Committee, *Tier 1 (Investor) Route: Economic Benefits and Thresholds* (London: February 2014), p 22.
66. Home Office, *Tier 1 (Investor)* (12 April 2016), available at: https://www.gov.uk/government/uploads/system/uploads/attachment_data/file/516302/Tier-1-investor-v8.pdf
67. Global Witness, *Blood Red Carpet* (March 2015), available at: https://www.global witness.org/en/reports/surrey-mansion-used-hide-suspect-funds/
68. Ibid.

69. 'Rakhat Aliyev: Businessman and Diplomat who Exploited his Connections to Make a Fortune but was Due to Stand Trial for Murder', *Independent* (26 February 2015).

70. 'The 10 Most Expensive Luxury Real Estate Sales in Los Angeles for 2013', *Pinnacle List* (13 February 2014), available at: http://www.thepinnaclelist.com/2014/02/13/13463/the-10-most-expensive-luxury-real-estate-sales-in-los-angeles-for-2013/

71. 'Prince Andrew and the Kazakh Billionaire', *Guardian* (29 November 2010).

72. Global Witness, *Mystery on Baker Street*.

73. See Stephen Kotkin, *Uncivil Society: 1989 and the Implosion of the Communist Establishment* (New York: Random House, 2009). Kotkin's provocative argument is that the term 'civil society' is hardly appropriate for describing the relatively small number of political dissidents and protestors, with little history of meaningful organisation, who were mythologised by the 1989 anti-Communist mass protests. By contrast, Kotkin argues that the Communist Party members, especially the apparatchiks, could aptly be termed an actual 'uncivil society', numbering in the millions, positioning themselves within their respective agencies and bureaucracies, gaining access to international perks, and trading support and political favours with each other.

74. The claim that NGOs are part of greater principled transnational networks that disrupt state sovereignty is most forcefully made in Margaret Keck and Kathryn Sikkink, *Activists Beyond Borders: Advocacy Networks in International Politics* (Ithaca: Cornell University Press, 1997).

75. See Cooley, *Great Games, Local Rules*, Appendix 1 for a list of NGO restrictions by country.

76. See Human Rights in China (HRIC), 'Counter-Terrorism and Human Rights: The Impact of the Shanghai Cooperation Organization' (March 2011), available at: http://www.hrichina.org/sites/default/files/publication_pdfs/2011-hric-sco-whitepaper-full.pdf; and International Federation for Human Rights (FIDH), 'Shanghai Cooperation Organisation: A Vehicle for Human Rights Violations' (Paris: September 2012), available at: https://www.fidh.org/IMG/pdf/sco_report.pdf

77. HRIC, 'Counter-Terrorism and Human Rights'; FIDH, 'Shanghai Cooperation Organisation'.

78. Andrei Soldatov and Irina Borogan, *The New Nobility: The Restoration of Russia's Security State and the Enduring Legacy of the KGB* (New York: Public Affairs, 2011).

79. Interpol, 'Fact Sheet: Red Notice System', available at: http://www.interpol.int/en/News-and-media/Publications2/Fact-sheets/International-Notices-system

80. Fair Trials International, *Strengthening Respect for Human Rights, Strengthening INTERPOL* (November 2013), available at: https://www.fairtrials.org/wp-content/uploads/Strengthening-respect-for-human-rights-strengthening-INTERPOL5.pdf; see also the account of outspoken Kremlin critic Bill Browder, who adopts 'Red Notice' as the title of his account of corruption in Russia: William Browder, *Red Notice: A True Story of High Finance, Murder and One Man's Fight for Justice* (New York: Simon & Schuster, 2014).

81. Keith A. Darden, 'Blackmail as a Tool of State Domination: Ukraine under Kuchma', *East European Constitutional Review* 10 (Spring/Summer 2001), pp. 67–71.

82. 'French Court Rules against Libel Claim from Uzbekistan 'Dictator's Daughter', *Telegraph* (1 July 2011).

83. 'Uzbekistan: Karimova Libel Trial Delivers More Scandals; MPs Demand EU Probe', *Eurasianet* (10 June 2011), available at: http://www.eurasianet.org/node/63664

84. Casey Michel, 'Kazakhstan Goes After Opposition Media in New York Federal Court', *Diplomat* (7 August 2015), available at: http://thediplomat.com/2015/08/kazakhstan-goes-after-opposition-media-in-new-york-federal-court/

85. Edward Lemon and Daniel Rosset, 'Offshore Central Asia: Switzerland as a Site for Political Struggles between Kazakh Elites', *Perspectives on Central Asia* (7 May 2015), pp. 9–13.

86. Casey Michel, 'Dismissing Disclosure and Free Agent Diplomacy' (MA thesis, Harriman Institute, Columbia University, 2015).
87. David Trilling, 'Tajikistan Using DC Proxies to Build Support for Rogun Dam', *Eurasianet* (13 February 2014), available at: http://www.eurasianet.org/node/68042
88. Ibid.
89. See 'Kazakhstan: Conflict-of-Interest Debate Flares in Washington', *Eurasianet* (2 June 2009), available at: http://www.eurasianet.org/departments/insightb/articles/eav060309b.shtml; and 'Chuck Hagel's Think Tank, Its Donors, and Intellectual Independence', *New Republic* (12 February 2013), available at: https://newrepublic.com/article/112398/chuck-hagels-atlantic-council-foreign-donors-and-independence.
90. 'Jack Straw Criticised for Accepting Part-Time Job Paid for by Kazakhstan', *Independent* (15 February 2015), available at: http://www.independent.co.uk/news/world/politics/jack-straw-criticised-for-accepting-part-time-job-paid-for-by-kazakhstan-10057426.html
91. See Adrien Fauve, 'Global Astana: Nation Branding as a Legitimization Tool for Authoritarian Regimes', *Central Asian Survey* 34:1 (2015), pp. 110–24.
92. Cooley, *Great Games, Local Rules*, Chapter 6.
93. This is an extension of the argument found in Heathershaw, 'Tajikistan amidst Globalization'.

Chapter 2: Kazakhstan's Most Wanted: Economic Fugitive or Democratic Champion? The Case of Mukhtar Ablyazov

1. See Sally Cummings, *Kazakhstan: Power and the Elite* (London: I.B. Tauris, 2002); and Martha Brill Olcott, *Kazakhstan: Unfulfilled Promise* (Washington, DC: Carnegie Endowment, 2010).
2. See the favourable portrayal in Jonathan Aitken, *Nazarbayev and the Making of Kazakhstan: From Communism to Capitalism* (London: Bloomsbury Publishing, 2009).
3. For critical exposés authored by exiled members of the regime's inner circle, see the books published by the president's late former son-in-law, Rakhat Aliyev, *The Godfather-in-Law: The Real Documentation* (Berlin: Trafo, 2009); and the former mayor of Almaty and energy minister, Viktor Khrapunov, *Nazarbayev – Our Friend the Dictator: Kazakhstan's Difficult Path to Democracy* (Stuttgart: ibidem-Verlag, 2015).
4. Edward Schatz and Elena Maltseva, 'Kazakhstan's Authoritarian Persuasion', *Post-Soviet Affairs* 28:1 (2012), pp. 45–65; Edward Schatz, 'Transnational Image Making and Soft Authoritarian Kazakhstan', *Slavic Review* 67:1 (2008), pp. 50–62.
5. See especially Schatz, *Modern Clan Politics*; and Sebastien Peyrouse, 'The Kazakh Neopatrimonial Regime: Balancing Uncertainties Among the "Family", Oligarchs and Technocrats', *Demokratizatsiya* 20:4 (2012), pp. 301–24.
6. See, for instance, Nariman Gizitdinov and Jason Corcoran, 'The \$5 Billion Heist', *Bloomberg Markets* (September 2012), pp. 71–8.
7. See 'How Far will Nazarbayev go to Take Down Ablyazov?', *RFE/RL* (7 June 2013), available at: http://www.rferl.org/content/kazakhstan-nazarbaev-ablyazov/25010488.html
8. International Centre for Settlement of Investment Disputes (ICSID), *KT Asia Investment Group (Claimant) v Republic of Kazakhstan (Defendant)*, ICSID Case No. ARB/09/8 (17 October 2013), paragraph 15.
9. *KT Asia Investment Group v Republic of Kazakhstan*, paragraph 15.
10. See Philip Alexander, 'One Bank, Two Stories', *The Banker* (August 2010); and Gizitdinov and Corcoran, 'The \$5 Billion Heist'.
11. Alexander, 'One Bank, Two Stories'.

12. 'Kazakh Bank Lost Billions in Western Investments', *New York Times* (27 November 2009).
13. Ibid.
14. Ibid.
15. Gizitdinov and Corcoran, 'The $5 Billion Heist', p. 73.
16. US Embassy Astana, 'Kazakhstan: The Ablyazov Factor', 09ASTANA1762_a (2 October 2009), available at: https://wikileaks.org/plusd/cables/09ASTANA1762_a. html
17. Marchenko estimates that these actions constitute the origins of the embezzlement allegations. US Embassy Astana, 'Kazakhstan: The Ablyazov Factor'.
18. 'Kazakh Bank Lost Billions in Western Investments'.
19. 'Billions Vanish in Kazakh Banking Scandal', *Wall Street Journal* (1 January 2014).
20. Ibid.
21. Ibid.
22. *KT Asia Investment Group v Republic of Kazakhstan*.
23. 'Mr. Ablyazov testified that he wished to protect his 75% interest in BTA from expropriation by President Nazarbayev by holding it through different companies situated outside of Kazakhstan.' *KT Asia Investment Group v Republic of Kazakhstan*, paragraph 13.
24. Ibid., paragraph 14. Further, according to the transcript: 'Given the position of trust between Mr. Ablyazov and his associates, the latter would implement any decision of the former by way of instructions to the nominee director of the relevant company.'
25. Ibid., paragraph 13.
26. Ibid., paragraph 179.
27. Ibid., paragraph 182.
28. Ibid., paragraph 90. Interestingly enough, in the tribunal itself, the panel found that though Ablyazov maintained the right to bring the case against BAT under the Dutch–Kazakh BIT, given KT Asia's registry in the Netherlands, KT Asia was not entitled to protections from BTA under the BIT because the company had made no 'investment', implying a 'transborder flux of capital', nor any contribution nor 'intention of future contribution' that could qualify as investment in BTA.
29. As recounted in ibid., paragraph 26.
30. Ibid.
31. In an interview with the *Guardian*, Ablyazov claimed 'For a long time the president was asking me to transfer 50% of the bank to him, free of charge. Requests were followed by threats that if I did not do it I would be imprisoned and they would take away my business. This situation dragged on for years. Finally, using the excuse of the financial crisis, the president took over. He kept telling me directly he was afraid of me and that I would seize power. "If I control your business, I control you," he said.' See 'Court Documents Allege "corrupt" Kazakhstan Regime's Link to FTSE Firms', *Guardian* (2 December 2010).
32. International Consortium of Investigative Journalists, 'Secrecy for Sale: Inside the Global Offshore Money Maze' (Center for Public Integrity, 2013), p. 11, available at: http://cloudfront-files-1.publicintegrity.org/documents/pdfs/ICIJ%20Secrecy%20 for%20Sale.pdf
33. Philip, 'One Bank, Two Stories'.
34. 'Sleuths Hunt for Kazakh Bank's Missing $6 Billion', *Bloomberg* (9 January 2014).
35. As reported in 'Kazakh Banks: Crippled by Bad Debts', *Financial Times* (1 August 2013).
36. 'Sleuths Hunt for Kazakh Bank's Missing $6 Billion'.
37. Elliot Wilson, 'The Hunt for Mukhtar Ablyazov: Banker, Criminal, Fugitive, Victim?', *Euromoney* (January 2014).

38. Ibid. The article further notes that: 'Receivers say it's the most complex case they've worked on in decades. More new law has been written as a result of five years of almost constant written and verbal testimony, rebuttal witnesses, and cloak-and-dagger surveillance than any case in living memory.'

39. See Jean Pierre Brun et al., *Public Wrongs, Private Actions: Civil Lawsuits to Recover Stolen Assets* (World Bank Publications, 2014), Box 5.4, p. 75. Ablyazov's court judgments are showcased in the World Bank's Stolen Asset Recovery report.

40. High Court of Justice, *JSC BTA Bank v Mukhtar Ablyazov & Ors*, EWHC 2833 (QB) (2009), paragraph 5, available at: http://www.bailii.org/ew/cases/EWHC/QB/2009/2833.html

41. Brun et al., *Public Wrongs*, Box 9.2, p. 113.

42. High Court of Justice, *JSC BTA Bank v Mukhtar Ablyazov and others*, EWHC 27883 (Comm) (2014), paragraphs 19 and 21, available at: http://www.bailii.org/ew/cases/EWHC/Comm/2014/2788.html

43. 'Arrest Warrant for Kazakh Billionaire Accused of One of the World's Biggest Frauds', *Guardian* (16 February 2012).

44. 'Banker Mukhtar Ablyazov "Fled to France on coach"', *Telegraph* (24 February 2012).

45. Quoted in 'Court Rules Against Ablyazov in $2bn Suit', *Financial Times* (23 November 2012).

46. 'Billions Vanish in Kazakh Banking Scandal'.

47. Gizitdinov and Corcoran, 'The $5 Billion Heist'.

48. Ibid.

49. 'Fugitive Oligarch's £25m Mansion Sold to Pay Creditors', *Telegraph* (29 April 2015).

50. Barbara Junisbai and Azamat Junisbai, 'The Democratic Choice of Kazakhstan: A Case Study in Economic Liberalization, Intraelite Cleavage, and Political Opposition', *Demokratizatsiya* 13:3 (2005), pp. 373–92.

51. Ibid. Also see Barbara Junisbai and Azamat Junisbai, 'A Tale of Two Kazakhstans: Sources of Political Cleavage and Conflict in the Post-Soviet Period', *Europe-Asia Studies* 62:2 (2010), pp. 235–69.

52. Junisbai and Junisbai, 'Democratic Choice of Kazakhstan', p. 374.

53. 'Political Turmoil Hits Kazakhstan as Nazarbayev Sacks Top Officials', *Eurasianet* (26 November 2001), available at: http://www.eurasianet.org/departments/insight/articles/eav112701.shtml

54. A European Parliament resolution on Kazakhstan in 2003 characterised the sentencing of Ablyazov and Zhakiyanov 'on politically motivated charges relating to so-called "abuse of office" and "misappropriation of state funds"'. European Parliament, 'Resolution on Kazakhstan' (13 February 2003), available at: http://www.europarl.europa.eu/sides/getDoc.do?pubRef=-//EP//TEXT+TA+P5-TA-2003-0064+0+DOC+XML+V0//EN&language=CS

55. In an interview with *RFE/RL*, Yevgeny Zhovtis, the head of the Kazakhstan International Bureau for Human Rights and Rule of Law, commented: 'Nazarbaev to a certain extent felt betrayed ... Because he thinks that he provided them the space to become wealthy, to become well-known, to make a career in state service or in business, and they challenged him. When he pardoned Ablyazov in 2003 and allowed him to return to business in exchange for a promise not to be involved in politics and then found out that he was again involved in politics, of course Nazarbayev felt betrayed twice.' See 'How Far will Nazarbayev go to Take Down Ablyazov?'.

56. US Embassy London, '(C) Kazakhstan: Ousted BTA Bank Head Ablyazov Seeks Regime Change from London', 09LONDON712 (23 March 2009), reprinted at: http://www.telegraph.co.uk/news/wikileaks-files/london-wikileaks/8305198/C--KAZAKHSTAN-OUSTED-BTA-BANK-HEAD-ABLYAZOV-SEEKS-REGIME-CHANGE-FROM-LONDON.html

57. 'How Far will Nazarbayev go to Take Down Ablyazov?'.
58. US Embassy Astana, 'Alga Leader Discusses Ablyazov, Two New Administrative Cases Against His Unregistered Party', 09ASTANA870 (21 May 2009), available at: https://wikileaks.org/plusd/cables/09ASTANA870_a.html
59. US Embassy London, 'Ousted BTA Bank Head Ablyazov Seeks Regime Change from London'.
60. Ibid.
61. 'Billions Vanish in Kazakh Banking Scandal'.
62. 'Court Documents Allege "Corrupt" Kazakhstan Regime's Link to FTSE Firms'.
63. Detailed in 'Kazakh Spat Casts Light on China Deals: Exiled Banker Alleges Chinese Oil Firm Routed $166 Million to Associate of Top Oil Executive, as Part of 2003 State Sale', *Wall Street Journal* (26 March 2010).
64. These denials are quoted in the article: 'In a statement, Magwells, a London-based law firm representing Mr. Kulibayev, said its client is not, and has never been, a shareholder in Darley, and wasn't involved in the Aktobe Munaigaz transaction.' London lawyer David Price, the representative of Mr Arvind Tiku, the business associate named in the story, said Mr Ablyazov's account of the deal 'does not provide a true reflection of the transaction', and the facts as stated in it were 'incomplete and inaccurate'. Price's response (quoted in ibid.) continues:

    In part ... the account does not reflect economic conditions which played an important part in the outcome of the Aktobe Munaigas transaction, including oil prices he says trebled between 2003 and 2005. Mr. Tiku said he had made full and open disclosure to the Kazakh investigating authorities, but said that 'due to confidentiality obligations' he was unable to provide further comment.

65. 'CNPC said Mr. Ablyazov's claims were "groundless and libelous." In a statement, the company's Hong Kong- and New York-listed subsidiary PetroChina said it "conducts its international business according to best business practice, with high integrity and in full compliance with regulations."' Quoted in ibid.
66. Quoted in ibid.
67. Ibid.
68. See 'Freedom of the Press in Kazakhstan', *BBC Kyrgyz.com* (22 February 2010), available at: http://www.bbc.com/kyrgyz/news/story/2010/02/100222_pressfreedom.shtml
69. See 'Kazakhstan: The News Weekly that Won't be Silenced', *Eurasianet* (29 March 2011), available at: http://www.eurasianet.org/node/63176
70. For background, see Human Rights Watch, *Striking Oil, Striking Workers: Violations of Labor Rights in Kazakhstan's Oil Sector* (2012).
71. Myles Smith, 'Zhanaozen Trials Set to Leave Many Unanswered Questions', *CACI Analyst* (30 May 2012).
72. Ibid.
73. See Freedom House, *Kozlov Case File: Final Monitoring Report on the Trial of Vladimir Kozlov, Akzhanat Aminov, and Serik Sapargali* (December 2012); and Human Rights Watch, *Striking Oil*.
74. Freedom House, *Kozlov Case File*, p. 2.
75. Ibid., pp. 7–8.
76. As quoted in ibid., p. 9.
77. For the transcript, see ibid., Appendix 7.
78. In one passage (ibid., pp. 43–4), Ablyazov reportedly says:

    In general, I mean, here I've been fighting constantly against the authorities for ten years. But within myself, I am convinced that no earlier and no later than by the end of the next year, the government must fall. And that's it. In principle, this is real. We just have to work on this. I was especially convinced at the beginning of this year, when we all started together to stir things up, and the authorities started to come loose, they were incapable. They were incapable last year. And right now it's very important [to build] on these dissatisfactions, the huge quantity, not to get scared and then our ranks will increase. And that's why I'm sure that by the end of the next year, if we continue, we will be able to break the government. That's why just yesterday I said, from here I can see that the regime will fall. *I'm also convinced that by the end of next year we can topple this government* [italics in original]. That's why I think that we have to find the weak spots in the government: oil workers, miners, debtors and everyone in order to merge them all into one, into one place, and that will have enormous force. And set the government aside. And from there – the most important is that we will integrate ourselves into this government.

79. 'Kazakhstan in Legal Move to Ban Opposition Parties and Media', *Reuters* (21 November 2012).

80. Dossym Satpayev and Tolgany Umbetaliyeva, 'The Protests in Zhanaozen and the Kazakh Oil Sector: Conflicting Interests in a Rentier State', *Journal of Eurasian Studies* 6 (2015), p. 127.

81. 'Main Opposition Media Silenced in Space of a Month', *Reporters Without Borders* (28 December 2012), available at: http://en.rsf.org/kazakhstan-main-opposition-media-silenced-in-28-12-2012,43751.html

82. Quoted in 'Foreign Minister Reveals the Ugly Truth on Exile Banker Mukhtar Ablyazov', *Tengrinews* (1 February 2013), available at: http://en.tengrinews.kz/politics_sub/Foreign-Minister-reveals-ugly-truth-on-exile-banker-Mukhtar-16549/

83. '"Trojan Horse" Raid Ends 18-Month Hunt for Kazakh Banker Mukhtar Ablyazov', *Independent* (4 August 2013).

84. See Adam Hug (ed.), *Shelter from the Storm? The Asylum, Refuge and Extradition Situation Facing Activists from the Former Soviet Union in the CIS and Europe* (London: Foreign Policy Centre, 2014). Moreover, the security services of these countries have conducted several operations and renditions on each other's territory even without legal justification (see Chapter 2).

85. 'French Court Cancels Kazakh Tycoon Ablyazov's Extradition to Russia', *Reuters* (9 December 2016), available at: http://www.reuters.com/article/us-bta-ablyazov-extradition-idUSKBN13Y2FC

86. On Kazakhstan's use of the Red Notice system for political ends, see Mario Savino, 'Global Administrative Law Meets Soft Powers: The Uncomfortable Case of Interpol Red Notices', *NYU Journal of International Law and Politics* 43 (2010), pp. 263–336.

87. European Parliament, Subcommittee on Human Rights, 'Question to the EEAS/ Commission' (Brussels, 10–11 July 2013), p. 1.

88. See Human Rights Watch, *Italy's 'Extraordinary Rendition to Kazakhstan'* (22 July 2013), available at: https://www.hrw.org/news/2013/07/22/dispatches-italys-extraordinary-rendition-kazakhstan; and Amnesty International, *Italian Government Must Ensure Accountability for Illegal Expulsion to Kazakhstan* (16 July 2013), available at: https:// www.amnesty.org/en/latest/news/2013/07/italian-government-must-ensure-accountability-illegal-expulsion-kazakhstan/

89. 'UN Human Rights Experts Urge Italy to Seek Return of Illegally Deported Kazakh Mother and Daughter', United Nations Human Rights, Office of the High Commissioner for Human Rights (18 July 2013), available at: http://www.ohchr.org/FR/NewsEvents/Pages/DisplayNews.aspx?NewsID=13559&LangID=E

90. Cooley, *Great Games, Local Rules*, pp. 103–8.

91. 'Deportation of Kazakhs Frays Italy's Government', *New York Times* (18 July 2013).

92. 'Silvio Berlusconi's Ally "Rendered Dissident's Family to Kazakhstan"', *Independent* (9 July 2013).

93. Riccardo Bellandi, 'Who Decides Foreign and Defense Policy in Italy?', *Italian Politics* 29 (2014), pp. 201–3.

94. 'Kazakh Dissident Ablyazov's Family Allowed Back in Italy', *BBC News* (28 December 2013).

95. 'Kazakh Envoys in Rome Accused of Kidnap', *Financial Times* (24 September 2013).

96. Amnesty International, *Spain Set to Extradite Man to Kazakhstan Despite Torture Risk* (8 November 2013), available at: https://www.amnesty.org/en/latest/news/2013/11/aleksandr-pavlov-extradition/

97. 'Isabel Santos in Madrid to Discuss the Extradition Case of Aleksandr Pavlov', *OSCE Newsroom* (18 October 2013), available at: http://www.osce.org/pa/111151

98. As mentioned in 'Kazakh Fugitive's Associate Freed From Czech Jail', *RFE/RL* (20 March 2014), available at: http://www.rferl.org/content/kazakhstan-czech-release-paraskevich-ablyazov-case/25304021.html; for the story, see 'Hay un avión esperando para llevarse a Pavlov', *El País* (1 March 2014), available at: http://politica.elpais.com/politica/2014/03/01/actualidad/1393692630_197617.html

99. 'Ablyazov's Former Head of Security Seeks Political Asylum in Spain', *TengriNews* (13 August 2014), available at: http://en.tengrinews.kz/politics_sub/Ablyazovs-former-head-of-security-seeks-political-asylum-in-Spain-255354/

100. 'As Clock Ticks, Ablyazov Associate Waits For Czech Asylum Ruling', *RFE/RL* (15 October 2013), available at: http://www.rferl.org/content/kazakhstan-ablyazov-pareskevich-czech-extradition/25137599.html

101. 'Kazakh Fugitive's Associate Freed From Czech Jail'.

102. 'Kazakhstan Accuses Russian Nationalist Of Inciting Hatred', *RFE/RL* (18 November 2014), available at: http://www.rferl.org/content/kazakh-belov-potkin-ablyazov-arrests-extradition-france-russia-ukraine/26697449.html

103. 'Police Say He Helped Steal $5 Billion, But Russia's Opposition Wants to Save Alexander Belov', *Global Voices* (11 November 2014), available at: https://globalvoicesonline.org/2014/11/11/police-say-he-helped-steal-5-billion-dollars-but-the-russian-opposition-wants-tosave-alexander-belov/

104. See 'Nichevo natsionalistichnovo prosto biznes [Nothing to Do with Nationalism, Just Business]', *Kommersant* (15 October 2014), available at: http://www.kommersant.ru/doc/2590480

105. 'For Exiled Activist, Kazakhstan Is Out Of Sight, But Never Out Of Mind', *RFE/RL* (22 June 2014), available at: http://www.rferl.org/content/kazakhstan-ketebaev-exiled-activist/25431090.html

106. See 'Spanish Court Approves Arrest of Kazakh Opposition Figure', *RFE/RL* (29 December 2014), available at: http://www.rferl.org/content/kazakhstan-opposition-spain/26767375.html

107. See 'Muratbek Ketebayev Left Spain and Went Back to Poland. Spain Rejected the Kazakh Request for Extradition', *Open Dialogue Foundation* (3 March 2015), available at: http://en.odfoundation.eu/a/6074,muratbek-ketebayev-left-spain-and-went-back-to-poland-spain-rejected-the-kazakh-request-for-extradition

108. For a timeline, see http://www.rferl.org/content/kazakhstan-rakhat-aliev-timeline/26867151.html

109. 'Interpol Drops Arrest Warrant against Kazakhstani Opposition Leader', *Eurasianet* (25 June 2002), available at: http://www.eurasianet.org/departments/insight/articles/eav062602a.shtml

110. 'Kazakhstan City Sues Former Mayor with U.S. Ties Alleging $300 Million Fraud, International Money Laundering Scheme Including Beverly Hills Mansions, Luxury Cars', *Business Wire* (14 May 2014).

111. 'Kazakh City Claims Mayor Looted It', *Courthouse News Service* (14 May 2014), available at: http://www.courthousenews.com/2014/05/14/67858.htm

112. 'Kazakhstan: Is US Lawsuit Against Ex-Mayor Selective Justice?' *Eurasianet* (15 May 2014), available at: http://www.eurasianet.org/node/68373

113. 'Oil, Cash and Corruption', *New York Times* (5 November 2006). On the emergence of the scandal and discovery of the bank accounts, see details in 'Kazakhstan is Suspected of Oil Bribes in the Millions', *New York Times* (28 July 2000).

114. See 'A Banished Member of Kazakhstan Royalty Has Died by Apparent Suicide', *qz.com* (24 February 2015), available at: http://qz.com/349695/a-banished-member-of-kazakhstan-royalty-has-died-by-apparent-suicide/

115. 'After Seven Years, "Kazakhgate" Scandal Ends with Minor Indictment', *RFE/RL* (10 August 2010), available at: http://www.rferl.org/content/After_Seven_Years_Kazakhgate_Scandal_Ends_With_Minor_Indictment_/2123800.html

116. The comments of Judge William Pauly III are quoted in Matthew G. Yeager, 'The CIA Made Me Do It: Understanding the Political Economy of Corruption in Kazakhstan', *Crime, Law and Social Change* 57:4 (2012), pp. 441–57, at 454.

117. 'Kazakh Officials Investigating "Godfather-In-Law" Book', *RFE/RL* (21 May 2009), available at: http://www.rferl.org/content/Aliev_Welcomes_Efforts_To_Ban_Book_On_Nazarbaev/1736354.html; a spokesman from the office of the prosecutor general further warned that: 'If we find out that any one of our citizens is involved in possessing, buying, or reproducing this book, they will be prosecuted for collaborating with this criminal, Rakhat Aliev, who is now running from justice. Apart from that, the book contains state secrets. If individuals are not [officially] allowed access to these secrets, they don't have the right to know the contents of the book.' Quoted in 'Former Kazakh Presidential Son-in-Law Publishes Tell-All Book', *RFE/RL* (22 May 2009), available at: http://www.rferl.org/content/Former_Kazakh_Presidential_SoninLaw_Publishes_TellAll_Book/1737423.html

118. See http://www.viktor-khrapunov.com

119. 'Amities Kazakh', *Le Monde* (2 November 2013).

120. See Khrapunov, *Nazarbayev – Our Friend the Dictator*, pp. 138–9.

121. Igor Savchenko, 'The Report: The Interpol System is in Need of Reform', *Open Dialogue* (14 February 2015), available at: http://en.odfoundation.eu/a/5947,the-report-the-interpol-system-is-in-need-of-reform

122. Lemon and Rosset, 'Offshore Central Asia', pp. 10–11.

123. Fauve, 'Global Astana'.

124. 'Kazakhstan: Conflict-of-Interest Debate Flares in Washington', *Eurasianet* (2 June 2009), available at: http://www.eurasianet.org/departments/insightb/articles/eav060309b.shtml

125. Michel, 'Dismissing Disclosure and Free Agent Diplomacy'.

126. Lemon and Rosset, 'Offshore Central Asia'.

127. See Human Rights Watch, *Blair's Kazakhstan Odyssey, Two Years On* (30 October 2013), available at: https://www.hrw.org/news/2013/10/30/blairs-kazakhstan-odyssey-two-years; see also 'Tony Blair Gives Kazakhstan's Autocratic President Tips on How to Defend a Massacre', *Telegraph* (24 August 2014).

Chapter 3: Tajikistan: The President of the Warlords and his Offshore State

1. US Embassy Dushanbe, 'Back in the USSR at TALCO', 08DUSHANBE516_a (14 April 2008), paragraphs 10–11, available at: https://wikileaks.org/plusd/cables/08DUSHANBE516_a.html

2. In reality, these figures of the formal economy are highly unreliable and fail to capture the majority of informal economic activity linked to transnational labour migration and shuttle-trading. See ibid.

3. Talco paid $.01/kilowatt hour in 2008 when the market rate was around $.045/kilowatt hour. A USAID study estimates that Tajikistan could make much more from exporting this electricity than using it to fuel the aluminium smelter. Ibid., paragraph 3.
4. High Court of Justice, *Tajik Aluminium Plant v Ermatov & Ors*, EWHC 2241 (21 October 2005), paragraphs 22–3, available at: http://www.bailii.org/cgi-bin/format. cgi?doc=/ew/cases/EWHC/Ch/2005/2241.html&query=(EWHC)+AND+(2241)
5. John Helmer, 'Cover off Tajikistan's Missing Millions', *Asia Times Online* (11 January 2008), available at: http://www.atimes.com/atimes/Global_Economy/JA11Dj03.html
6. High Court of Justice, *Tajik Aluminium Plant v Ermatov & Ors*, paragraph 59.
7. Ibid., paragraphs 28, 60.
8. Driscoll, *Warlords*, especially pp. 89–90.
9. Kirill Nourzhanov, 'Saviours of the Nation or Robber Barons? Warlord Politics in Tajikistan', *Central Asian Survey* 24:2 (2005), p. 117.
10. 'Tajikistan passes law designating Rahmon the "leader of the nation"', *Asia Plus* (9 December 2015), available at: http://news.tj/en/news/tajikistan-passes-law-designating-rahmon-leader-nation
11. High Court of Justice, *Tajik Aluminium Plant v Ermatov & Ors*, paragraph 61.
12. International Court of Arbitration, *Hamer Final Award, In The Matter Of An Arbitration Pursuant To The Swiss Rules Of International Arbitration*, case no. 600097-20079 (October 2013), paragraph 188.
13. High Court of Justice, *Tajik Aluminium Plant v Ermatov & Ors*, paragraphs 81–5.
14. In fact the barter agreements of 2000 and 2003 were made under the jurisdiction of English law in the form of the London Court of International Arbitration. Ibid., paragraph 23.
15. In particular, the judgment of Justice Blackburne of 21 October 2005, High Court of Justice, *Tajik Aluminium Plant v Ermatov & Ors*, and the subsequent *Settlement Agreement between Hydro Aluminium and Tajik Aluminium Company* (20 December 2006), available at: http://johnhelmer.net/wp-content/uploads/2008/12/taj-trial-hydro-Talco-agreement-of-dec-20-2006.pdf
16. John Helmer, 'Tajik Aluminium Case Gets Nearer Judgment', *Dances with Bears* (2 August 2008), available at: http://johnhelmer.net/?p=479; it seems that these moves began in at least 2003 as Ermatov, by his subsequent testimony, was pressured by Sadullayev to transfer Talco accounts to Orienbank. High Court of Justice, *Tajik Aluminium Plant v Ermatov & Ors*, paragraph 63.
17. Ibid.
18. High Court of Justice, 'Witness Statement of Khasan Asadullozoda' (13 April 2008), paragraph 38.
19. Arbitration in the Stockholm Chamber of Commerce, *CDH v Albaco*, case no. 145/2007 (2007). High Court of Justice, 'Witness Statement of Sherali Olimovich Kabirov', paragraph 103.
20. Ibid., paragraphs 74, 191.
21. Ibid., paragraphs 75, 76.
22. Although the Talco case did not involve extraterritorial rendition or assassination, this happened in other instances around this time. Mahmadruzi Iskandarov, a former opposition leader and head of the state oil and gas servicing company Tajikkommunservis, was abducted from Russia on 15 April 2005 and rendered to Tajikistan where on 5 October 2005 he was sentenced to thirty-two years in prison on terrorism charges. The European Court of Human Rights concluded in 2010 that 'the applicant was arrested by Russian State agents and that he remained under their control until his transfer to the Tajik authorities'. European Court of Human Rights, *Case Of Iskandarov v Russia*, application no. 17185/05, judgment (23 September 2010), available at: http://hudoc. echr.coe.int/sites/eng/pages/search.aspx?i=001-100485. See also Chapter 7.

23. CDH, for example, was formerly owned by a nominee director, Mr Marinov, resident in Cyprus. However, according to the testimonies of Sadullayev and his subordinate Sherali Kabirov, CDH was managed by Kabirov under the instruction of Sadullayev. Arbitration in the Stockholm Chamber of Commerce, *CDH v Albaco*.
24. This 'breach of contract' action referred to a 2003 barter agreement between the two parties: Talco subsequently failed to deliver $128 million in aluminium shipments.
25. Justice Blackburne states: 'TadAz [Talco] claims that CDH is ultimately owned by Orienbank. The evidence lends support to the view that Orienbank is controlled by close members and/or associates of President Rahmon's family.' High Court of Justice, *Tajik Aluminium Plant v Ermatov & Ors*, paragraph 180.
26. Ibid., paragraph 182.
27. Justice Blackburne states: 'It is difficult to see why Talco should have wished to enter into an agreement of this kind with an off-shore shell company, as CDH was, which had no track record in alumina, aluminium or any other kind of dealings.' Ibid., paragraphs 181, 183–4.
28. 'Witness Statement of Sherali Olimovich Kabirov', paragraph 103.
29. US Embassy Dushanbe, 'A Minor Miracle? Tajik Settlement with Norsk Hydro Could Be Major Victory for Potential Investors', 06DUSHANBE2243_a (22 December 2006), paragraph 4, available at: https://wikileaks.org/plusd/cables/06DUSHANBE2243_a.html
30. Ibid.
31. Ibid.
32. Ibid.
33. The agreement also includes 'settlement sums' totalling $94 million made in instalments from 31 December 2006 to 31 December 2010. High Court of Justice, *Settlement Agreement between Hydro Aluminium and Tajik Aluminium Company*, pp. 5, 21–5. See also Helmer, 'Tajik Aluminium Court Case ends in London defeat for President Rahmon'.
34. US Embassy Dushanbe, 'A Minor Miracle?' (2006), paragraph 5.
35. US Embassy Dushanbe, 'Will Rogun Ever Get Built? Tajikistan and Rusal Engage in War of Words', 06DUSHANBE1545_a (11 August 2006), paragraph 8, available at: https://wikileaks.org/plusd/cables/06DUSHANBE1545_a.html
36. High Court of Justice, *Tajik Aluminium Plant v Ermatov & Ors*, paragraphs 29, 99. Martha Brill Olcott, *Tajikistan's Difficult Development Path* (Washington, DC: Carnegie Endowment, 2012), pp. 183–214 has a thorough discussion of the Talco–Hydro relationship.
37. US Embassy Dushanbe, 'Ambassador's Farewell Call on President Rahmon', 06DUSHANBE1420_a (24 July 2006), paragraph 14, available at: https://wikileaks.org/plusd/cables/06DUSHANBE1420_a.html
38. Hydro, 'Report Regarding Hydro's Trade in Tajikistan' (statement to the Norwegian Ministry of Trade, Industry and Fisheries, 2 March 2016), p. 7.
39. Ibid.
40. Ibid., paragraph 14.
41. US Embassy Dushanbe, 'A Minor Miracle', paragraph 2.
42. Herbert Smith LLP, 'Hydro Aluminium AS and Tajik Aluminium Plant: Settlement Agreement', paragraph 9.6, pp. 12–13, available at: http://johnhelmer.net/wp-content/uploads/2008/11/taj-trial-hydro-tadaz.pdf
43. Transparency International, 'Corruption Perception Index', available at: http://www.transparency.org/research/cpi/cpi_2006/0/
44. 'Witness Statement of Khasan Asadullozoda' (13 April 2008), paragraph 48.
45. High Court of Justice, 'Third Witness Statement of Sherali Olimovitch Kabirov', *Tajik Aluminium Company v Ansol Ltd* (14 April 2008), paragraph 232.
46. US Embassy Dushanbe, 'Back in the USSR at TALCO', paragraph 10.

47. The other two individuals were Ismatullo Hayoyev and Jamshed Abdulov – each owning 10 per cent.

48. US Embassy Dushanbe, 'The Orima Defence Team Speaks; But what are they saying?', 08DUSHANBE515_a (14 April 2008), available at: https://wikileaks.org/plusd/cables/08DUSHANBE515_a.html

49. US Embassy Dushanbe, 'Tajikistan – Conviction of Prominent Entrepreneur Reminds Business Community of Who is the Boss', 08DUSHANBE512_a (10 April 2008), available at: https://wikileaks.org/plusd/cables/08DUSHANBE512_a.html

50. John Helmer, 'Hydro Aluminium in Trouble over Tajikistan Corruption Concerns', *MineWeb* (12 November 2007), available at: http://www.mineweb.com/archive/hydro-aluminium-in-trouble-over-tajikistan-corruption-concerns/

51. Brill Olcott, *Tajikistan's Difficult Development Path*, p. 192.

52. John Helmer, 'Other Side of the TALCO Saga', *Dances with Bears* (19 September 2008), available at: http://johnhelmer.net/?p=518

53. Emomali Rahmon to Dominique Strauss-Khan, 'Tajikistan: Letter of Intent', 19 April 2011, p. 2.

54. Justice Blackburne states that 'a "near irresistible" inference of all of this is that, in the period between 1996 to the end of 2000, there was a fraudulent scheme similar to the scheme between Talco and Ansol after that time'. High Court of Justice, *Tajik Aluminium Plant v Ermatov & Ors*, paragraph 35.

55. Ibid., paragraphs 175, 177.

56. John Helmer, 'IMF Blows Whistle on Tajik Corruption', *Asia Times Online* (26 March 2008), available at: http://www.atimes.com/atimes/Central_Asia/JC26Ag01.html; similar arrangements are described with respect to the 1996–2004 partnership with Ansol in the 2005 judgment: High Court of Justice, *Tajik Aluminium Plant v Ermatov & Ors*, paragraph 163.

57. 'Tajikistan: Suit Settlement Brings No Resolution', *Eurasianet* (1 December 2008), available at: http://www.eurasianet.org/departments/insightb/articles/eav120208a.shtml

58. John Helmer, 'IMF attacks Tajikistan Aluminium Co – Orders International Audit', *MineWeb* (11 September 2008); IMF, *Republic of Tajikistan: Staff-Monitored Program: Letter of Intent, Memorandum of Economic and Financial Policies, and Technical Memorandum of Understanding* (10 June 2008), available at: http://www.imf.org/external/np/loi/2008/tjk/061008.pdf

59. Kabirov claims that since 2007 the new agreement with TML has 'produced (over time) a substantial improvement in the fee paid' to Talco. 'Witness Statement of Sherali Olimovich Kabirov', paragraph 234.

60. Nazarov's lawyer, John Doctor QC, estimated Talco's losses to be $450 million from 2005 to 2007 while the profits of CDH/TML were around $500 million, all of which were transferred directly to CDH/TML's unknown owners. John Helmer, 'President Rahmon Forced to End Tajik Aluminium Court Case in London', *Dances with Bears* (27 November 2008), available at: http://johnhelmer.net/?p=626

61. Farangis Najibullah, 'Tajikistan: "Disappearance" of President's Brother-In-Law Sparks Rumors', *RFE/RL* (15 May 2008); 'Tadzhikistan: Po nepodtverzhdennym dannym, ubit vliyatelnyi banker Kh. Sadullayev [Tajikistan: Unconfirmed Reports that Influential Banker H. Sadullayev is Dead]', *Ferghana News* (9 May 2008), available at: http://www.fergananews.com/news.php?id=9117

62. Wild conspiracy theories included claims that Hasan had a non-identical twin, Hussein Sadullayev, who underwent plastic surgery in Germany so he could impersonate his brother. Why he (or the German government, which would have had to issue a visa for this purpose) would want to enable this plot is unclear. However, the very existence of such conspiracy theories tells us about the effects on political society of the secret state.

63. John Helmer, 'Tajik Aluminium Witness "Must Appear"', *Asia Times* (5 August 2008), available at: http://atimes.com/atimes/Central_Asia/JH05Ag01.html

64. Rukhshona Ibragimova, 'IMU continues to threaten Central Asia', *Central Asia Online* (18 February 2010), available at: http://www.centralasiaonline.com/cocoon/caii/xhtml/en_GB/features/caii/features/main/2010/02/18/feature-02

65. Talco, 'Press-reliz po auditu' (3 August 2010), available at: http://www.talco.com.tj/index.php?l=2&action=newslist&id=153&page=1

66. Ibid.

67. Thanks once again go to the incomparable David Trilling.

68. Grant Thornton JSC (Yerevan), *Consolidated Financial Statements and Independent Auditor's Report, Talco Management Limited JSC* (31 December 2011).

69. This had risen to $363 million by May 2014. ICC International Court Of Arbitration, *Alumina & Bauxite Company Ltd. (British Virgin Islands) v Cdh Investments Corp. (British Virgin Islands)*, 15002/Cco/Jrf/Ca/Mhm, final award (29 May 2013); International Court of Arbitration, *Hamer Final Award*; see also David Trilling, 'Russian Aluminum Giant Pries Open Books at Tajikistan's Largest Factor', *Eurasianet* (9 June 2014), available at: http://www.eurasianet.org/node/68466

70. 'Folie de Grandeur: A President with an Edifice Complex is Screwing the Motherland', *The Economist* (27 July 2013), available at: http://www.economist.com/news/asia/21582325-president-edifice-complex-screwing-motherland-folie-de-grandeur

71. CA-News (TJ), 'MinFin Tadzhikistana obvinil v sokriytie dokhoda v $1.1 Mlrd krup-neishii alyuminiya zavod v Tsentralnoi Azii TALCO [Ministry of Finance of Tajikistan Accuses the Leading Aluminium Factory in Central Asia of Hiding $1.1 billion]', 28 October 2016, available at: http://ca-news.org/news:1340167

72. Talco, 'Tomorrow', available at: http://www.talco.com.tj/en/aboutus/tomorrow

73. International Court of Arbitration, *Hamer Final Award*, paragraphs 286–324.

74. Ibid., paragraph 276.

75. These were reported in 2006 hearings before Justice Cresswell and are summarised in Brill Olcott, *Tajikistan's Difficult Development Path*, p. 199.

76. Ibid., p. 277.

77. International Court of Arbitration, *Hamer Final Award*, paragraph 316.

78. Ibid., paragraph 317.

79. Ibid., paragraph 194.

80. Ibid., paragraph 199.

81. Ibid., paragraph 8.

82. Trilling also provided these documents to the authors.

83. US Embassy Dushanbe, 'Tajikistan – Boeing makes a deal with Somon Air', 09DUSHANBE1112_a (30 September 2009), available at: https://wikileaks.org/plusd/cables/09DUSHANBE1112_a.html; Trilling, 'Russian Aluminum Giant Pries Open Books at Tajikistan's Largest Factory'.

84. David Trilling, 'Tajikistan's Cash Cow: Enough Milk to Go Around?', *Eurasianet* (10 June 2014), available at: http://www.eurasianet.org/node/68491

85. Fabiani & Company, 'Short Form Registration Statement' (US Department of Justice, 19 July 2013), available at: http://www.fara.gov/docs/6045-Short-Form-20130719-28.pdf

86. David Trilling, 'Tajikistan Using DC Proxies to Build Support for Rogun Dam'.

87. Fabiani & Company, 'Amendment to Registration Statement' (US Department of Justice, 30 January 2014), available at: http://www.fara.gov/docs/6045-Amendment-20140130-3.pdf

88. Alexander Botting admitted as much on the telephone in three separate conversations with Helmer, Trilling and Heathershaw in January and February 2014.

89. John Helmer, 'Camelflage – Tajik President Emomali Rahmon and James Fabiani Hide Expensive Washington Lobbying Secrets', *Dances with Bears* (26 February 2014), available at: http://johnhelmer.net/?p=10302

90. Alessandra Colarizi, 'A "China Town" in Northern Tajikistan', *Diplomat* (20 October 2015), available at: http://thediplomat.com/2015/10/a-china-town-in-northern-tajikistan/
91. Catherine Putz, 'Tajik Leader in China, Building Roads', *Diplomat* (3 September 2015), available at: http://thediplomat.com/2015/09/tajik-leader-in-china-building-roads/
92. Freedom House, *Tajikistan: Nations in Transit* (2016), available at: https://freedomhouse.org/report/nations-transit/2016/tajikistan
93. See the *Dagens Næringsliv* newspaper's website, available at: http://www.dn.no/
94. Hydro, 'Report regarding Hydro's trade in Tajikistan'.
95. Ibid., p. 2.
96. Ibid., p. 8.
97. Ibid., p. 10.
98. Ibid.
99. Ibid., p. 7.
100. Ibid.
101. International Court of Arbitration, *Hamer Final Award*, paragraph 255.
102. Zayd Saidov was arrested and convicted of corruption and various other offences in 2014 following his announcement of a new political party that would contest the 2015 presidential election. Umarali Kuvvatov was killed and his wife and children poisoned in Istanbul in March 2015 following several unsuccessful attempts to extradite him back to Tajikistan (see Chapter 7).
103. International Court of Arbitration, *Hamer Final Award*, paragraph 285.

Chapter 4: Uzbekistan's Closed Polity and Global Scandal

1. Donald S. Carlisle, 'Power and Politics in Soviet Uzbekistan: From Stalin to Gorbachev' in W. Fierman (ed.), *Soviet Central Asia: The Failed Transformation* (Oxford: Westview Press, 1991), pp. 93–129.
2. See Nancy Lubin, *Labour and Nationality in Soviet Central Asia* (London: Macmillan, 1984).
3. James Critchlow, '"Corruption", Nationalism, and the Native Elites in Soviet Central Asia', *Journal of Communist Studies and Transition Politics* 4:2 (1988), pp. 142–61.
4. See James Critchlow, *Nationalism in Uzbekistan: A Soviet Republic's Road to Sovereignty* (Boulder: Westview Press, 1991), pp. 39–52; and Gregory Gleason, 'Nationalism or Organized Crime? The Case of the "Cotton Scandal" in the USSR', *Corruption and Reform* 5:2 (1990), pp. 87–108.
5. Neil Melvin, *Uzbekistan: Transition to Authoritarianism on the Silk Road* (Amsterdam: Harwood Academic Publishers, 2000).
6. McGlinchey, *Chaos, Violence, Dynasty*.
7. Laura Adams, *The Spectacular State: Culture and National Identity in Uzbekistan* (Durham: Duke University Press, 2010).
8. Lawrence P. Markowitz, *State Erosion: Unlootable Resources and Unruly Elites in Central Asia* (Ithaca: Cornell University Press, 2013).
9. Alisher Ilkhamov, 'Neopatrimonialism, Interest Groups and Patronage Networks: The Impasses of the Governance System in Uzbekistan', *Central Asian Survey* 26:1 (2007), pp. 65–84.
10. Deniz Kandiyoti (ed.), *The Cotton Sector in Central Asia: Economic Policy and Development Challenges: Proceedings of a Conference Held at SOAS University of London, 3–4 November 2005* (School of Oriental & African Studies, University of London, 2007).
11. Bakhodyr Muradov and Alisher Ilkhamov, 'Uzbekistan's Cotton Sector: Financial Flows and Distribution of Resources', working paper (New York: Open Society Foundations, October 2014).
12. Sabahi and Ziyaeva, 'Investor State Arbitration in Central Asia'.

13. World Bank, 'Doing Business', data for Uzbekistan, available at: http://www.doing business.org/data/exploreeconomies/uzbekistan
14. George Gavrilis, *The Dynamics of Interstate Boundaries* (New York: Cambridge University Press, 2008).
15. Cooley, *Great Games, Local Rules*; David Lewis, *The Temptations of Tyranny in Central Asia* (New York: Columbia University Press, 2008).
16. Luca Anceschi, 'Integrating Domestic Politics and Foreign Policy Making: The Cases of Turkmenistan and Uzbekistan', *Central Asian Survey* 29:2 (2010), pp. 143–58.
17. See Cooley, *Great Games, Local Rules*; and Stephen Grey, *Ghost Plane: The True Story of the CIA Torture Program* (New York: Macmillan, 2006).
18. Matteo Fumagalli, 'Alignments and Realignments in Central Asia: The Rationale and Implications of Uzbekistan's Rapprochement with Russia', *International Political Science Review* 28:3 (2007), pp. 253–71.
19. 'U.S Gives Uzbekistan Military Equipment Boost', *Voice of America* (22 January 2015).
20. The Andijan crackdown, in particular, posed severe dilemmas for Washington and Brussels. The US government was split over whether to criticise the Uzbek government, with the Pentagon fearing that Tashkent would curtail its basing rights (which proved correct when US troops were evicted from the country in July 2005). The European Union imposed sanctions and a travel ban on upper-level officials, but almost immediately softened its position after a more conciliatory bloc, led by Germany, moved for their lifting and proposed continuing 'engagement'. In doing so, the whole question of cooperating with the Uzbek regime ignited larger questions within the EU over whether Brussels should be a strategic or normative actor in the region. See Alexander Cooley, 'Principles in the Pipeline: Managing Transatlantic Values and Interests in Central Asia', *International Affairs* 84:6 (2008), pp. 1173–88.
21. 'Bitter Divorce Threatens Unlikely Alliance at the Heart of War on Terror', *Telegraph* (18 April 2004); see also 'Life Tasted Good for Coke Bottler in Tashkent Until He Separated from President's Daughter', *Wall Street Journal* (21 August 2001).
22. See US Embassy Tashkent, 'Uzbekistan: From A to Zeromax', 10TASHKENT27_a (20 January 2010), available at: https://wikileaks.org/plusd/cables/10TASHKENT27_a. html; and Farangis Najibullah, 'The Demise of Uzbekistan's Cash Cow Zeromax', *RFE/RL* (16 June 2010), available at: http://www.rferl.org/content/Zeroing_In_On_ The_Demise_Of_Uzbekistans_Cash_Cow/2073867.html
23. US Embassy Tashkent, 'Resource Nationalism: Grab What You Can', 07TASHKENT2029_a (26 November 2007), available at: https://wikileaks.org/plusd/ cables/07TASHKENT2029_a.html
24. 'NDN Operator: We Have No Connection to Gulnara Karimova', *Eurasianet* (7 December 2010), available at: http://www.eurasianet.org/node/62519; 'Setting the Record Straight, Again, on the NDN and the Karimovs', *Eurasianet* (16 December 2010), available at: http://www.eurasianet.org/node/62582
25. 'Zeromax's Woes in Tashkent: GooGoosha's Swan Song from Politics?', *Eurasianet* (20 November 2010), available at: http://www.eurasianet.org/node/61110
26. 'Zeromax GmbH Creditors to Meet in Switzerland', *Uznews.net* (8 August 2011).
27. See 'WikiLeaks Cables: US keeps Uzbekistan President Onside to Protect Supply Line', *Guardian* (12 December 2010).
28. US Embassy Tashkent, 'Gulnora Karimova Looks to Improve Her Image', 05TASHKENT2473_a (5 September 2005), available at: https://wikileaks.org/plusd/ cables/05TASHKENT2473_a.html
29. As of 2015, Uzbekistan ranks outside the 100 leading countries in the World Bank's 'Doing Business Survey'. The country also consistently appears near the bottom of Transparency International's 2015 'Corruption Perceptions Index', ranking 153 out of 168 countries. Available at: https://www.transparency.org/country/#UZB

30. ITU, 'Measuring the Information Society Report' (2014), available at: http://www.itu.int/en/ITU-D/Statistics/Pages/publications/mis2014.aspx
31. 'U.S. Seeks to Seize $1 Billion in Telecom Probe', *Wall Street Journal* (13 August 2015).
32. Ibid.
33. 'U.S. Can Seize $300 Million Allegedly Linked To Russian-Uzbek Bribery Scandal', *RFE/RL* (13 July 2015), available at: http://www.rferl.org/content/uzbekistan-karimova-justice-department-bribery-scandal/27124827.html.
34. US Department of Justice, 'Letter to Honorable Judge Andrew Carter, Re: *United States v Any and All Assets Held in Account Numbers 102162418400, 102162418260, and 102162419780 at Bank of New York Mellon SA/NV, et al.*, 15 Civ. 05063' (1 July 2015), available at: http://star.worldbank.org/corruption-cases/sites/corruptioncases/files/Uzbek_Telecom_SDNY_DOJ_Letter_Request_Arrest%20in%20Rem_Jul1_2015.pdf. The letter states:

> As alleged in the Complaint, from 2004 until in or around 2011, two international telecommunications companies paid more than $500 million to shell companies beneficially owned by Government Official A. The telecom companies made these payments to induce Government Official A to use his or her influence, including Government Official A's influence over other Uzbek government officials, to assist the telecom companies in entering and operating in the Uzbek telecommunications market.

35. OCCRP, 'Uzbekistan: How the President's Daughter Controlled the Telecom Industry' (21 March 2015), available at: https://www.occrp.org/corruptistan/uzbekistan/gulnara_karimova/the-prodigal-daughter/how-the-presidents-daughter-controlled-the-telecom-industry.php
36. Ibid.
37. OCCRP, 'Articles of Association' document, Registrar of Companies Gibraltar (22 December 2003), available at: https://cdn.occrp.org/projects/corruptistan/documents/uzbekistan/Takilant_01.pdf; a 2005 filing, listing the additional two directors from St Kitts and Nevis who resigned on 2 November 2005, is available here: https://cdn.occrp.org/projects/corruptistan/documents/uzbekistan/Takilant_07.pdf; all source documents available at: https://www.occrp.org/en/corruptistan/uzbekistan/gulnarakarimova/documents.html
38. 'Uzbekistan's Gulnara Karimova Linked to Telecoms Scandal', *BBC News* (27 November 2012).
39. Ms Akayan could not be reached for comment. See 'Uzbekistan: The Leading Lady', *Financial Times* (7 March 2013).
40. OCCRP, 'Uzbekistan: How the President's Daughter Controlled the Telecom Industry'.
41. OCCRP, 'The Billion Dollar Payoff', available at: https://www.occrp.org/en/corruptistan/uzbekistan/gulnarakarimova/payoff.html
42. 'TeliaSonera CEO Quits Amid Criticism', *Wall Street Journal Blog* (1 February 2013), available at: http://blogs.wsj.com/corruption-currents/2013/02/01/teliasonera-ceo-quits-amid-criticism/
43. 'TeliaSonera Negotiated Directly with the Karimov-Regime', *svt.se* (12 December 2012), available at: http://www.svt.se/ug/teliasonera-negotiated-directly-with-the-karimov-regime
44. Ibid.
45. US Embassy Tashkent, 'Scandinavian-Turkish Firm May Buy Coscom and Sister Companies in Central Asia', 07TASHKENT769_a (13 April 2007), available at: https://wikileaks.org/plusd/cables/07TASHKENT769_a.html
46. 'Fresh Allegations Link Gulnara Karimova to Shady Telecoms Deal', *Eurasianet* (13 December 2012).

47. In September 2007 the Scandinavian company paid an initial $30 million sum to Teleson Mobile, a local Uzbek company which had been formed only seventeen days earlier, to acquire a 3G licence. Teleson was also owned by Avakyan, who was the registered director of Takilant. In December 2007, TeliaSonera AB paid Takilant $80 million through Parex Bank in Latvia, ostensibly to purchase 1800 MHz/UMTS frequencies and numbering block, while later that same day Takilant transferred TeliaSonera's subsidiary $50 million for a 26 per cent share of TeliaSonera Uzbek Holding. In 2010, TeliaSonera bought back 20 per cent of Takilant shares via a trust account and a Hong Kong bank for the princely sum of $220 million. Later that year, TeliaSonera Uzbek Holding B.V. paid $55 million to Takilant for additional frequency licences. See https://www.occrp.org/en/corruptistan/uzbekistan/gulnarakarimova/payoff.html

48. 'TeliaSonera under Fire over Uzbek Bribe Claims', *Local* (20 September 2012), available at: http://www.thelocal.se/20120920/43344

49. 'TeliaSonera Negotiated Directly with the Karimov-Regime'.

50. Mannheimer Swartling, 'Rapport till styrelsen i TeliaSonera AB' (Stockholm, 31 January 2013), available at: http://www.dn.se/Images/Utredning%20slutlig.pdf; see English-language summary of findings in Mannheaimer Swartling, 'Reviewer Criticizes Teliasonera', press release (1 February 2013), available at: http://www.mannheimer-swartling.se/en/news/news/reviewer-criticises-teliasonera/

51. 'TeliaSonera CEO Quits Amid Criticism'.

52. Ibid.

53. Quoted in 'Swiss Announce Karimova Money-Laundering Probe', *RFE/RL* (12 March 2014), available at: http://www.rferl.org/content/switzerland-karimova-investigation-uzbekistan-money-laundering/25294326.html

54. Swiss Federal Council, 'La fille du président ouzbek dans la ligne de mire de la justice suisse' (12 March 2014), available at: https://www.admin.ch/gov/fr/start/dokumentation/medienmitteilungen.msg-id-52278.html

55. 'La justice française s'intéresse à la fille du dictateur ouzbek' *Rue89* (31 July 2013), available at: http://rue89.nouvelobs.com/2013/07/31/justice-francaise-sinteresse-a-fille-dictateur-ouzbek-244641; 'Uzbekistan: Pressure Mounts in Europe's Gulnara-Linked Corruption Probes', *Eurasianet* (31 July 2013), available at: http://www.eurasianet.org/node/67325

56. 'Documents Link Uzbekistan's Karimova To Money-Laundering Suspect', *RFE/RL* (12 October 2012), available at: http://www.rferl.org/content/uzbekistan-karimova-linked-to-money-laundering/24736143.html

57. 'Telia Faces $1.4 billion Fine for Corruption in Uzbekistan', *Compliance Weekly* (19 September 2016), available at: https://www.complianceweek.com/blogs/enforcement-action/telia-faces-14-billion-fine-for-corruption-in-uzbekistan#.V-kjFFfjKS0

58. US Securities and Exchange Commission (SEC), 'VimpelCom to Pay $795 Million in Global Settlement for FCPA Violations' (18 February 2016), available at: https://www.sec.gov/news/pressrelease/2016-34.html

59. Under the terms of the settlement, the company was required to pay $167.5 million to the SEC, $230.1 million to the US Department of Justice and $397.5 million to Dutch regulators, and it was required to retain an independent corporate monitor for three years.

60. 'Takilant Found Guilty of Taking Bribes From Telia, VimpelCom', *Bloomberg* (20 July 2016).

61. SEC, 'VimpelCom to Pay $795 Million in Global Settlement for FCPA Violations'.

62. Ibid.

63. US Department of Justice, Southern District of New York, 'Global Telecommunications Company and Its Subsidiary Charged in Massive Bribery Scheme Involving Uzbek Official; Company to Pay $795 Million in Penalties', press release (18 February 2016),

available at: https://www.justice.gov/usao-sdny/pr/global-telecommunications-company-and-its-subsidiary-charged-massive-bribery-scheme

64. Ibid.
65. Ibid.
66. Ibid.
67. As identified by the statement, the major players in the corruption scheme were 'Foreign Official', who was 'an Uzbek government official and a close relative of a high-ranking Uzbek government official', along with 'Associate A', a 'close associate' of 'Foreign Official', and 'Associate B', 'chief executive of one of Unitel's primary executives in Uzbekistan', who nevertheless 'represented Shell Company and Foreign Official in their business dealings with VIMPELCOM and Unitel'. US Attorney's Office (USAO), Southern District of New York, 'Attachment A: Statement of Fact' (18 February 2016), p. A-3, lines 7–10, available at: https://www.justice.gov/usao-sdny/file/826456/download
68. The schemes included: 1) Shell company purchase: an individual payment of $60 million to acquire Burtzel, a company in which VimpelCom officials knew that Foreign Official had an indirect stake via the shell company; 2) Fraudulent buyout: a 2006 agreement to allow Foreign Official an indirect ownership in Unitel that would later be repurchased by VimpelCom at a guaranteed profit, thereby paying a $37.5 million bribe to Foreign Official; 3) 3G licensing bribes: a 2007 bribe payment via a shell company to Foreign Official, 'purportedly to obtain 3G frequencies'; 4) Fake consulting contracts: in 2008 and 2011 knowingly entering into fake consulting contracts with the shell company in order to provide $32 million to Foreign Official 'in exchange for valuable telecommunications assets and to allow Unitel to continue to conduct business in Uzbekistan'; 5) Fake reseller agreements: in 2011 and 2012 bribe payments to Foreign Official through 'purposefully non-transparent transactions with purported "reseller companies"'. Ibid., pp. A-3, A-4 and A-5, lines 11–13, available at: https://www.justice.gov/usao-sdny/file/826456/download
69. Alexei Malashenko, *Exploring Uzbekistan's Potential Political Transition* (Moscow: Carnegie Center, 2014), p. 8.
70. 'Uzbek TV Channels Controlled by Karimova Stop Broadcasting', *RFE/RL* (22 October 2013), available at: http://www.rferl.org/content/uzbekistan-karimova-tv-channels-broadcasts-stop/25144301.html; 'Bank Accounts Of Holding Group Linked To Karimova Frozen', *RFE/RL* (30 October 2013), available at: http://www.rferl.org/content/uzbekistan-karimova-bank-accounts-frozen/25152801.html
71. 'More Uzbek TV Channels Cease Broadcasting', *RFE/RL* (12 November 2013), available at: http://www.rferl.org/content/uzbekistan-karimova-more-tv-channels-closed/25165546.html
72. 'First Daughter's Charity Network Reportedly Under Fire', *Eurasianet* (27 October 2013), available at: http://www.eurasianet.org/node/67684
73. 'V kvartire docheri prezidenta Uzbekistana proshyol obysk [Uzbek President's Daughter's flat was searched]' (18 February 2014), available at: http://russian.rt.com/article/22407
74. 'Uzbek Authorities Acknowledge Karimova Under House Arrest', *RFE/RL* (24 September 2014), available at: http://www.rferl.org/content/uzbekistan-gulnara/26601995.html
75. 'Associates of Uzbekistan's Gulnara Karimova Reportedly Sentenced', *RFE/RL* (14 July 2014), available at: http://www.rferl.org/content/karimova-avakian-uzbekistan-madumarov-trial-sentence-reportedly/25455961.html
76. US Embassy Tashkent, 'Ambassador's May 28 Meeting with Uzbek Intelligence Chief', 08TASHKENT610_a (30 May 2008), available at: https://www.wikileaks.org/plusd/cables/08TASHKENT610_a.html
77. Reported in 'New Woes for Gulnara', *Eurasianet* (8 November 2013), available at: http://www.eurasianet.org/node/67741

78. Ibid.
79. As quoted in 'Karimova Mocks National Security Chief', *RFE/RL* (1 November 2013), available at: http://www.rferl.org/content/uzbekistan-karimova-mocks-security-chief/25154821.html
80. Natalia Antelava, 'Suspected Gulnara Karimova Letter Smuggled to BBC', *BBC News Magazine* (24 March 2014), available at: http://www.bbc.com/news/magazine-26713383
81. Ibid.
82. 'Uzbekistan's First Family; Too Sexy for the Catwalk', *The Economist* (29 August 2014).
83. 'Amid Rumors Of Her Demise, A Question: Does Gulnara Matter?', *RFE/RL* (2 November 2013), available at: http://www.rferl.org/content/does-gulnara-karimova-matter/25155794.html.
84. 'Uzbekistan's Feuding Family Elite', *Global Voices, Central Asia* (31 January 2014), available at: https://iwpr.net/global-voices/uzbekistans-feuding-family-elite
85. 'Uzbekistan: US Court Seizes Millions in Karimov Family-Linked Case' (10 July 2015), available at: http://www.eurasianet.org/node/74186
86. US Department of Justice, Office of Public Affairs, 'VimpelCom Limited and Unitel LLC Enter into Global Foreign Bribery Resolution of More Than $795 Million; United States Seeks $850 Million Forfeiture in Corrupt Proceeds of Bribery Scheme', press release (18 February 2016), available at: https://www.justice.gov/opa/pr/vimpelcom-limited-and-unitel-llc-enter-global-foreign-bribery-resolution-more-795-million
87. 'U.S. Demands Uzbek Leader's Daughter Turn Over $550 Million', *RFE/RL* (23 April 2016), available at: http://www.rferl.org/a/us-prosecutors-demand-karimova-turn-over-550-million/27692833.html
88. Swiss Federal Council, 'La fille du président ouzbek'.
89. Swiss Federal Police, 'Annual Report' (2014), available at: http://star.worldbank.org/corruption-cases/sites/corruption-cases/files/Swiss%20Federal%20Police%20Annual%20Report%202014_Pub%20May%202015_0.pdf
90. 'Uzbekistan: Frozen Millions on Agenda as Minister Holds Talks in U.S.?' *Eurasianet* (20 January 2016), available at: http://www.eurasianet.org/node/76896
91. Ibid.
92. Ibid.
93. Ibid.
94. 'Telecoms Forfeiture Case Moved into U.S.-Uzbekistan Negotiations', *Wall Street Journal* (28 April 2016), available at: http://blogs.wsj.com/riskandcompliance/2016/04/28/telecoms-forfeiture-case-moved-into-u-s-uzbekistan-negotiations/
95. Emile van der Does de Willebois et al., *The Puppet Masters: How the Corrupt Use Legal Structures to Hide Stolen Assets and What to Do About It* (World Bank Publications, 2011).
96. See I.M. Jimu, 'Managing Proceeds of Asset Recovery: The Case of Nigeria, Peru, the Philippines and Kazakhstan', Basel Institute on Governance Working Paper Series 6 (2009).

Chapter 5: Kyrgyzstan's Prince Maxim and the Switzerland of the East

1. 'Kyrgyz President Attacks UK for "Hosting a Guy who Robbed Us"', *Guardian* (14 July 2013).
2. US Embassy Bishkek, 'Lunch with Max: Soup to Nuts', 09BISHKEK1065_a (22 September 2009), available at: https://wikileaks.org/plusd/cables/09BISHKEK1065_a.html
3. Global Witness, *Grave Secrecy* (June 2012), available at: https://www.globalwitness.org/en/campaigns/corruption-and-money-laundering/anonymous-company-owners/grave-secrecy/

4. 'Kyrgyzstan Demands Extradition of Deposed President's Son', *Telegraph* (11 May 2010).
5. Global Witness, 'Former Kyrgyz President's Son Lives in £3.5m Surrey Mansion Despite Convictions for Attempted Murder of UK Citizen and Grand Corruption at Home' (24 March 2015), available at: https://www.globalwitness.org/en/archive/former-kyrgyz-presidents-son-lives-35m-surrey-mansion-despite-convictions-attempted-murder/
6. 'U.S. Ends Case Against Ex-Kyrgyz Leader Bakiev's Son', *Bloomberg* (9 May 2013), availableat:http://www.bloomberg.com/news/articles/2013-05-09/u-s-case-ends-against-ex-kyrgyz-leader-Bakiev-s-son
7. John Anderson, *Kyrgyzstan: Central Asia's Island of Democracy?* (Amsterdam: Harwood Academic, 1999).
8. Ibid., p. 65.
9. Ulan Sarbanov, board member, National Bank of the Kyrgyz Republic, discussant at 'Challenges to Economies in Transition: Stabilization, Growth, and Governance: International Conference in Honor of the Kyrgyz Som', Bishkek (27–28 May 1998), p. 2, available at: https://www.imf.org/external/np/eu2/kyrgyz/pdf/sarbanov.pdf
10. McGlinchey, *Chaos, Violence, Dynasty*, pp. 84–5.
11. See Dinissa Duvanova, *Building Business in Post-Communist Russia, Eastern Europe and Eurasia* (Cambridge University Press, 2013), p. 52.
12. See Kang, *Crony Capitalism*; see also Radnitz, *Weapons of the Wealthy*.
13. Johan Engvall, 'The State as Investment Market: An Analytical Framework for Interpreting Politics and Bureaucracy in Kyrgyzstan' (PhD dissertation, University of Uppsala, 2010).
14. For a long list see Rina Prizhivoit, 'Prezident izdal ukaz vsekh otmyt' v poslednyi raz', *Moya Stolitsa Novosti* (8 February 2005).
15. For more detail see Cooley, *Great Games, Local Rules*; McGlinchey, *Chaos, Violence, Dynasty*; and Kemel Toktomushev, 'Regime Security, Base Politics and Rent-Seeking: The Local and Global Political Economies of the American Air Base in Kyrgyzstan, 2001–2010', *Central Asian Survey* 34:1 (2015), pp. 57–77.
16. The main cause for the protest was the arrest of Azimbek Beknazarov, the prominent figure from the south. The protest in support of his release in Aksy in 2002 left six people dead. For more, see Cornelius Graubner and Alexander Wolters, 'Kirgisischer Feldversuch Demokratie: Zwischen Schattenstaat and Tulpen Revolution', in Manfred Sapper, Volker Weichsel and Andrea Huterer (eds.), *Machtmosaik Zentralasien: Traditionen, Restriktionen, Aspirationen* (Bonn: Bundeszentrale für politische Bildung, 2007), p. 200.
17. McGlinchy, *Chaos, Violence, Dynasty*, pp. 99–100.
18. Radnitz, *Weapons of the Wealthy*, p. 204.
19. Private communication to authors, 2006.
20. US Embassy Bishkek, 'Maxim Bakiev's Influence Becomes Official', 09BISHKEK1199_a (13 November 2009), available at: https://wikileaks.org/plusd/cables/09BISHKEK1199_a.html. Blackpool FC made major investments in players under the Belokon/Bakiyev partnership and were promoted to the English Premier League, the most lucrative football league in the world. Belokon is reputedly a friend of the heir to the British throne, Prince Charles, and sits on the board of The Prince's Foundation. See 'Pool President Belokon: "I'm Innocent"', *Blackpool Gazette* (14 January 2013).
21. For the summary of the findings of the investigation, see 'V Kyrgyzstane budut paspro-dani aktsii natsionalizirorovannikh kompanii [In Kyrgyzstan There Will be a Sale of Shares in a Nationalised Company]', InoZpress.kg, *Business New Europe*; for analysis of this structure may have worked see Global Witness, *Grave Secrecy*, p. 57.
22. 'Kyrgyz Commission: 30 Contract Killings During Bakiev Presidency', *RFE/RL* (12 April 2011), available at: http://www.rferl.org/content/kyrgyz_commission_report_30_contract_killings_under_bakiev/3555238.html.

23. See Philip Shishkin, *Restless Valley: Revolution, Murder, and Intrigue in the Heart of Central Asia* (New Haven & London: Yale University Press, 2013).
24. The Kyrgyz court reported this as £4 million in cash and 4 million shares in the company while Oxus's CEO Bill Trew claimed under oath in the London Court that he was asked to pay $15 million to the Bakiyevs, a request he refused. Pervomaisky District Court, Case No. UD-352/14 B3, Sentence (Bishkek, Kyrgyz Republic, 4 April 2014), p. 7; Royal Courts of Justice, London, Case No. HQ14P04904, transcript, Day 6, p. 38.
25. Royal Courts of Justice, London, Case No. HQ14P04904, transcript, Day 6, p. 38.
26. 'Gold Miner Oxus Stops Glittering in Central Asia', *The Sunday Times* (27 August 2006).
27. High Court, London, Case No. HQ14P04904, Before the Honourable Mr Justice Supperstone, Judgment Approved, paragraph 18.
28. Ibid., paragraph 19.
29. High Court, London, Case No. HQ14P04904, transcript, Day 3, p. 116.
30. 'Global Gold in Deal with Kazakh Investment Group over Jerooy', *MineWeb* (21 August 2007).
31. Ibid.; the well-researched William Hogan and Federico Sturzenegger (eds.), *The Natural Resources Trap: Private Investment Without Public Commitment* (Cambridge, MA: MIT Press, 2010), p. 18, includes Oxus's experience in Kyrgyzstan as one of the 'expropriation cases' among others that took place around the world in the years of 2006–07.
32. Pervomaisky District Court, Case No. UD-352/14 B3, Sentence, p. 7.
33. Ibid.
34. Ibid., p. 2.
35. Later, Oxus Resource Corporation received compensation from a succeeding investor, Visor Holding, and the dispute between Oxus and the Kyrgyz government was settled by an amicable agreement. See 'Claims Against the Kyrgyz Government', *Oxus* (11 September 2006).
36. 'Jerooy Project', *Kyrgyzaltyn.kg* (2011), available at: http://www.kyrgyzaltyn.kg/en/invest-proekti/47-proekt-djerui
37. 'Global Gold in Deal'.
38. Royal Courts of Justice, London, Case No. HQ14P04904, transcript, Day 6, pp. 28–30.
39. In turn, this company is 50 per cent owned by Lagun Investment and Iman Financial, both registered in the British Virgin Islands. *Compromat.ru* claims that the owner of these two companies is Alexander Turkot of the company Salford Capital Partners. Turkot is known as a manager of two other investment funds, New World Value Fund and Bary Discovered Partners, which operate various interests across the post-Soviet space. Finally, *Compromat.ru* alleges, both funds belonged to Berezovsky. See 'Kak Berezovsky sunul palku v muraveinik [How Berezovsky Put a Stick into an Anthill]', *Compromat.ru* (25 August 2006).
40. 'Kto razoril Borisa Berezovskogo? [Who Ruined Boris Berezovsky?]', *Forbes.ru* (8 May 2013).
41. 'Kirgizskaia oppozicia: Berezovsky taino posetil Bishkek [Kyrgyz Opposition: Berezovsky's Secret Visit to Bishkek]', *NEWSru* (12 September 2006). A recent report on the death of Boris Berezovsky by Russia-24, a large media outlet, also makes allegations about Berezovksy's interests in the Kyrgyz gold-mining sector; see 'Russia States There are Links between Ex-President of Kyrgyzstan Bakiev and Boris Berezovsky', *News-Asia* (25 March 2013).
42. 'Berezovsky planiroval napravit $7,4 mln na reidersky zahvat zolotogo mestorojdenia Jerooy v Kyrgyzstane [Berezovksy Planned to Direct $7.4 million to a Raid Occupation of the Jerooy Gold Deposit in Kyrgyzstan]', *News Fiber*.
43. 'Kto razoril Borisa Berezovskogo?'
44. Visor acquired 60 per cent of a joint venture with the Kyrgyz state under the Bakiyev government. After Bakiyev was deposed, the government annulled the licence, leading

Visor to press its case against Kyrgyzstan in the International Court of Arbitration. See Nariman Gizitdinov, 'Kazakh Dealmaker Finds Profit, Peril in Central Asian Stans', *Bloomberg Markets* (12 August 2015), available at: http://www.bloomberg.com/news/articles/2015-08-11/kazakh-dealmaker-karibzhanov-finds-riches-peril-in-central-asia

45. High Court, London, Case No. HQ14P04904, transcript, Day 3, pp. 156–8.

46. In Azerbaijan, for example, partial adoption of and weaknesses in the Extractive Industries Transparency Initiative have enabled such corruption. See Global Witness, *Azerbaijan Anonymous: Azerbaijan's State Oil Company and Why the Extractive Industries Transparency Initiative Needs to Go Further* (December 2013), p. 8; and Jonathan E. Turner, *Money Laundering Prevention: Deterring, Detecting, and Resolving Financial Fraud* (Hoboken: John Wiley, 2011).

47. US Embassy Bishkek, 'Candid Discussion with Prince Andrew on the Kyrgyz Economy and the "Great Game"', 08BISHKEK1095_a (29 October 2008), available at: https://wikileaks.org/plusd/cables/08BISHKEK1095_a.html

48. US Embassy Bishkek, 'Maxim Bakiev's Influence becomes Official'.

49. US Embassy Bishkek, 'Kyrgyz Elite Fawn Over President's Son', 09BISHKEK700_a, (20 June 2009), available at: https://wikileaks.org/plusd/cables/09BISHKEK700_a.html

50. US Embassy Bishkek, 'Kyrgyzstan: Dinner at Maxim's', 09BISHKEK744 (15 July 2009), available at: http://cables.mrkva.eu/cable.php?id=216680

51. Tierney, *Mystery at Manas*, p. 3.

52. Ibid.

53. 'Kyrgyz Elite Fawn Over President's Son'.

54. Cited in Shishkin, *Restless Valley*, p. 120.

55. Asel Otorbayeva, 'Mikhail Nadel: National Bank of Kyrgyzstan Tries to Justify its Actions by Deliberately False Accusations against AUB', *24.kg* (8 June 2011).

56. See Global Witness, *Drug Cartels, Terrorist Financing Risk and Sanctioned Regimes also on HSBC's Books Under Lord Green* (11 February 2015).

57. Global Witness, *Grave Secrecy*, p. 12.

58. Ibid.

59. Ibid., p. 4.

60. Ibid., pp. 17–18.

61. Personal communication with authors, 2013.

62. Shishkin, *Restless Valley*, p. 126.

63. 'US Freezes Assets of Kyrgyz Fugitive Maxim Bakiev', *bne IntelliNews* (18 July 2013).

64. 'Bakiev, Maksim Kurmanbekovitch', Interpol Red Notice (2010), available at: http://www.interpol.int/notice/search/wanted/2010-20244

65. 'Kyrgyzstan: Former "Prince" Dodges US Prosecution', *Eurasianet* (15 May 2013).

66. Ibid.

67. Central Bank of Russia, 'O provedenii somnitelnikh operatsii po schetam Aktsionernogo kommercheskogobanka "Aziya Universal Bank" [On The Conducting of Doubtful Operations with Regard to the Share Auction of Private Bank "Asia Universal Bank"]', 10 February 2006?, available at: http://www.cbr.ru/Press/Archive_get_blob.aspx?doc_id=060213_1014031.htm

68. US Embassy Bishkek, 'Embassy Cautions Against OPIC Role in Kyrgyzstan', 08BISHKEK386_a (18 April 2008), available at: https://wikileaks.org/plusd/cables/08BISHKEK386_a.html

69. Interview with Baktygul Jeenbaeva, National Bank of the Kyrgyz Republic, Bishkek (4 June 2015).

70. Blackpool FC would join fourteen of twenty English Premier League clubs in being owned by opaque offshore companies in 2010, according to the report by Christian Aid, *Blowing the Whistle: Time's Up for Financial Secrecy* (May 2010).

71. 'Kyrgyz President Attacks UK'.
72. House of Commons debate, c634W (13 July 2010).
73. Philip Shishkin, 'Kyrgyzstan's Most Wanted: The Curious Case of Eugene Gourevitch', *Foreign Affairs* (31 October 2013).
74. Global Witness, *Grave Secrecy*.
75. Shishkin, 'Kyrgyszstan's Most Wanted'.
76. 'Fallen Tsars', *The Economist* (15 October 2012).
77. 'Kyrgyz Ex-Leader Bakiev's Son Held in UK for Fraud', *BBC News* (13 October 2012).
78. Shishkin, 'Kyrgyszstan's Most Wanted'.
79. Ibid.
80. Christie Smythe, 'Ex-Kyrgyz Regime Adviser Gets Five Years for Wire Fraud', *Bloomberg* (16 June 2014).
81. Pervomaisky District Court, Case No. UD-352/14 B3, Sentence.
82. 'The decision has been taken to refuse your request because it is likely that its execution would prejudice our order public [public policy]', according to a November 2013 letter written by senior lawyer Busola Johnson. 'Why Surrey is the Hardest Word . . .', *Private Eye* 1418 (May 2016), available at: http://www.private-eye.co.uk/issue-1418/news
83. British Embassy Bishkek, 'Criminal Justice Dialogue: Sharing Legal Expertise in Bishkek' (23 June 2014), available at: https://www.gov.uk/government/world-location-news/uk-home-office-lawyer-participated-in-star-seminar-in-bishkek
84. Hickman & Rose homepage, available at: http://www.hickmanandrose.co.uk/
85. High Court, London, Case No. HQ14P04904, transcript, Day 6, p. 78.
86. High Court, London, Case No. HQ14P04904, Before the Honourable Mr Justice Supperstone, Judgment Approved, paragraph 178.
87. Ibid., paragraphs 185 and 196.
88. High Court, London, Case No. HQ14P04904, transcript, Day 6, p. 61.
89. While no cases of money laundering through AUB have been proved in court, the US had apparently brought charges of extortion against Gourevitch related to his time as the broker and financial officer of the Bakiyev regime. See Shishkin, 'Kyrgyszstan's Most Wanted'.

Chapter 6: The New Offshore Silk Roads

1. 'Secretary of State Clinton at New Silk Road Ministerial Meeting', US Department of State (22 September 2011), available at: http://iipdigital.usembassy.gov/st/english/texttrans/2011/09/20110923160643su0.3639272.html#axzz3yMiVUG68
2. 'Clinton Says Building New Silk Road Is Critical for Afghanistan', US Department of State (23 September 2011), available at: http://iipdigital.usembassy.gov/st/english/article/2011/09/20110923170112eiznekcam0.5790216.html#axzz3yMiVUG68
3. Cooley, *Great Games, Local Rules*, Chapter 3.
4. 'President Xi Jinping Delivers Important Speech and Proposes to Build a Silk Road Economic Belt with Central Asian Countries', Ministry of Foreign Affairs of the People's Republic of China (7 September 2013), available at: http://www.fmprc.gov.cn/mfa_eng/topics_665678/xjpfwzysiesgjtfhshzzfh_665686/t1076334.shtml
5. '"One Belt, One Road" will Define China's Role as a World Leader', *South China Morning Post* (2 April 2015).
6. Stephen Kotkin notes that the significance of these empires was to leave a regional legacy of 'imperial exchange', bequeathing practices of despotism and patrimonialism, in contrast to the centralised bureaucracies and national identities formed in the European state-building project. Stephen Kotkin, 'Mongol Commonwealth? Exchange and Governance Across the Post-Mongol Space', *Kritika: Explorations in Russian and Eurasian History* 8:3 (2007), pp. 487–531.

7. Halford John Mackinder, 'The Geographical Pivot of History', *Royal Geographical Society* (1904), p. 434.
8. Other NATO countries also reached deals to stage troops and transport supplies in the region, including Germany – which operated an air base from the Uzbek town of Termez on the Afghanistan border – and France, which used Dushanbe international airport in Tajikistan.
9. See Kucera, *US Military Aid to Central Asia*; and Cooley, *Great Games, Local Rules*.
10. Alexander Cooley, 'Base Politics', *Foreign Affairs* 84:6 (2005), pp. 79–92.
11. Shishkin, *Restless Valley*.
12. Information on the routes is given in Andrew C. Kuchins, Thomas M. Sanderson and David A. Gordon, *The Northern Distribution Network and the Modern Silk Road: Planning for Afghanistan's Future: A Report of the CSIS Transnational Threats Project and the Russia and Eurasia Program* (Washington, DC: CSIS, 2009).
13. United States Senate Committee on Foreign Relations, 'Central Asia and the Transition in Afghanistan' (Washington, DC: Majority Staff Report Prepared for the Use of the Committee on Foreign Relations, 11 December 2011), p. 5.
14. 'Pentagon Paid Airport Fees to Turkmenistan, But Can't Say How Much', *Eurasianet* (12 July 2010), available at: http://www.eurasianet.org/node/61514; 'Documents Highlight Problems with Uzbek Corridor of Afghan Supply Route', *Eurasianet* (28 June 2010), available at: http://www.eurasianet.org/node/61427
15. 'Wikileaks Cables: US Keeps Uzbekistan President Onside to Protect Supply Line', *Guardian* (12 December 2010).
16. John F. Tierney, *Warlord, Inc.: Extortion and Corruption Along the U.S. Supply Chain in Afghanistan* (Washington, DC: United States Congress, House of Representatives, Committee on Oversight and Government Reform: Subcommittee on National Security and Foreign Affairs, June 2010).
17. On the various US-proposed New Silk Route concepts developed in the post-Cold War era, see Marlene Laruelle, 'The US Silk Road: Geopolitical Imaginary or the Repackaging of Strategic Interests?', *Eurasian Geography and Economics* 56:4 (2015), pp. 360–75.
18. Kuchins, Sanderson and Gordon, *The Northern Distribution Network and the Modern Silk Road*; Andrew C. Kuchins, Thomas M. Sanderson and David A. Gordon, 'Afghanistan: Building the Missing Link in the Modern Silk Road', *Washington Quarterly* 33:2 (2010), pp. 33–47; Andrew C. Kuchins, et al., *The Northern Distribution Network and Afghanistan* (Washington, DC: CSIS Report, January 2010).
19. Graham Lee, 'The New Silk Road and the Northern Distribution Network: A Golden Road to Central Asian Trade Reform?', Open Society Foundations Central Eurasia Project Occasional Paper 8 (October 2012).
20. Ibid., pp. 27–31.
21. Ibid., p. 35.
22. As quoted in ibid., p. 30.
23. See the data on comparative regional import and export times in Cooley, *Great Games, Local Rules*, p. 155.
24. As reported in 'Kyrgyz Contracts Fly Under the Radar', *Washington Post* (1 November 2010).
25. Toktomushev, 'Regime Security, Base Politics and Rent-Seeking', p. 61.
26. Tierney, *Mystery at Manas*, p. 12.
27. David Cloud, 'Pentagon's Fuel Deal Is Lesson in Risks of Graft-Prone Regions', *New York Times* (5 November 2015).
28. Aram Roston, 'A Crooked Alliance in the War on Terror?', *NBC News* (30 October 2006), available at: http://www.nbcnews.com/id/15448018/print/1/displaymode/1098/40955459

29. Toktomushev, 'Regime Security, Base Politics and Rent-Seeking', p. 62.
30. Deirdre Tynan, 'Deconstructing Manas Fuel Suppliers' Corporate Structures', *Eurasianet* (3 May 2010), available at: http://www.eurasianet.org/departments/business/articles/eav042010.shtml
31. 'Kyrgyz Contracts Fly Under the Radar'.
32. Tierney, *Mystery at Manas*.
33. Ibid., p. 12.
34. Representatives of the rival IOTC claimed that their bid for the contract, which they claim was lower, was not considered by DLA. 'Kyrgyzstan: Manas Fuel Supply Contract to be Re-Opened?', *Eurasianet* (22 December 2010).
35. Aram Roston, 'Fueling the Afghan War', *Nation* (10 May 2010).
36. 'Kyrgyz Contracts Fly Under the Radar'.
37. Tierney, *Mystery at Manas*.
38. Ibid., p. 5.
39. Reproduced in ibid., p. 38.
40. Ibid., p. 37.
41. Ibid., pp. 42–50.
42. Robert M. Gates, *Duty: Memoirs of a Secretary at War* (New York: Knopf Doubleday, 2014), p. 194.
43. 'The New Silk Road', *The Economist* (12 September 2015).
44. National Development and Reform Commission of the People's Republic of China (NDRC), *Vision and Actions on Jointly Building Silk Road Economic Belt and 21st-Century Maritime Silk Road* (28 March 2015), available at: http://en.ndrc.gov.cn/newsrelease/201503/t20150330_669367.html
45. Wang Jisi, 'March West: China's Geopolitical Strategy of Rebalancing', *Global Times* (17 October 2012).
46. See Steven Liao and Daniel McDowell, 'Redback Rising: China's Bilateral Swap Agreements and Renminbi Internationalization', *International Studies Quarterly* 59:3 (2015), pp. 401–22.
47. Rilka Dragneva and Kataryna Wolczuk, 'Eurasian Economic Integration: Institutions, Promises and Faultlines', *The Geopolitics of Eurasian Economic Integration, Special Report* 19 (2014), pp. 8–22.
48. See Michael Clarke and Douglas Smith (eds.), *China's Frontier Regions: Ethnicity, Economic Integration and Foreign Relations* (London: I.B. Tauris, 2016); and Michael Clarke, 'Beijing's March West: Opportunities and Challenges for China's Eurasian Pivot, *Orbis* 60:2 (2016), pp. 296–313.
49. 'Central Asia Powers Machinery Revival', *China Daily* (5 September 2013).
50. 'China's UnionPay Prepares for Significant Move into Kazakhstan and Central Asia', *South China Morning Post* (12 June 2015).
51. See also Sebastien Peyrouse and Gaël Raballand, 'Central Asia: The New Silk Road Initiative's Questionable Economic Rationality', *Eurasian Geography and Economics* 56:4 (2015), pp. 405–20.
52. Monica Beuran, Marie Castaing Gachassin and Gael Raballand, 'Are There Myths on Road Impact and Transport in Sub-Saharan Africa?', *Development Policy Review* 33 (2015), pp. 673–700.
53. See Asian Development Bank (ADB), *CAREC CPMM Corridor Performance, Measurement & Monitoring Report* (2014), p. 5. Available at: http://cfcfa.net/images/downloads/CPMM%20AR2014%20ENG.pdf
54. 'A freight forwarder operating in Altynkol reports that container trains can be processed within two hours or can take as long as 7 days, depending on the incentives provided to expedite processing.': ibid., p. 9, fn. 4.
55. Ibid., pp. 10–11.

56. Crisis Group, *Central Asia: Decay and Decline* (Brussels: Report No. 201, 3 February 2011), pp. 17–18.

57. 'Tajik President's Son-in-Law Denies Ties to Company', *RFE/RL* (12 July 2010), available at: http://www.rferl.org/content/Tajik_Presidents_SonInLaw_Denies_Ties_To_Company/2097815.html

58. Thomas Stephan Eder, *China-Russia Relations in Central Asia: Energy Policy, Beijing's New Assertiveness and 21st Century Geopolitics* (Wiesbaden: Springer VS, 2014); Keun-Wook Paik, *Sino-Russian Oil and Gas Cooperation: The Reality and Implications* (Oxford Institute for Energy Studies, 2012).

59. Erica Strecker Downs, *Inside China, Inc.: China's Development Bank's Cross-Border Energy Deals* (Washington, DC: John L. Thornton China Center at Brookings, 2011).

60. 'Special Report: Inside Xi Jinping's Purge of China's Oil Mandarins', *Reuters* (25 July 2014).

61. Ibid.; 'Powerful Oil Clique at Center of Chinese Probes', *Wall Street Journal* (5 September 2013).

62. Ibid.

63. Downs, *Inside China, Inc.*

64. Henry Sanderson and Michael Forsythe, *China's Superbank: Debt, Oil and Influence – How China Development Bank is Rewriting the Rules of Finance* (New York: Bloomberg, 2012).

65. Downs, *Inside China, Inc.*

66. 'China's State-Owned Firms Warned to Keep Closer Watch on Overseas Investments', *South China Morning Post* (18 June 2015).

67. Paik, *Sino-Russian Oil and Gas Cooperation*, p. 282.

68. ICIJ, 'China's Scandal-Torn Oil Industry Embraces Tax Havens' (22 January 2014), available at: http://www.icij.org/offshore/chinas-scandal-torn-oil-industry-embraces-tax-havens

69. Ibid.

70. Edward Wong, 'Investigative Stories Delve Into the Use of Offshore Companies by Chinese', *New York Times Sinophere* (14 January 2014), available at: http://sinosphere.blogs.nytimes.com/2014/01/23/investigative-stories-delve-into-the-use-of-offshore-companies-by-chinese/?_r=0

71. ICIJ, 'China's Scandal-Torn Oil Industry Embraces Tax Havens'.

72. Ibid.

73. 'Kazakh Spat Casts Light on China Deals', *Wall Street Journal* (26 March 2010).

74. Ibid. The same article notes that 'Magwells, a London-based law firm representing Mr. Kulibayev, said its client is not, and has never been, a shareholder in Darley, and wasn't involved in the Aktobe Munaigaz transaction'. The article further notes that Tiku's lawyer stated that 'Mr. Ablyazov's account of the Aktobe Munaigas deal "does not provide a true reflection of the transaction", and the facts as stated in it were "incomplete and inaccurate"', and 'CNPC said Mr. Ablyazov's claims were "groundless and libelous". In a statement, the company's Hong Kong- and New York-listed subsidiary Petrochina said it "conducts its international business according to best business practice, with high integrity and in full compliance with regulations".'

75. Paik, *Sino-Russian Oil and Gas Cooperation*, p. 308.

76. Juan Pablo Cardenal and Heriberto Araújo, *China's Silent Army: The Pioneers, Traders, Fixers and Workers Who Are Remaking the World in Beijing's Image* (New York: Crown Archetype, 2013), p. 111.

77. Ibid., p. 112.

78. 'Corruption Clampdown on CNPC Nets Two More Executives', *Caixin* (17 May 2014), available at: http://english.caixin.com/2014-05-17/100678740.html

79. 'Jennifer Lopez Turkmenistan Gig Shines Light on Chinese Oil Firm', *Wall Street Journal* (1 July 2013).

80. Ibid.

81. See Wong, 'Investigative Stories Delve Into the Use of Offshore Companies by Chinese'.

82. William Vlcek, 'Byways and Highways of Direct Investment: China and the Offshore World', *Journal of Current Chinese Affairs* 39:4 (2011), pp. 111–42.

Chapter 7: Political Exiles and Extraterritorial Repression

1. The Central Asian Political Exiles (CAPE) database available at: http://blogs.exeter.ac.uk/excas/exiles/

2. David Trilling, 'Uzbekistan's President Attacks "Lazy" Labor Migrants', *Eurasianet* (21 June 2013), available at: http://www.eurasianet.org/node/67157

3. World Bank, migration and remittances data (2014), available at: http://www.worldbank.org/en/topic/migrationremittancesdiasporaissues/brief/migration-remittances-data

4. Statistics as of 2014 from the Russian Federal Migration Service. See http://www.fms.gov.ru/about/activity/stats/Statistics

5. See Human Rights Watch, *'Are You Happy to Cheat Us?' Exploitation of Migrant Construction Workers in Russia* (10 February 2009), available at: https://www.hrw.org/report/2009/02/10/are-you-happy-cheat-us/exploitation-migrant-construction-workers-russia

6. Robert Owen, *The Litvinenko Inquiry: Report into the Death of Alexander Litvinenko* (January 2016), available at: https://www.litvinenkoinquiry.org/files/Litvinenko-Inquiry-Report-web-version.pdf

7. Alexander Litvinenko, *The Uzbek File*, INQ017397 (undated), a document submitted to the Litvinenko Inquiry (2016), available at: https://www.litvinenkoinquiry.org/files/2015/04/INQ017384wb.pdf

8. For a discussion of the relationship between governments and organised crime across the region see Alexander Kupatadze, *Organized Crime, Political Transitions and State Formation in Post-Soviet Eurasia* (Basingstoke: Palgrave Macmillan, 2012).

9. David Lewis, ' "Illiberal Spaces": Uzbekistan's Extraterritorial Security Practices and the Spatial Politics of Contemporary Authoritarianism', *Nationalities Papers* 43 (2015), p. 146.

10. Alexander Cooley, 'The League of Authoritarian Gentlemen', *Foreign Policy* (30 January 2013), available at: http://foreignpolicy.com/2013/01/30/the-league-of-authoritarian-gentlemen/

11. Both India and Pakistan were due to accede to the organisation in 2017 after signing a memorandum of understanding in June 2016.

12. HRIC, 'Counter-Terrorism and Human Rights'.

13. UN Human Rights Council, *Report of the Special Rapporteur on the Promotion and Protection of Human Rights and Fundamental Freedoms While Countering Terrorism, Martin Scheinin*, A/HRC/10/3 (4 February 2009), available at: http://www2.ohchr.org/english/issues/terrorism/rapporteur/docs/A.HRC.10.3.pdf

14. The Ministry of Foreign Affairs of the Russian Federation, *The Convention Against Terrorism of the Shanghai Cooperation Organization* (2001), Article 18, original available at: http://www.mid.ru/bdomp/ns-rkonfl.nsf/ac72b85191b0db0643256adc002905c1/baf6836c773da9b2c325786400292549!OpenDocument; unofficial translation, FIDH International Federation for Human Rights (15 February 2012), available at: http://www.fidh.org/The-Convention-Against-Terrorism

15. Fair Trials International, *Strengthening Respect for Human Rights, Strengthening INTERPOL*.

16. Lewis, ' "Illiberal Spaces" ', p. 142.

17. In September 2015, the final move was made against Kabiri and the Islamic Revival Party with the arrest of the entire presidium of the party – except Kabiri, who remained in exile – on charges of terrorism following the apparent rebellion of a deputy defence

minister with minimal links to the party who had fled after being targeted for arrest. The government of Tajikistan accused the IRPT of launching a coup d'état and applied to Interpol for a Red Notice for Kabiri's arrest.

18. Constitution of the ICPO-INTERPOL adopted by the General Assembly at its twenty-fifth session (Vienna, 1956).
19. Fair Trials International, *Strengthening Respect for Human Rights, Strengthening INTERPOL*.
20. Ibid., p. 3.
21. Ibid., p. 13–14.
22. Joanna Lillis, 'Kazakhstan: Coup Trial May Have Government's Image', *Eurasianet* (30 March 2008), available at: http://www.eurasianet.org/departments/insight/articles/eav033108a.shtml
23. 'Austria Investigates Bid to Kidnap Kazakh Exile', *Wall Street Journal* (26 September 2008).
24. Article 3 of the European Convention on Human Rights, to which Russia and Turkey – two of one of the main destinations for Central Asian exiles – are signatories, forbids *refoulement*. The European Court introduced its Rule 39 to require members not to deport or extradite at-risk persons before a final judgment is made by the court on the likelihood of torture.
25. European Court of Human Rights, *Case of Zokhidov v Russia*, judgment (5 February 2013), available at: http://hudoc.echr.coe.int/eng?i=001-116330
26. Ibid.
27. Ibid.
28. Ibid.; see also Amnesty International, *Return to Torture: Extradition, Forcible Returns and Removals to Central Asia* (London, 2013), pp. 38–9.
29. In addition to the explicit violation of the European Convention on Human Rights, Russia is also often in violation of the UN's Refugee Convention which requires it to consult with UNHCR in cases of the deportation or extradition of a UNHCR-registered refugee. Amnesty International, *Return to Torture*, p. 40.
30. Murat Sadykov, 'Uzbekistan: No Former Soviet State a Safe Place for Uzbek Refugees', *Eurasianet* (24 April 2013), available at: http://www.eurasianet.org/node/66873; Joanna Lillis, 'Kazakhstan: Last Ditch Appeal from Uzbek Asylum Seekers Facing Extradition', *Eurasianet* (30 November 2010), availllable at: http://www.eurasianet.org/node/62472
31. Alisher Ilkhamov, 'Ten Years after Uzbekistan's Massacre, the Tragedy Continues to Unfold', *Ferghana News* (13 May 2015), available at: http://enews.fergananews.com/articles/2920
32. Ibid.
33. Martha Brill Olcott and Marina Barnett, *The Andijan Uprising, Akramiya and Akram Yuldashev* (Washington, DC: Carnegie Endowment, 25 June 2006), available at: http://carnegieendowment.org/2006/06/22/andijan-uprising-akramiya-and-akram-yuldashev
34. Ilkhamov, 'Ten Years After Uzbekistan's Massacre'; Sarah Kendzior, 'Inventing Akromiya: The Role of Uzbek Propagandists in the Andijon Massacre', *Demokratizatsiya* 14:4 (2006), pp. 545–62.
35. Human Rights Watch, *'Saving Its Secrets': Government Repression in Andijan* (2008).
36. European Court of Human Rights, *Case of Ismoilov and Others v Russia*, judgment (24 April 2008), available at: http://hudoc.echr.coe.int/eng?i=001-86086
37. European Court of Human Rights, *Case of Ermakov v. Russia*, judgment (7 November 2013), paragraph 14, available at: http://hudoc.echr.coe.int/eng?i=001-127816
38. Ibid., paragraph 79.
39. Ibid., paragraph 81.
40. Ibid., paragraph 88.
41. Ibid., paragraph 98.

42. Ibid., paragraphs 99–100.
43. Ibid., paragraph 155.
44. Ibid., paragraph 182.
45. Sadykov, 'Uzbekistan'.
46. Ilkhamov, 'Ten Years After Uzbekistan's Massacre'.
47. Sarah Kendzior, 'Digital Distrust: Cynicism and Solidarity in the Internet Age', *American Ethnologist* 38 (2011), p. 561.
48. Association for Human Rights in Central Asia, 'The Karimov Regime is Accused of Terrorist Activities: An Attempt on the Life of Political Émigré Obidkhon Nazarov' (29 February 2012), available at: http://www.ahrca.eu/index.php/uzbekistan/refugees/693-the-karimov-regime-is-accused-of-terrorist-activities-n-attempt-on-the-life-of-political-emigre-obidkhon-nazarov
49. 'Prominent Uzbek Cleric In Critical Condition After Sweden Shooting', *RFE/RL* (22 February 2012), available at: http://www.rferl.org/content/exiled_uzbek_cleric_survives_attack/24493065.html
50. 'Interview: Refugee Uzbek Imam Calls For Religious Freedom', *RFE/RL* (8 April 2006), available at: http://www.rferl.org/content/article/1067544.html
51. 'Sweden Sheltering Terrorist Cleric: Uzbek TV', *Local* (29 May 2010), available at: http://www.thelocal.se/20100529/26918
52. Lewis, '"Illiberal Spaces"', p. 154.
53. 'Swedish Court Rules "Innocent" Suspects in Attempt on Uzbek Imam's Life', *Ferghana News* (2 July 2013), available at: http://enews.fergananews.com/news.php?id=2651
54. 'Man Jailed for Attempted Murder of Uzbek Dissident in Sweden', *BBC News* (15 December 2015), available at: http://www.bbc.co.uk/news/world-europe-35100353
55. 'Swedish Court Rules "Innocent" Suspects'.
56. Sirojiddin Tolibov and Johannes Dell, 'Uzbek Assassination Plot Rocks Quiet Swedish Town', *BBC News* (26 July 2012), available at: http://www.bbc.co.uk/news/world-europe-18998039
57. Association for Human Rights in Central Asia, 'The Karimov Regime is Accused of Terrorist Activities'.
58. European Court of Human Rights, *Case of Mukhitdinov v Russia: Judgment* (21 May 2015), available at: http://hudoc.echr.coe.int/rus?i=001-155007#{%22itemid%22:[%22001-155007%22]}
59. For more detail on each of these cases see Appendix 2 and the full Central Asian Political Exiles (CAPE) database, available at: http://blogs.exeter.ac.uk/excas/exiles/
60. European Court of Human Rights, *Case of Iskandarov v Russia*, paragraph 13.
61. Ibid., paragraphs 25–32.
62. 'Controversial Tajik Tycoon Falls From Grace', *RFE/RL* (25 December 2013), available at: http://www.rferl.org/content/tajikistan-zayd-saidov-convicted/25212375.html
63. 'Tajikistan: Opposition Leader Kidnapped?', *Global Voices* (26 March 2013), available at: https://globalvoicesonline.org/2013/03/26/tajikistan-opposition-leader-kidnapped/
64. Nargis Hamroboyeva, 'Umarali Quvvatov Expected to Be Extradited to Tajikistan Soon', *Tajikistan News* (25 January 2013), available at: http://news.tj/en/news/umarali-quvvatov-expected-be-extradited-tajikistan-soon
65. Nadejda Atayeva, 'Turkey: The Leader of Group 24 Umarali Kuvatov is Detained' (20 December 2014), available at: http://nadejda-atayeva-en.blogspot.fr/2014/12/turkey-leader-of-goup-24-umarali.html
66. Mehrangez Tursunzoda, 'Verkhovnyii Sud Tadzhikistana obyavil Gruppu 24 ekstremistskoi [High Court of Tajikistan Declares Group 24 Extremist]', *Tajikistan News* (9 October 2014), available at: http://news.tj/ru/news/verkhovnyi-sud-tadzhikistana-obyavil-gruppu-24-ekstremistskoi

67. David Trilling, 'Terrified Tajikistan Declares Obscure Facebook Critics "Extremist"', *Eurasianet* (9 October 2014), available at: http://www.eurasianet.org/node/70386

68. Edward Lemon, 'Tajikistan Extradites Opposition Leader, Arrests Sympathizers', *Eurasianet* (2 February 2014), available at: http://www.eurasianet.org/node/71916

69. 'Opublikovani imena zaklyuchennikh chlenov OO Moldezh Tadzhikistana za Vozrozhdedniye [Published Names of Detained Members of Social Organisation Youth for the Revival of Tajikistan]', *Toj News* (27 January 2015), available at: http://tojnews.org/ru/news/opublikovany-imena-zaklyuchennyh-chlenov-oo-molodezh-tadzhikistana-za-vozrozhdenie

70. 'Tadzhikskii Sud utochnil prigovor oppozitsioneru Maksudu Ibragimovu: 17 let zaklyucheniya [Tajik Court Hands Downs Sentence of Oppositionist Maksud Ibragimov: 17 Years of Detention]', *Ferghana News* (23 July 2015), available at: http://www.fergananews.com/news/23671

71. Freedom House, *Tajikistan Opposition Leader Kuvvatov Facing New Dangers* (21 January 2015), available at: https://freedomhouse.org/article/tajikistan-opposition-leader-kuvvatov-facing-new-dangers#.VbC-oflVhBd

72. 'Ubiistvo Umarali Kuvvatova v Stambule: Reakstiya iz Dushanbe [The Killing of Umarali Kuvvatov in Istanbul; Reactions from Dushnabe]', *RFE/RL* (6 March 2015), available at: http://rus.ozodi.org/content/article/26884830.html

73. 'Three Arrested As Tajik Opposition Tycoon Buried In Istanbul', *RFE/RL* (9 March 2015), available at: http://www.rferl.org/content/slain-tajik-opposition-tycoon-to-be-buried-in-istanbul/26889471.html

74. 'Sulaimon Kayumov baroi katli Umarali Kuvatov ba habsi abad mahkum shud [Sulaimon Kayumov Was Sentenced to Life Imprisonment for the Murder of Umarali Kuvvatov]', *Radio Ozodi* (26 February 2016), available at: http://www.ozodi.org/a/umarali-quvvatovs-killer-sentenced-to-life-term-prison/27575897.html

75. For more detail on each of these cases, see Appendix 3 and the full Central Asian Political Exiles (CAPE) database, available at: http://blogs.exeter.ac.uk/excas/exiles/

76. Lewis, '"Illiberal Spaces"', p. 146.

77. Amnesty International, *Return to Torture*, p. 44.

Conclusion: Confronting the Challenge of Global Authoritarianism

1. United Nations General Assembly, Resolution 68/262 (adopted 27 March 2014), available at: http://www.un.org/en/ga/search/view_doc.asp?symbol=A/68/PV.80

2. 'Rating World Leaders: What People Worldwide Think of the U.S., China, Russia, the EU and Germany', *Gallup* (July 2015), p. 11, available at: http://www.gallup.com/services/182771/rating-world-leaders-report-download.aspx

3. See e.g. Lincoln Mitchell, *The Democracy Promotion Paradox* (Washington, DC: Brookings, 2016).

4. European Stability Initiative, 'Caviar Diplomacy: How Azerbaijan Silenced the Council of Europe', *ESI Reports* 24 (2012), available at: http://www.esiweb.org/pdf/esi_document_id_131.pdf

5. 'Foreign Powers Buy Influence at Think Tanks', *New York Times* (4 September 2014).

6. 'Gaddafi Donation to LSE May Have Come from Bribes, Inquiry Finds', *Guardian* (30 November 2011).

7. Jason Sharman, 'For Research, We Pretended to Be Crooks and Terrorists and Tried to Buy Shell Companies. The Results Were Disturbing', *Washington Post* (11 April 2014).

8. 'Treasury Announces Key Regulations and Legislation to Counter Money Laundering and Corruption, Combat Tax Evasion', US Department of the Treasury (5 May 2016), available at: https://www.treasury.gov/press-center/press-releases/Pages/jl0451.aspx

9. Johann Graf Lambsdorff, 'Corrupt Intermediaries in International Business Transactions: Between Make, Buy and Reform', *European Journal of Economic Law* 35 (2013), pp. 349–66.
10. Adam Hug (ed.), *Institutionally Blind? International Organisations and Human Rights Abuses in the Former Soviet Union*, Foreign Policy Centre report (February 2016); Hug (ed.), *Sheltering from the Storm?*; Amnesty International, *Return to Torture*; Fair Trials International, *Strengthening Respect for Human Rights, Strengthening Interpol*.
11. Hug (ed.), *Institutionally Blind?*, pp. 49–50.
12. Interpol Red Notice, Kabiri, Mukhiddin, available at: http://www.interpol.int/notice/search/wanted/2015-63685
13. Edward Schatz and Renan Levine, 'Framing, Public Diplomacy, and Anti-Americanism in Central Asia', *International Studies Quarterly* 54:3 (2010), pp. 855–69.

INDEX

Page numbers in italics indicate inclusion in figures and tables.

281

ILLUSTRATION CREDITS

1 Reuters/Vladimir Tretyakov. 2 Astana Economic Forum. 3 and 6 U.S. Department of State [Public Domain]. 5 Sulton1987. 7 World Economic Forum, Nader Daoud. 8 Ellgaard Holger. 9 DoD photo by Tech. Sgt. Kevin J. Gruenwald, U.S. Air Force. 10 Kyrgyz Presidential Website [Official Source]. 11 turkistanlilar.org. 12 Ola Westerberg/ TT/TT News Agency/Press Association Images.